Contributions to Finance and Accounting

The book series 'Contributions to Finance and Accounting' features the latest research from research areas like financial management, investment, capital markets, financial institutions, FinTech and financial innovation, accounting methods and standards, reporting, and corporate governance, among others. Books published in this series are primarily monographs and edited volumes that present new research results, both theoretical and empirical, on a clearly defined topic. All books are published in print and digital formats and disseminated globally. This book series is indexed in Scopus.

Fredrik Nilsson
Editor

Exploring Fund Management Expertise

 Springer

Editor
Fredrik Nilsson
Department of Business Studies
Uppsala University
Uppsala, Sweden

ISSN 2730-6038   ISSN 2730-6046 (electronic)
Contributions to Finance and Accounting
ISBN 978-3-032-08544-3   ISBN 978-3-032-08545-0 (eBook)
https://doi.org/10.1007/978-3-032-08545-0

This Springer imprint is published by the registered company Springer Nature Switzerland AG
The registered company address is: Gewerbestrasse 11, 6330 Cham, Switzerland

If disposing of this product, please recycle the paper.

Preface

It is a common standpoint among scholars and practitioners that fund managers do not create value for their stakeholders. With such a starting point, it is natural to argue that fund management is an area in which expertise does not matter. Hence, an investor is financially better off placing money in a passively managed fund. Still, the fund management industry continues to prosper, and fund managers are usually highly compensated for their services. Surprisingly, the extant literature does not provide an unambiguous answer to the intriguing question of whether fund managers actually create value and whether expertise exists in this field. This lack of clarity on a fundamental question in the accounting and finance field sparked our interest to explore what fund management expertise is and how it is used. Drawing on research on expertise in general, and in an accounting and finance in particular, we set out to explore the field through a series of literature reviews and interviews. The results of this research endeavour are presented in this edited volume.

I would like to thank all contributors for their highly rewarding and professional collaboration. Even as the plans for this volume were finalised, we were confident that this book project would build on and contribute to the ongoing research on expertise at the Department of Business Studies (e.g., Backman et al. 2024; Grant and Nilsson 2022, 2023; Grant et al. 2022), by opening up an exciting avenue for future research in a new context, namely, fund management. I would especially like to thank Martin Abrahamson, Katarzyna Cieslak, and Michael Grant, who were closely involved in the initial planning of the book project and contributed to the final book proposal submitted to Springer. Special thanks also go to our editor, Rocio Torregrosa, and to our language editor, Donald MacQueen. Finally, we gratefully acknowledge the financial support from the Jan Wallander and Tom Hedelius Foundation and the Tore Browaldh Foundation (P22-0239), which partially funded the research reported in this volume.

Järvsö, Sweden   Fredrik Nilsson
August 2025

References

Backman J, Grant M, Nilsson F (2023) Expertise in financial auditing. In: Marton J, Nilsson F, Öhman P (eds) Auditing transformation: regulation, digitalisation and sustainability. Routledge, Abingdon, New York, pp 338–359

Grant M, Nilsson F (2020) The production of strategic and financial rationales in capital investments: judgments based on intuitive expertise. Br Account Rev 52:100861

Grant M, Nilsson F (2023) Intuitive expertise and financial decision-making. Routledge, Abingdon, New York

Grant M, Nilsson F, Nordvall A-C (2022) Pre-merger acquisition capabilities: a study of two successful serial acquirers. Eur Manag J 40:932–942

Contents

Editor and Contributors

About the Editor

Fredrik Nilsson Ph.D., is a Professor (Chair) of Business Studies (Accounting) at Uppsala University, Sweden. His research focuses on how information systems, for example, related to financial accounting, management control, and enterprise risk management, are designed and used in formulating and implementing strategies. His research has been accepted for publication in scientific journals such as *Accounting, Auditing and Accountability Journal, Accounting & Finance, British Accounting Review, British Journal of Management, European Management Journal, Management Accounting Research, Qualitative Research in Accounting and Management* and *Scandinavian Journal of Management* as well as books (e.g., Routledge and Springer) and book chapters. He is a member of the Examination Council at the Swedish Inspectorate of Auditors, Chairman of the Swedish Research School of Management and Information Technology, and a former Chairman of the Swedish Academy of Auditing.

Contributors

Martin Abrahamson Department of Business Studies, Uppsala University, Uppsala, Sweden

Sajid Anwar School of Business and Creative Industries, University of the Sunshine Coast, Sippy Downs, QLD, Australia

Katarzyna Cieslak Department of Business Studies, Uppsala University, Uppsala, Sweden

Michael Grant Department of Business Studies, Uppsala University, Uppsala, Sweden

Frank Hartmann Northeastern University, Boston, MA, USA

Janina Hornbach Mälardalen University, Västerås, Sweden

Haojun Hu Department of Business Studies, Uppsala University, Uppsala, Sweden

Melissa Innes School of Business and Creative Industries, University of the Sunshine Coast, Sippy Downs, QLD, Australia

Inna Neskorodieva Department of Business Studies, Uppsala University, Uppsala, Sweden;
Karazin Business School, V.N. Karazin Kharkiv National University, Kharkiv, Ukraine

Fredrik Nilsson Department of Business Studies, Uppsala University, Uppsala, Sweden

Anna-Carin Nordvall Department of Business Studies, Uppsala University, Uppsala, Sweden

List of Tables

Performance and Fund Managers' Expertise

Expertise in Fund Management

Fredrik Nilsson⬤

Abstract The chapter starts with a rationale for why expertise in fund management is important and why we need to increase and improve our knowledge about it. It presents a concise overview of the current and limited scientific knowledge on expertise in fund management. With that as a starting point, the contributions to the literature are outlined. The chapter ends with a presentation of how the book is structured and short chapter descriptions.

Keywords Expertise · Financial decision-making · Fund management · Judgment · Performance

1   Introduction and Rationale

Why are some professionals more successful than their peers? How is it that they consistently outperform them? These are questions that seem to intrigue professionals, many of whom have been dedicated to their profession for a long time. The results from the judgments and decisions made by these experts should be visible. Still, it is rather difficult to describe what expertise consists of and how expertise translates into high and consistent performance. In fund management, where the financial results of judgments and decisions can be followed in real time, performance is always in focus. Since actively managed funds charge a great deal for their services, it is not surprising that their performance is scrutinised. A critical article in the *New York Times* is representative for the type of scepticism that surrounds the question whether fund managers create any added value at all (Sommer 2022):

> It's very hard to beat the stock or bond markets with any regularity. Each year, some investors manage to do it, of course, but can they do it consistently? A new study of actively managed mutual funds by S&P Dow Jones Indices asked that question and came up with a startling result. It found that not a single mutual fund – not one – managed to beat its benchmark in either the U.S. stock or bond markets regularly and convincingly over the last five years.

F. Nilsson (✉)
Department of Business Studies, Uppsala University, Uppsala, Sweden
e-mail: fredrik.nilsson@fek.uu.se

© The Author(s), under exclusive license to Springer Nature Switzerland AG 2025
F. Nilsson (ed.), *Exploring Fund Management Expertise*, Contributions to Finance and Accounting, https://doi.org/10.1007/978-3-032-08545-0_1

These results are even worse than those of 2014 and 2015, when I last examined this subject closely.

Sommer (Ibid.) points out that the conclusion from this study[1] is not new and is in line with research conducted over many decades. One well-cited paper from that period, written by Michael Jensen (1968), has conclusions that are similar to those reported by the *New York Times*. Jensen writes (Ibid., p. 415):

> The evidence on mutual fund performance discussed above indicates not only that these 115 mutual funds *were on average* not able to predict security prices well enough to outperform a buy-the-market-and-hold policy, but also that there is very little evidence that any *individual* fund was able to do significantly better than that which we expected from mere random chance. It is also important to note that these conclusions hold *even* when we measure the fund returns gross of management expenses (that is assume their bookkeeping, research, and other expenses except brokerage commissions were obtained free). Thus, on average the funds apparently were not quite successful enough in their trading activities to recoup even their brokerage expenses.

Even though there is considerable research showing that actively managed funds do not create added value, common sense would lead us to question if such a conclusion could be entirely correct; the simple reason being that the fund management industry is huge and prosperous. In other words, how can it survive if no added value is created? This type of common-sense argumentation is put forward by researchers like Berk (2005). He explains why value-creation by fund manager experts are not clearly visible, and how this has led to incorrect conclusions regarding the existence of expertise (Berk 2005, p. 31):

> An important insight is that returns cannot be used to measure managerial skill. Because researchers generally use return to measure skill, they have drawn the erroneous conclusion that active managers add little value. Given the overall levels of manager compensation, one would expect that managers in aggregate should have significant levels of skill and thus add considerable value. I show that when skill is measured correctly, the data are indeed consistent with many skilled managers who add considerable value but capture this themselves in the fees they charge.

In addition, there is recent research showing that fund managers do indeed create added value. One of these papers that studied the development of US equity funds over a 45-year period clearly shows that fund management expertise exists and that fund managers are 'able to extract value from capital markets' (Barras et al. 2022, p. 635).

We can thus conclude that the literature does not provide a coherent and unambiguous answer to the question of whether, and to what extent, fund managers create value. Even so, few would maintain that expertise in fund management does not

---

[1] The study, part of the so-called persistence scorecard series, was carried out by a team at the S&P Dow Jones (i.e., S&P Dow Jones Indices). They analysed 2132 actively managed funds selecting the top 25% best-performing funds in 2018 for further analyses. The performance of these funds, for the coming four-year period, led to the conclusions presented in the New York Times article. Persistence scorecards, from the US and other countries, can be downloaded from the S&P Global webpage (www.spglobal.com).

exist (see for example, Berk 2005). With these starting points, we argue that, irrespective of the position taken in this matter, there is a clear need to problematise and study fund management expertise in greater detail. Surprisingly, and to the best of our knowledge, not a single book explicitly discusses fund management expertise. However, there are books and papers that cover expertise in general (e.g., Ericsson et al. 2006; Gobet 2016; Ward et al. 2020) and in an accounting context; such as auditing (e.g., Backman et al. 2024; for an overview see Mala and Chand, 2015) and financial decision-making (for an overview see Grant and Nilsson 2023).

The present book adds a significant and novel contribution to this stream of research. More specifically, the book explores what fund management expertise is and how it is used. This is related to how recent and significant developments in society, e.g., sustainability, artificial intelligence and multiple accountabilities, affect what expertise consist of today and how it can be expected to develop in the future. To facilitate that discussion, the following theoretical starting points from the extant literature—as summarised by Grant and Nilsson (2023, p. 9)—will be used to define experts and expertise.

First, an expert shows highly superior performance, consistently over a long period of time, within a specific domain and its related tasks. A domain is often similar to a profession, for example a university professor, a CFO, or other senior executives. Second, the acquisition of expertise requires a long period of deliberate practice, typically 10 years or more. Pursuing such practice is highly demanding and requires motivation and persistence. Staying an expert is an everyday challenge with the overall objective to maintain and develop expert knowledge. Third, the effects of deliberate practice are supported by neural research. It shows that effects on the size and function of the brain are associated with the tasks related to expertise. Moreover, research shows that experts and novices cognitively 'see' things differently, affecting how they store and recall experiences.

2   Contributions and Chapter Overview

We apply these theoretical starting points to all chapters of the book. Each chapter explores a particular aspect or area of fund management expertise. Aspects and areas covered are: The performance of expert fund managers (chapter 'Performance and Fund Managers' Expertise'); the skills and characteristics of expert fund managers (chapter 'Searching for Expert Fund Managers'); judgments and decisions by expert fund managers (chapter 'Judgments and Decisions by Expert Fund Managers'); foresight and fund management expertise (chapter 'Individual Foresight and Fund Management Expertise'); fund managers' expertise and artificial intelligence (chapter 'Artificial Intelligence in Discretionary Fund Management'); fund managers' expertise and ESG investments (chapter 'Integrating ESG Information in Active Fund Management'); the behavioural effects of expert fund managers' accountability (chapter 'Analysing Fund Managers' Accountability'); and the final chapter, which discusses whether expertise really does matter in fund management (chapter 'Does Expertise Matter? Concluding Reflections'). The remainder of this introductory chapter will give a detailed overview of each chapter starting with the chapter 'Performance and Fund Managers' Expertise.'

The chapter 'Performance and Fund Managers' Expertise' is written by Martin Abrahamson and Michael Grant. As pointed out in the introduction to this book, fund manager performance has long been a subject of interest for both practitioners and scholars. Two key areas for debate are to what extent fund managers create added value for investors and how value creation (i.e., performance) should be measured. Since fund manager expertise is shown through consistently delivering a high level of performance these two questions are fundamental to any informed discussion exploring fund management expertise. The chapter contributes to that discussion by critically scrutinising and building on the stream of literature in the areas of finance and expertise. In their overview of the literature the authors put an emphasis on difficulties of measuring and assessing expertise of an individual fund manager. Some examples of these difficulties are the strong stochastic character of the stock market, how to choose a benchmark and how to address survival bias. The authors utilise these insights from the literature as their theoretical starting points for an explorative interview study with recruiters, rating agencies, fund industry organisations and fund managers, providing multiple perspectives on expert fund managers' performance and tasks. By combining existing knowledge from the field with findings from their empirical study, the authors explore and problematise performance of expert fund managers beyond simple and often-used measures like stock portfolio returns.

The chapter 'Searching for Expert Fund Managers' is written by Martin Abrahamson and Michael Grant. The literature almost always uses high performance over a long period of time as an indicator of expertise. As clearly shown in the previous chapter such an operationalisation of expertise has some inherent problems. It also shows that expertise exists and does matter, even though it can be difficult to measure. Therefore, it is important to know more about what constitutes skills and characteristics of an expert fund manager. The literature review in this chapter demonstrates that we know a lot about general skills of fund management in areas such as stock-picking, market-timing, data acquisition and analysis, and the implementation of a disciplined investment strategy. However, and perhaps a bit surprisingly, the extant literature does not contribute much that enhances our knowledge of the individual fund manager, the reason being that the level of analysis in most of the papers reviewed is the fund itself. Therefore, the authors conducted an exploratory interview study with recruiters and CEOs from fund management companies to examine their views on the characteristics they look for in expert fund managers. The chapter demonstrates that recruiters use a combination of criteria—such as abilities, interests, education, personality, and a sense of deliberate practice—when identifying experts in the field. Thus, they appear to search for more general characteristics of expertise that can be applied to the fund industry and the specific tasks of fund managers.

The chapter 'Judgments and Decisions by Expert Fund Managers' is also written by Martin Abrahamson and Michael Grant. In the finance literature, fund management practices are often described as highly rational. Analytical tools and models are thus important when judgments and decisions are made. The use of intuition and heuristics is often considered to introduce biases into fund management decision-making and is therefore to be avoided. As shown by the authors, however, there is a burgeoning stream of literature in financial decision-making in areas such as auditing and mergers and acquisitions which reveals that experts use both analysis and intuition (i.e., intuitive expertise) when making judgments and decisions. Surprisingly, this research shows that experts do not seem to use formal analytical models to the extent that is often claimed in the finance literature and elsewhere. The reason for this, the authors argue, is that experts are relying on their long experience in the domain. The domain of fund management is also characterised by a high level of uncertainty which, according to cognitive research, makes heuristics suitable. Adding to the stream of literature studying intuitive expertise, the authors have conducted an exploratory study of how expert fund managers make judgments and decisions. The results show, in contrast to many earlier studies in the field of finance, that intuition and heuristics are important and that expert fund managers use qualitative and quantitative assessments. It also shows the importance of emotions and how to manage them in an environment characterised by a high level of uncertainty.

The chapter 'Individual Foresight and Fund Management Expertise' is written by Melissa Innes and Sajid Anwar. An expert fund manager is usually characterised as having deep industry knowledge and long experience of conducting financial analyses. In a situation when a significant and unexpected event occurs, this knowledge and experience is put to the test. However, it is far from certain that the expertise acquired by the fund manager is useful for making judgments and decisions in a non-routine situation. The authors of the chapter argue that in such a scenario the fund manager could also benefit from individual foresight. This refers to the ability to envision future scenarios by drawing on past experiences, planning future actions, and evaluating those actions to predict potential success. The authors show that foresight is closely related to intuitive expertise (i.e., a fund manager's personal knowledge, experience, and ability to intuit). But to be able to develop and use foresight the fund manager will also need to engage with collaborative learning mechanisms, draw on formal and informal social networks, take time for reflection, and engage in future-thinking and other cognitive strategies to arrive at beneficial outcomes for investors. This chapter discusses how the unique skills and abilities of expert fund managers, and the process of individual foresight, can be acknowledged and planned for in future fund management development opportunities.

The chapter 'Artificial Intelligence in Discretionary Fund Management' is written by Haojun Hu. The rapid development of data-analytical tools, such as artificial intelligence, has spurred a discussion of how these tools will affect what is considered to be expertise and how it is used. This discussion is very much alive in fund management, an industry considered to be at the forefront of using advanced analytical tools. The author argues that the empirical reality of discretionary fund management still requires a human in the loop. Therefore, it is still the implementation and use of the tools that are important when discussing discretionary fund management expertise. Professional judgment is necessary in order to make an informed decision, for example, when inputting data and interpreting signals acquired. That said, the literature does not provide many insights into how these decisions are made in practice, whether advanced analytical tools are used, and if so, how this interacts with human fund management expertise. To fill the identified gap in the literature, the author has conducted an exploratory interview study with professionals in discretionary fund management. Specifically, it provides the reader with empirical insights into the fundamental question of whether the development of new analytical tools and the use of advanced information technology solutions have changed how fund managers make judgments and decisions. Based on the findings the author critically examines and problematises the relationship between machine—in the form of artificial intelligence—and human expertise.

The chapter 'Integrating ESG Information in Active Fund Management' is written by Katarzyna Cieslak, Inna Neskorodieva and Fredrik Nilsson. Sustainable investments have become one of the major fund management trends in recent years, spurring a discussion on the performance of these investments. As argued by the authors of the chapter it is reasonable to assume that active management of sustainable investments, in contrast to reliance on ESG ratings, can have positive effects. However, it is not well understood how sustainable investments are made by fund managers. Following this line of reasoning, and based on interviews with experienced and successful fund managers, the chapter explores how ESG information is integrated into the active management of sustainable investments. Somewhat surprisingly, the findings indicate that sustainability investing is strongly grounded in the paradigm of financial materiality with negative screening being a pervasive investment approach. Key skills in ESG-focused investments include selecting financially material ESG information, validating this information and balancing over- and underreaction to ESG information.

The chapter 'Analysing Fund Managers' Accountability' is written by Frank Hartmann, Janina Hornbach and Anna-Carin Nordvall. Accountability is a fundamental concept in the accounting and finance literature. In the fund management industry, the overall objective is to create added value for investors. Thus, fund managers are held accountable for reaching that objective. Lately this long-standing and taken-for-granted objective has been challenged. Other objectives, related to ESG aspects, have also become prominent. The chapter provides an analysis of how this development, creating a complex performance environment, affects fund managers' accountability towards external and internal stakeholders and their subsequent behaviour. The authors start by suggesting that performance pressures are influenced by competitive dynamics among funds, as well as societal pressures for sustainability and other non-financial performance dimensions. These pressures make it difficult to reconcile what should be achieved and how performance should be measured. The authors draw on research in the fields of behavioural and cognitive sciences to analyse how multiple accountabilities impact fund management behaviour. It especially addresses how formal and informal accountabilities can be expected to influence how fund managers think and act.

The chapter 'Does Expertise Matter? Concluding Reflections' is written by Fredrik Nilsson, Martin Abrahamson, Katarzyna Cieslak, Michael Grant, Haojun Hu, Melissa Innes, Inna Neskorodieva and Anna-Carin Nordvall. The final chapter of the book provides the reader with a holistic analysis of the chapters 'Performance and Fund Managers' Expertise', 'Searching for Expert Fund Managers', 'Judgments and Decisions by Expert Fund Managers', 'Individual Foresight and Fund Management Expertise', 'Artificial Intelligence in Discretionary Fund Management', 'Integrating ESG Information in Active Fund Management', and 'Analysing Fund Managers' Accountability' and how they together contribute to our understanding of fund management expertise. The objective of the final chapter is thus to show what fund management expertise is, how it is used and why it matters. The chapter concludes by presenting avenues for future research and some practical implications.

The book is structured to cover different aspects of what constitutes fund management expertise in the early chapters. How this expertise is applied in various areas and situations is discussed next. Although the intention is to follow a certain logic in the structure of the book, each chapter is also a complete and stand-alone contribution. This means that it is possible to begin with whichever chapter seems most interesting. We now turn to the second chapter, which explores the fundamental question of fund manager performance.

References

Backman J, Grant M, Nilsson F (2024) Expertise in financial auditing. In: Marton J, Nilsson F, Öhman P (eds) Auditing transformation: regulation, digitalisation and sustainability. Routledge, Abingdon, New York, pp 338–359

Barras L, Gagliardini P, Scaillet O (2022) Skill, scale, and value creation in the mutual fund industry. J Financ 77(1):601–638

Berk JB (2005) Five myths of active portfolio management. J Portfolio Manag 31(3):27–31

Ericsson KA, Charness N, Feltovich PJ, Hoffman RR (eds) (2006) The Cambridge handbook of expertise and expert performance. Cambridge University Press, Cambridge

Gobet F (2016) Understanding expertise: a multi-disciplinary approach. Red Globe Press, London

Grant M, Nilsson F (2023) Intuitive expertise and financial decision-making. Routledge, Abingdon, New York

Jensen MC (1968) The performance of mutual funds in the period 1945–1964. J Financ 23(2):389–416

Sommer J (2022) Strategies: mutual funds that consistently beat the market? Not one of 2,132. The New York Times, 2 Dec

Ward P, Schraagen JM, Gore J, Roth EM (eds) (2020) The Oxford handbook of expertise. Oxford University Press, Oxford

References

Performance and Fund Managers' Expertise

Martin Abrahamson⊙ and Michael Grant⊙

Abstract This chapter explores what constitutes performance of an expert fund manager in actively managed equity funds. Drawing on literature from finance and expertise, and exploratory interviews with actors in different roles in the fund industry, we problematise performance and explore it beyond the simple stock portfolio return. The findings highlight three areas, starting with the fundamental difficulty of assessing and measuring long-term performance of a fund manager in relation to a fund's excess returns. Hence, approximate ways of assessing and measuring the performance of fund managers were used such as comparison with an index, or a 'good enough' rating from a rating agency, combined with a proven investment strategy and process. Second, fund managers' tasks were not limited to generating excess returns; ability to market the fund and being a good representative and colleague for the fund were also important. This indicates a potential agency issue for the investors with the owners of the fund. Third, the findings suggest a difference in fund managers and organisational types. For example, funds that were owned by larger organisations such as banks or insurance companies could not provide equal or better remuneration or visibility for the individual fund manager compared with privately-owned fund companies, suggesting that privately owned funds have an advantage in recruiting and keeping expert fund managers.

Keywords Expertise · Financial management · Fund manager · Performance · Value

M. Abrahamson (✉) · M. Grant
Department of Business Studies, Uppsala University, Uppsala, Sweden
e-mail: martin.abrahamson@fek.uu.se

M. Grant
e-mail: michael.grant@fek.uu.se

© The Author(s), under exclusive license to Springer Nature Switzerland AG 2025
F. Nilsson (ed.), *Exploring Fund Management Expertise*, Contributions to Finance and Accounting, https://doi.org/10.1007/978-3-032-08545-0_2

1 Introduction

This chapter explores what constitutes performance of an expert fund manager in actively managed equity funds. Hence, it focuses on exploring typical fund manager tasks and how the performance and expertise of fund managers are assessed. It draws on literature from finance and expertise, and exploratory interviews with actors in different roles in the fund industry. Attention is paid to actors who are key in assessing fund managers' expertise; thus, performance is problematised and explored beyond the simple stock portfolio return.

Performance as seen from the perspective of expertise is defined by Ericsson and Lehmann (1996, p. 277) as: 'consistently superior performance on a specified set of representative tasks for a domain.' For financial decision-making Grant and Nilsson (2023) has suggested that *superior performance* should be seen as a continuum going from 'somebody who obtains results that are vastly superior to those obtained by the majority of the population' to 'somebody whose performance is vastly superior to the majority of experts' (Gobet 2016, p. 5). Consequently, we consider an expert fund manager a person who consistently over a long period of time demonstrates superior performance related to representative or typical tasks.

Early on, finance researchers questioned whether expert fund managers exist. Studies showed that funds were not able to generate positive alpha (excess financial returns, outperforming their benchmark), thus inferring that expertise did not exist in fund management (e.g., Carhart 1997; Fama 1970; Jensen 1968). This is consistent with the random walk theory, meaning that future prices are hard to predict and that it should be impossible on a risk-adjusted basis to consistently outperform the market over a longer period of time. This commonly held belief is also prevalent in the area of expertise. For example, in their seminal article Kahneman and Klein (2009) describe stock picking as an area not lending itself to expertise because: 'it is unlikely that there is publicly available information that could be used to predict how well a particular stock will do—if such valid information existed, the price of the stock would already reflect it' (Ibid., p. 520).[1] In contrast to this Berk and Green (2004), Kosowski et al. (2006), Berk and Van Binsbergen (2015), Barras et al. (2022) and Harvey and Liu (2022), show that funds can create value and generate positive returns, and hence that fund management expertise exists. This also resonates with the way investors and other stakeholders act and reason. Fund managers are among the highest paid jobs (Böhm et al. 2023) and investors still choose active funds, emphasising that there is expectation and belief in expertise within fund management. For example, in Sweden although passive funds have increased, actively managed equity funds still dominate. At the end of 2024, the value of actively managed equity funds based

---

[1] Kahneman and Klein base their conclusion on the random walk theory. Furthermore, they refer to Shanteau (1992), who describes stockbrokers as a profession not lending itself to expertise due to an unpredictable environment. Shanteau (Ibid.) states in his article that poor expert performance has been observed for stockbrokers, without providing any references supporting this. However, in a later article Shanteau (2015) reiterates this statement referring to two earlier studies, which in a closer reading prove to be studies about clinical psychologists, not stockbrokers.

Table 1 Longevity of fund managers (source: Citywire)

Year	Managers	%
1	48,362	96.7
5	22,493	45.0
10	8,732	17.5
15	3,020	6.0
20	807	1.6
25	191	0.38
30	59	0.12
35	15	0.03
37	11	0.02

in Sweden amounted to SEK 4,491 billion (out of SEK 5,839 billion of total equity fund value, according to Statistics Sweden 2025). This corresponds to approximately 70% of the Swedish annual GDP, with a net inflow, primarily to index funds, over the past 5 years of SEK 391 billion (Swedish Investment Fund Association 2025).

While there is a quantum of research on fund performance, surprisingly there is a dearth of knowledge about fund managers and their performance. A reason for this is that the finance field is dominated by quantitative studies and that there is a lack of available data at the level of fund managers. Moreover, fund managers typically have short longevity, which makes it difficult to measure their performance over a longer period of time.[2] Consequently, little is known about individual expert fund managers' superior performance and how we can assess it. This also applies to understanding the tasks that comprise fund managers' work. While the task of generating portfolio returns can be seen as a core task, we can discern in studies of fund performance that marketing to generate capital inflow to the fund can be seen as an additional task.

Hence, this study explores what constitutes performance for an expert fund manager by examining how performance is measured and assessed and what tasks an expert fund manager deals with. The study builds on seven exploratory interviews with recruiters, rating agencies, fund industry organisations and fund managers, providing multiple perspectives on expert fund managers' performance and tasks. For a detailed description of the method and interviewees, see the book's Appendix.

The findings highlight three areas. First, there is the sheer difficulty of assessing and measuring long term consistent performance of a fund manager in relation to a fund's excess returns. In addition, there is a high turnover of fund managers, and many of them leave their profession as fund manager. Moreover, there is a large stochastic element in the stock market, and interviewees were well aware of the

---

[2] Table 1 shows the short longevity of fund managers, that is how long fund managers stay in their profession. The table is based on secondary data we have received from Citywire and is based on a global population of 48,362 managers (equity and fixed-income funds) covering the period through 2018. If a manager is managing more than one fund, each fund is counted as a manager. It shows that after 5 years only 45% of the fund managers remain. The corresponding number for 10 years is 17.5%.

difficulty, or impossibility, of generating excess returns every single year. Hence, approximate ways of assessing and measuring the performance of fund managers were used such as comparison with an index, or a 'good enough' rating from a rating agency, combined with a proven investment strategy and process. Second, fund managers' tasks were not limited to generating excess returns; ability to market the fund and being a good representative and colleague for the fund were also important. This indicates a potential agency issue for the investors with the owners of the fund. The owners could benefit by selecting a manager with strong marketing ability rather than prioritising a manager with strong ability to generate excess returns and less marketing skills. Third, the findings suggest a difference in fund managers and type of organisation. For example, funds that were owned by and part of larger organisations such as banks or insurance companies could not provide equal or better remuneration or visibility for the individual fund manager as privately-owned fund companies. In a competitive market for expert fund managers this suggests that privately owned funds have an advantage in recruiting and keeping expert fund managers.

2 Literature Review

During the last couple of decades there have been a multitude of studies about fund performance and whether actively managed funds can persistently show outperformance. Related to this are discussions whether fund managers can possess expertise and, if so, the question how superior performance can be identified and described. In this section we provide an overview of current knowledge pertaining to these questions, building on a selection of seminal and recent influential studies in finance. Our focus is on active equity mutual funds, which are the main consideration of these studies.

2.1 Fund Performance Studies

In a seminal paper, Carhart (1997) studied the performance of equity mutual funds during the 1962–1993 period. The results show that outperformance could be explained by common stock return factors and investment costs (expenses and transaction costs). The study does not support the existence of fund managers' expertise above investment costs on average. Since then, a multitude of studies have further examined the question of outperformance of funds and whether fund managers possess expertise. A critical element in these studies pertains to methodological development, since it is inherently difficult to measure outperformance of funds. Thus, in the following text we discuss and conclude what we can learn from the most salient of these studies, namely, Berk and Green (2004), Kosowski et al. (2006), Fama and French (2010), Berk and Van Binsbergen (2015), Barras et al. (2022), and Harvey and Liu (2022).

Berk and Green (2004) developed an economic model showing that in an efficient competitive market, in equilibrium and under certain conditions, lack of persistence in positive returns does not imply lack of expertise among fund managers. Rather, the model shows that there can be high average returns by fund managers, even if the fund market shows an average alpha of zero. One reason is decreasing returns to scale in deploying the expertise, something which also several later studies have shown.[3] Kosowski et al. (2006) use a bootstrap (resampling of data) statistical technique on domestic mutual funds in the US covering the period 1975 to 2002. They show that for active equity mutual funds: 'a sizable minority of managers pick stocks well enough to more than cover their costs. Moreover, the superior alphas of these managers *persist*' (Ibid., p. 2551). Fama and French (2010) apply in line with Kosowski et al. (2006) bootstrap simulation on a sample of US equity mutual funds including the period from 1984 to 2006. However, in contrast, their results suggest that 'most fund managers do not have enough skill to produce benchmark-adjusted net returns that cover costs' (Fama and French 2010, pp. 1931–1932). Nevertheless, they do not dismiss expertise, as they write that the result 'suggests that some fund managers have enough skill to produce expected benchmark-adjusted net returns that cover costs' (Ibid., p. 1929). Consequently, based on their measure there should be some, though few, fund managers characterised as experts. In comparison with Kosowski et al. (2006), Fama and French also note that their sample is based on another time period and since then the financial market(s) has developed and become more efficient over the years, something which they argue partly can explain the difference between the studies.

Berk and van Binsbergen (2015) take a microeconomic perspective on fund managers' skill and measure the added value a fund manager extracts. The study measures the fund returns, in line with previous studies. However, it more directly targets the fund managers in comparison with measuring alpha as it measures value added, defined as 'the fund's gross excess return over its benchmark multiplied by assets under management' (Ibid., p. 2). The data they use is US mutual funds covering the period 1977 to 2011. The result shows that the average mutual fund extracts a value of about $3.2 million per year, excluding fees. How the fund company distributes this value to the fund managers, overhead costs, and to the fund owners is not measured owing to lack of data. Moreover, they show persistence of value added up to 10 years. Consequently, their study convincingly demonstrates that fund managers on average have expertise, in line with the economic model of Berk and Green (2004). Berk and van Binsbergen also detect that by using a tradable benchmark they 'no longer find evidence of the under-performance previously shown in the literature' (Ibid., p. 3),

---

[3] Studies show that there are diseconomies of scale at the industry and fund level (Pástor et al. 2015, 2022; Zhu 2018). This is explained by liquidity constraints. At the fund level this means: as a fund becomes larger it has a bigger impact on asset prices, which limits the fund's performance. Moreover, diseconomies of scale have implications for what the fund's alpha means. Zhu (2018, p. 115) writes: 'Decreasing returns to scale at the fund level imply that the fund alpha and the fund size are not two independent entities. Thus, neither provides a complete picture of managerial skill.' Consequently, Zhu argues that the model of Berk and van Binsbergen (2015), which measures value added, is the appropriate way to measure managerial skill.

that is, negative alpha. This highlights the difficulty and sensitivity of choosing suitable benchmarks, even for researchers. A critique is that several benchmarks used when measuring alpha of funds, such as Fama-French factor models are not available for investment.

Using the method from Berk and van Binsbergen (2015), Barras et al. (2022) measure the value added in US equity funds covering the period from 1975 to 2019. They analyse the two components of value added, that is, the excess return which they translate to skill and the size of the fund. Their findings show that most funds (60%) generate value over the period and that 'funds are highly sensitive to diseconomies of scale—on average, a one-standard-deviation increase in size reduces the gross alpha by 1.3% per year' (Ibid., p. 603). Taken together Barras et al. (2022) strongly support that there is expertise among fund managers and that many fund managers can be qualified as experts, but that it is difficult to scale up good investment ideas.

Harvey and Liu (2022) re-examine the studies by Kosowski et al. (2006) and Fama and French (2010), by using a developed statistical method which takes into consideration Type I errors, falsely claiming fund outperformance, and Type II errors, falsely claiming no outperformance. By using their method, they reconcile the findings of the two contradicting studies and claim that 'our evidence on mutual fund outperformance lies somewhere between Kosowski et al. (2006) and Fama and French (2010)' (Harvey and Liu 2022, p. 1922). Conducted by highly reputable established researchers aiming at separating luck from skill, these three studies, like Carhart (1997), try to answer the question whether outperforming funds exist. The studies point to the difficulty of measuring outperformance. As they apply different methods, each provides slightly different answers. Consequently, if we use these studies to infer the extent of fund management expertise, the answer will vary from many experts in fund management (Kosowski et al. 2006) to a few (Fama and French 2010), or somewhere in between (Harvey and Liu 2022).

Taken together, these studies support the existence of fund management expertise, albeit by inferring this from data at the level of the fund (see further discussion in the paragraphs below). The studies also suggest that a substantial part of the funds deliver positive alpha, that is, generate excess returns to its investors. Furthermore, some funds consistently outperform their benchmarks over time. This contrasts with early seminal studies that showed and argued that funds were not able to generate positive alpha, thus inferring that expertise did not exist in fund management (e.g., Carhart 1997; Fama 1970; Jensen 1968). Arguably methodological developments, as evidenced in the studies discussed above, have led to findings which resonate with the way investors and the fund market act and reason. As Berk (2005, p. 27) rhetorically illustrates, if fund managers cannot have expertise 'why do we have active portfolio managers at all?' Moreover, 'If active managers cannot pick stocks or time the market, what rare skill do they have that makes them among the highest paid members of society? […] Why do investors continue to invest with active managers in the face of this evidence?'

2.2 Performance of the Expert Fund Manager

The fund performance studies show the methodological difficulties of measuring and inferring fund managers' performance. Cuthbertson et al. (2016) show the lack of research focusing on the fund manager rather than the fund. In a quest to measure the performance of individual fund managers, Clare et al. (2022) highlight other ambiguities when using fund performance as a measure. First, the level of analysis. Fund performance can reside at the organisational level and/or at the individual fund manager's level. Hence, does superior fund performance reflect expertise at the level of the organisation or at the level of the individual fund manager? Second, there is significant turnover among fund managers. This means that a fund's performance over a longer period of time includes the performance of several fund managers. Consequently, they suggest that performance should be measured at the individual level of the fund manager. Further, in contrast to our research, their focus on performance is primarily to understand if and how differences in fund manager characteristics such as age, gender and education affect performance. Moreover, they use alpha to measure performance, so the methodological difficulties of measuring fund performance remain, although they follow funds' performance for each respective fund manager.

The value-added measure, introduced by Berk and van Binsbergen (2015) suggests that performance of an expert fund manager is related to several stakeholders and tasks. Value added is defined as 'the fund's gross excess return over its benchmark multiplied by assets under management' (Ibid., p. 2). Consequently, it measures the value added of the fund before overhead costs of the fund, remuneration of the fund manager(s) and returns to the fund owners. The remaining value added (positive or negative) is for the investors of the fund. Hence, apart from the task of generating excess returns, increasing the size of the fund can be seen as an additional task. However, as there are diminishing rate of returns, there is likely a balance of how large the fund can become before value added starts deteriorating (Barras et al. 2022).

2.3 Performance, Agency and the Fund Organisation

Studies in management and financial research have shown the importance of organisational structure for performance in general, using empirics from the mutual fund industry. For example, Csaszar (2012) and Adams et al. (2018) show that the organisation of the fund affects the performance of the fund. However, the results are not conclusive, and Adams et al. (2018) show the necessity of close monitoring from fund boards, if the organisation consists of a team of fund managers rather than a single fund manager. Adams et al. (2018) also state that previous research has not been clear on whether the extra cost of a team of managers might be covered by performance or not.

One way of trying to align the interest of the fund manager with the interest of fund investors is to have each fund manager invest in their own fund. Khorana et al. (2007) show that when fund managers are personally invested in the fund, this correlates positively with fund performance. Furthermore, they claim that for every basis point of fund manager ownership, the fund improves its performance by three basis points. This suggests agency issues connected to performance of the fund.

2.4 Key Insights from the Literature

Arguably, the studies discussed above show that fund management is an area that lends itself to expertise. This contrasts with the earlier established view that funds were not able to show positive alpha, thus inferring that expertise did not exist in fund management (Carhart 1997; Fama 1970; Jensen 1968). Still, outside finance, this seems to be partially an established view. For example, regarding the area of expertise, in their seminal article Kahneman and Klein (2009) describe stock picking as an area that does not lend itself to expertise.

The studies also demonstrate the difficulty of measuring superior performance at the level of the fund manager. For example, they point to methodological difficulties like selection of benchmark to compare performance with, a high turnover rate of fund managers, and problems in separating organisational level performance from performance of the individual fund manager. Other ways of assessing expertise and superior performance remain to be explored.

Moreover, the literature suggests that performance of expert fund managers is not only related to the task of generating superior returns but also about generating capital inflow to the fund and thus increasing the fund's size. Where generating superior returns can be viewed as generating inflow, this relation is likely more complex. One reason is that the value added generated by a fund is distributed not only to investors of the fund but also to fund manager(s) and fund owners. However, previous studies provide little knowledge about the role of these stakeholders and how this affects returns to the investors. Hence, by using explorative interviews with several stakeholders, this study contributes to problematising expert fund managers' performance from multiple perspectives.

3 Results

This section presents our findings on what constitutes performance for an expert fund manager, that is, what typical fund manager tasks we have identified and how their respective performance is assessed. The findings are presented in five subsections. In the first two we present findings related to what can be seen as the core task of a fund manager, generating portfolio returns. Thereafter follow additional tasks we identified as relevant to fund manager performance, such as marketing and sales (to generate inflows to the fund) and being a good representative and colleague. Finally, we discuss how requirements placed on fund managers can differ between funds owned by large organisations and privately held funds.

3.1 The Performance of the Fund and the Fund Manager

Clare et al. (2022) explicitly raise the issue of unit of analysis in their critique of previous research, where conclusions about fund managers' performance have been incorrectly drawn from studies of funds rather than managers. To single out the performance or expertise of the fund manager vis-a-vis the fund is a difficult task, especially in quantitative studies dependent on available quantitative data, whereas these are generally based on the fund and fund performance rather than the fund manager. Not only academics or investors struggle with the unit of analysis; when recruiters assess the expertise of candidates for a position, they face a similar problem. The recruiters describe it as follows:

> We have a part [in the interview] where we discuss performance in their previous roles, and in this case, it's more about performance in terms of hard facts. How well have you succeeded in your previous management of other assets/funds? (4)

> I mean, someone else has created that [the fund], so it's really about: 'When did you come in, what did it look like then, how has the market performed in general or compared to similar funds that are managed by others, and also in relation to what fees they have charged compared to what you are charging.' (5)

As the quotes above demonstrate, the recruiters describe the need to evaluate the performance in the context the fund manager was in at the time when her/his performance was measured. For example, the market conditions could have played in favour of the fund manager's performance (or the opposite). Hence, the performance could be explained by market movements rather than the fund manager's skill. Consequently, it might be necessary to evaluate the fund manager in comparison with for example other funds rather than the index chosen for the fund.

When searching for performance beyond financial returns, the recruiters had difficulties finding appropriate measures other than references from previous workplaces, as illustrated in the following quote.

> [Rating firm name] is, of course, an important tool to see what this person has managed in the past, whether they have a rating on [Rating firm name]. It's not the main part, absolutely not, but it gives a kind of starting point, to some extent. Often, the client has requirements for gender and diversity, especially when it comes to large organisations, they have a diversity component that is important, goals that we of course also need to consider. And then, together with the client, in this case the CEO and HR, we discuss whether we think these profiles have the qualifications for the role. Normally it's a big [leadership] role. We assess that they can handle the leadership aspects, so moving away from a purely specialised competence focus. (4)

It could also be difficult for the fund managers themselves to separate their own performance from that of the fund. Rating firms generally focus on fund performance rather than performance of the fund manager. Therefore, the data source issues raised by previous research might present a problem for the fund manager who attempts to dissociate from the fund. The following quote from one specialist recruiter illustrates it in the following way:

> Because that's really difficult. Many people… they live by their performance, they are their performance, to some extent. (1)

3.2 Fund Managers' Portfolio Returns

When we asked both recruiters and other interviewees how they assess the performance of a fund manager, they typically described that it should be assessed over a long period of time. They indicated that performance varies and therefore it is not possible for fund managers to overperform every consecutive year. But it is more reasonable that over a longer period of time someone can on average show superior performance. As two of the interviewees expressed:

> Generally speaking, I think you can only really say that a manager is good after analysing their performance over many years. There's always the possibility that it could be a fluke, or that they got lucky one year, or crashed and burned the next year, and so on. But a good manager is always somewhat up there – they don't need to be at the top every year. […] Rather, if you're going to evaluate someone, it should perhaps be over ten years. You rarely have that time though, there's movement in this industry, people change jobs and if someone is skilled, they get recruited somewhere else and so on. With that said, I think you have to give them time. (6)
>
> But this thing about beating the index over let's say business cycles and let's say volatility cycles, extremely few people can manage that. Extremely few can do it. […] many perhaps don't have a track record that… that spans an entire cycle. (1)

As the quotes above suggest, a long-term view is difficult in practice as it requires that fund managers stay for many years, whereas many do not have a track record covering a whole stock market cycle. When directly measuring fund manager performance over time, fund managers' portfolio performance was evaluated using the scores of rating agencies and qualitative assessments. One of the recruiters described the threshold as a 'sufficiently high rating,' that is, a minimum 3-star rating out of 5 from Morningstar. In essence it showed the historical performance of the portfolio returns versus an index.

Having a proven investment process that is systematic and structured was also mentioned by several of the interviewees as an important criterion. Arguably this concerned their future work on how to achieve high portfolio returns. But it also captured the ability to communicate this to investors. Two of the interviewees described it in the following way:

> Because it's also very much about what we should, what it is we deliver, what it is we say we deliver to our fund investors. (1)
>
> Have they done what they say they do, that's the part, so it's very much philosophy. What is their thinking about how they will outperform an index or similar products or whatever it might be. (7)

In line with the above, a common theme from the interviews was that performance fluctuates even for expert fund managers, as the market can be volatile and has a stochastic element. One of the interviewees described it as 'the market is like its own monster.' Still, it seems that expert fund managers can perform and are able to 'tame' or not be affected by 'the monster' as elaborated in the following quote:

> Performance, it fluctuates but often it's the case that people who have a structured process and work systematically and who are truly interested in what they're doing and can somehow… yes, separate different things from each other and be open and communicative about when times are tough and when things are going well and so on, without letting it affect them too much. That usually tends to be a more important component than whether you have three or four stars in Morningstar. You know that will vary over time and periodically all managers will have tough times because the market is like its own monster that moves around and so on. (1)

Another way to view it came from one of the fund managers, who explained that it was dangerous trying to be 100% right all the time. Instead, their aim is to be right 60% of the time and accept being wrong 40%:

> But it's difficult, then I also have to say that we had a kind of philosophy that we won't be one hundred percent right, if we can be sixty percent right and forty percent wrong then that's good because then we'll get this outperformance. (6)

3.3   Fund Managers' Marketing of the Fund

The funds' financial performance was only one task and aspect of the fund manager's work. Marketing and sales to new investors was another task, as new inflow into the fund is essential to the fund company. As an interviewee expressed it:

> For the client, it is performance that is relevant, for a fund company there are two aspects of a good manager, one is performance but it is also selling the product. So, you want a communicative person who can explain to the clients what they do and how they are going to make money for the client. (8b)

Typically, a high-performing fund attracts new capital through reputation both of the fund and its fund manager. Therefore, there is strong competition for recruiting these persons. As one of the interviewees described it:

> Everyone wants to recruit the person or people who have the best performance and who could potentially move to another place and attract new capital and continue with this good return under their management instead, to attract more capital and so on, and make more money. (1)

On the other hand, being strong in marketing and sales and building your own brand as a fund manager can sometimes overrule actual performance. This concerns the fund manager being visible and communicative in the media and hence being perceived as an expert. One interviewee illustrated it with an actual example in the following way:

> But if we take a person like [X] for example. [...] He has three stars in Morningstar so he is like an average fund really, he is an average manager, but he is a very important marketing channel for [the fund company]. He is very good at... these different types of... seminars, presentation contexts. He is like a brand in himself.... I mean, if you were to ask... he has almost gotten past this performance thing.... If you were to ask, like how many stars does [X] have in his Sweden fund, you are asking... a thousand random or a hundred randomly selected people who invest in his fund. I promise, I don't know how many would get it right, but I think it is far fewer than half anyway. (1)

The value of inflow to the fund versus fund performance could potentially lead to an agency issue, as the example above illustrates. This is based on the trade-off between having a manager skilled at marketing and selling the fund versus having a manager being an expert in producing high financial performance.

3.4 Fund Managers' Other Criteria

In addition to performance, the criteria of being a good representative for the fund and a good colleague were both described as essential. As one of the recruiters describes performance in the form of at least a three-star rating by Morningstar is 'a kind of hygiene level' whereas being a good representative is 'a hugely important aspect.' This included being up to date with and following regulation.

> Performance is just one component in my view when I talk to our clients. It's not unimportant, but there are other things that are at least as important, and it often becomes, let's say, some kind of hygiene level, so to speak; 'That we want people who have, let's say, at least three stars in Morningstar if we're going to recruit managers. But then there are many other factors that are... also important for us as an organisation when it comes to culture and how one behaves in general and things like that. (1)

> And that's also a hugely important aspect, being a good representative for the fund company. [...] So it's important to be a good colleague, to be fair, to have nothing to hide, to handle the compliance-related parts that... are extremely important when it comes to maintaining order... how you communicate, that you, well, behave properly both as a person and in terms of following regulations in a fair and good way. That's really important. (1)

The quotes above emphasise the importance of being a good representative and demonstrating good fit with the company's culture. However, at times, a fund manager may need the confidence to challenge the existing order, to create effective fund performance:

> Yes, well that's where it's important that you have the right personality too. On one hand, you should... you need to fit in properly with the client. They usually have a corporate culture or way of working with their managers that you need to match, or sometimes you shouldn't match it because they need someone of a different kind. I mean if you have the same fund manager on all funds it becomes, yes, then that's what becomes index-like and that doesn't turn out so well. [...] They also need to... be good at collaborating, so we put a high value on that in these cases since you have a lot of collaboration with the analysts. (2)

According to a UK recruiter, in the past being a good representative both externally and to employees wasn't always considered essential. Instead, a strong financial performance could take precedence over their ability to represent the organisation. However, being a good representative and colleague wasn't neglected and described as a requirement 'regardless of how skilled you are'. Still, the interviewee also provided an example when the behavioural component was clearly overridden by financial performance. However, this pertained to a particular environment in a US investment bank. As the interviewee explained 'it becomes less and less common.'

3.5 Fund Managers' Performances and Type of Organisation

Several interviewees mentioned differences in cultures between funds that are owned and part of large organisations like banks or insurance companies and privately-owned fund companies. An example was different demands on you as a person and in larger organisations the need of being able to communicate internally with different groups, as one of the interviewees described:

> When it comes to, for example, if you're a large bank, it can be quite a lot about what you're like as a person, if you're going to be part of a large team, if you're going to be someone who will be out meeting with bank branches and meeting with advisors and somehow representing them. (1)

Another difference between being part of a large organisation and a privately-owned fund concerned bonuses. Larger organisations had limited possibility of awarding expert fund managers high bonuses. This could pose a challenge as there is intense competition for expert fund managers in the market. The most talented individuals are highly sought after, making it difficult to attract and retain them without competitive compensation packages. One of the interviewees, a CEO of a fund company, illustrated it with an example from his work experience:

> I actually think that when it comes to equity management, it's difficult to retain skilled managers if you don't have bonus opportunities. [...] That was probably what, at my previous workplace, they had quite brutal departures for a while, because they only had fixed salaries and when you had outperformed the index by five percentage points in a year and then got a three percent salary increase, that's when some managers started getting restless. (7)

> Then he started working with me at [Insurance company] and I was his manager there for a few years, and there they only had fixed salaries for the managers, and he was a straightforward person who after about one and a half to two years, during one of our salary discussions, told me that if I were to do this on my own or become a partner in the fund somehow or do it some other way, then I realise I would earn more money doing this thing that I enjoy. [...] That was his motivation for leaving [Insurance company] and going to another place where he has completely different incentives to... [...] take a larger piece of the pie, so to speak. (7)

Privately-owned funds differed from funds being owned by larger companies in other aspects as well. One example is the role of marketing and sales. Large organisations hamper the visibility of their managers in media, for example due to internal rules, whereas privately owned funds can let their fund managers be visible. One of the interviewees described it as a mutual relationship between the manager and the fund, the fund being marketed while at the same time the fund manager building his or her reputation. In the interview it was expressed in the following way:

> Yes, but there's one thing that I think is really important actually, and that's allowing managers to be rock stars. Like letting them answer questions from Dagens Industri [The leading Swedish Business paper] and get some media exposure. I think this is really important actually, partly because from a sales perspective it's good to get out there and be visible because as a manager you're actually also a salesperson, you should say, you need to build capital and you have to contribute to that, it's an important part of the whole thing. But I think it's such an important thing, because there is, I believe, at least one large bank that hasn't allowed their fund managers to answer questions from Dagens Industri without all answers going through compliance and like quite long processes, and then Dagens Industri isn't so interested, they want quick answers and brief reflections like that. [...] I actually think this is an important thing, and as a manager you also need to be a person who wants to stand on stage and answer questions if you want to be employable in the long term and also contribute to building more capital in the products. I think that's one thing, that you have to allow them to be... a 'rock star' might be pushing it, but you still have to let them be visible. (7)

To conclude, in particular for fund managers in privately owned funds, receiving an attractive compensation package and building your 'social capital' can be viewed as complementary aspects that reinforce each other. In line with this, from the perspective of the fund, a well-reputed fund manager can increase inflow to the fund. On the other hand, there is a risk of having the fund too closely connected to a specific fund manager as this can grant them excessive bargaining power in relation to the fund. In addition, this increases the risk of losing the fund manager to competing funds. Consequently, there is likely a balance in how much funds allow fund managers to build their own 'social capital' and maintaining the distinct value and identity of the fund itself. From the interviews it seems that this balance is clearly different between privately owned funds, which allow fund managers to build their own 'social capital' to a much larger extent than funds owned by larger companies like banks which focus on the identity of the fund itself as being part of the larger company.

4 Conclusions

This study contributes to our knowledge of what constitutes performance for an expert fund manager. By moving from the level of fund performance to that of the individual fund manager we show that performance by expert fund managers is far more complex than simple stock portfolio returns. Based on our definition of expertise—*superior performance* related to *representative tasks* (Ericsson and Lehmann 1996, p. 277)—our findings suggest that in addition to the core task of fund managers, that is, to generate superior performance to investors, a fund manager also has tasks related to other stakeholders, each task requiring its own performance. Consequently, it reveals several perspectives and stakeholders, demonstrating that expertise and expert performance in fund management extend beyond the financial returns of funds, encompassing a complex interplay of factors. This complexity includes potential agency conflicts where fund managers' interests may not align with investors' goals.

In the following we discuss these findings, summarised in Table 2. The first column disaggregates financial returns to investors into fund managers' tasks related to the stakeholders we have identified in the study. Based on the model of Berk and van Binsbergen (2015) the return to investors can mathematically be seen as fund value created (excess returns × assets under management) less return to fund owners, less cost of fund organisation, less pay to fund managers. The second column summarises our findings on the fund managers' performance of the respective task. In the following text we discuss these findings in depth.

Interviewees were well aware of the difficulties of assessing and measuring the financial performance of fund managers, that is, excess returns created. Reasons mentioned were the stochastic nature of the market and lack of long track records for fund managers due to short longevity and high turnover among fund managers (see also footnote 2). In addition, the difficulty of separating the performance of the fund manager from the fund was discerned. In practice, returns compared to an index or a 'sufficiently high rating' from a rating agency together with a proven, systematic and structured investment process, seemed to be a key criterion. This is well in line with the literature, which shows the methodological complexities of measuring fund performance (e.g., Barras et al. 2022; Harvey and Liu 2022) and fund managers' performance (Clare et al. 2022).

Table 2 Findings of fund managers' tasks and performance in relation to stakeholders

Fund managers' tasks (stakeholders in italics)	Fund managers' performance

Fund value created = excess returns × assets under management (AUM)	• Excess returns are difficult to assess and measure.
	    – High turnover and short longevity.
	    – Sufficiently high ranking, strategy and investment process.
	• Diminishing returns of scale.

Less return to *fund owners*	• Potential agency conflict with investors, as prioritising marketing ability of fund manager over returns can yield more returns to owners. • Important to be a good representative of the fund.
Less cost of *fund organisation*	• The role and contribution of the other members of the fund organisation has yet to be examined. • Important to be a good colleague.
Less pay to *fund manager*	• Pay and visibility are two important criteria for fund managers. This can vary depending on the type of owners of the fund.
= Value to *investors*	• Generating value to the investors can be seen as the core task of a fund manager.

This difficulty of measuring fund performance is also supported by Dahlquist and Ødegaard (2018). They carried out an extensive review of The Norwegian Bank's active management of the Government's Pension Fund Global. Their review raised several methodological problems when assessing the fund's active management results. Nonetheless, by using different methods and drawing on the latest academic knowledge they concluded that the active management returns and value added had been positive and substantial over the period January 1998 to June 2017, and January 2013 to June 2017. However, they recognised that the review lacks 'great statistical precision' (p. 2) especially when evaluating performance over the last years. This shows that evaluating fund performance in practice is a challenging and approximate task involving judgments by the evaluators, even in this large and ambitious assessment, drawing on substantial resources and expertise.

Moreover, our findings show that recruiters conducted a qualitative assessment of the fund managers' strategy and investment process when they assessed their performance. This can be viewed as providing deeper knowledge and understanding of how the fund manager creates value, and thus being more forward orientated than measuring past performance. Consequently, this ties into the concept of individual foresight as discussed in chapter 'Individual Foresight and Fund Management Expertise' in this volume. Given the limited understanding of the strategy and investment process, we recommend further investigation in future research, as these elements likely play a crucial role in fund manager performance (see also Cremers et al. 2019).

One question related to the fund managers' performance is whether performance is about excess returns and/or assets under management. Fund value created is calculated as excess returns times assets under management. Further complicating this is the complexity of decreasing returns to scale which has been shown in several studies (Barras et al. 2022; Pástor et al. 2022). Zhu (2018) argues that decreasing returns to scale implies that expertise in fund management—consistently superior performance over a longer period of time—should be measured as value added in accordance with Berk and van Binsbergen (2015). The reason is that (Zhu 2018, p. 115): 'Decreasing returns to scale at the fund level imply that the fund alpha and the fund size are not two independent entities. Thus, neither provides a complete picture of managerial skill.'

Moreover, the practical implications of diseconomies of scale may vary considerably across different fund types and markets. Large-cap and small-cap funds, for instance, could experience distinct forms of scale-related challenges, a reason being that large cap funds likely have more liquid stocks than small-cap funds. Similarly diminishing returns due to scale effects could be more accentuated in a small market like Sweden, in comparison with the US market.

Taken together, whether superior performance of an expert fund manager should be seen as generating excess return and/or fund value raises several questions. For example, is expertise of a fund manager generating high returns in a small fund lower than that of a fund manager in a larger fund generating lower returns but higher value created?

In addition to the task of generating excess return and/or fund value, we identified other tasks of fund managers. These relate to the fund owners and fund organisation:

the task of marketing and generating inflow to the fund, and the task of being a good colleague and fund representative. Whereas these tasks are somewhat self-evident, interviewees provided examples where they conflicted with the interest of generating excess returns, thus pointing to potential agency issues between investors and fund owners. This is in line with and further developed in the elaborated theoretical discussion on fund managers' accountability in chapter 'Analysing Fund Managers' Accountability' in this volume.

The role of marketing for increasing the fund size is mentioned by Berk and van Binsbergen (2015) in the example of the Magellan fund managed by Peter Lynch. However, they do not discuss potential conflicts of interest. Increasing the size of a fund can generate high value to the fund owners. Hence, they can gain on employing a fund manager with strong marketing skills rather than one who has less marketing ability but is stronger in generating returns. This is accentuated by the difficulty in assessing the performance of funds. This is further aggravated by the complexity of diminishing rate of returns of scale.

Being a good colleague and representative of the fund was viewed by recruiters as a prerequisite. In the past, this was not as strong a requirement as today. The recruiters emphasised that today this is a requirement, even though one gave an example of an investment firm that only chose performance. Hence, indicating that it can potentially be a trade-off. This is discussed in more detail in chapter 'Searching for Expert Fund Managers' in this volume, which explores what characteristics and requirements recruiters look for in expert fund managers.

Moreover, the findings showed that for fund managers, remuneration and visibility were important. Funds owned by larger organisations like insurance companies or banks could not provide as good compensation as privately owned funds. Similarly, visibility for the fund manager in the business press, for example, was more restricted. In a competitive market for fund managers, this indicates that privately owned funds have an advantage in recruiting and keeping the best managers. We have not found any previous studies examining this. However, Ibert et al. (2018) investigate management pay and fund revenues, indicating an agency friction between fund managers and owners. Based on Swedish data, they show that a 1% increase in fund revenues increases managers' pay by 0.15%. Thus, an increase in the fund size—assets under management—only leads to a relatively minor increase in pay for the fund manager. Our findings, in line with Ibert et al. (2018), show that there are several multifaceted relationships between fund managers, owners of the fund and investors in the fund.

Taken together, even though our study is explorative, it arguably contributes to our knowledge of what constitutes performance for an expert fund manager in several ways. Theoretically it applies the concept of expertise to fund management. Consequently, as outlined in Table 2, this adds to the model of Berk and van Binsbergen (2015) by revealing several tasks related to different stakeholders, each task with its own respective perspective on performance. Hence, the study illuminates the intricacies of tasks involving other stakeholders than the investors in the fund, not least difficult trade-offs between the tasks. Furthermore, the findings add to the literature on expertise by applying it in a domain which to the best of our knowledge has not previously been studied by scholars in expertise. In contrast to previous views in expertise (Kahneman and Klein 2009) the study arguably shows that fund management is an area benign for expertise. Whereas fund management has a large stochastic element—to a degree distinctive to the fund management domain—we suggest that the criteria of superior performance in fund management should be viewed as an average over several years. However, taken together, and as detailed in chapter 'Does Expertise Matter? Concluding Reflections' in this volume, the most important contribution is that the study opens up several avenues for future research examining the relationship between fund managers' expertise in various tasks and their corresponding performance, including potential agency conflicts between fund managers, fund owners, and investors.

For practitioners, the findings provide a holistic view of fund managers' tasks and stakeholders affecting value generated to investors in the fund. Together with the discussion of the concept of expertise, this could perhaps serve as a basis to increase investors' understanding of the interests of different stakeholders and potential conflicts of interest within fund management. Furthermore, the study provides an overview of the latest research that arguably supports that fund management lends itself to expertise.

This study has several limitations. Bearing in mind its explorative nature and limited number of interviews, the findings should be interpreted with caution. Moreover, we have not interviewed investors and their views of fund managers' expertise. Likewise, as the perspective is at the level of the individual fund manager, the role of the fund organisation and what expertise it contributes has yet to be examined. Still, we hope to increase the interest in understanding the complexities of expert fund managers' tasks and performance.

Acknowledgements The authors acknowledge financial support from the *Jan Wallander and Tom Hedelius Foundation* and the *Tore Browaldh Foundation* (*project: P22-0239*). We are thankful for valuable comments from the editor and our fellow authors of the book. We are also thankful for the support of the *Ingmar Bergman Foundation*, which allowed us to focus on our thinking and writing in the magical environment of the home of the late Ingmar Bergman.

References

Adams JC, Nishikawa T, Rao RP (2018) Mutual fund performance, management teams, and boards. J Bank Finance 92:358–368

Barras L, Gagliardini P, Scaillet O (2022) Skill, scale, and value creation in the mutual fund industry. J Finance 77:601–638

Berk JB (2005) Five myths of active portfolio management. J Portfolio Manag 31:27–31

Berk JB, Green RC (2004) Mutual fund flows and performance in rational markets. J Polit Econ 112:1269–1295

Berk JB, Van Binsbergen JH (2015) Measuring skill in the mutual fund industry. J Financ Econ 118:1–20

Böhm MJ, Metzger D, Strömberg P (2023) Since you're so rich, you must be really smart': talent, rent sharing, and the finance wage premium. Rev Econ Stud 90:2215–2260

Carhart MM (1997) On persistence in mutual fund performance. J Finance 52:57–82

Clare A, Sherman M, O'Sullivan N, Gao J, Zhu S (2022) Manager characteristics: predicting fund performance. Int Rev Financ Anal 80:102049

Cremers KM, Fulkerson JA, Riley TB (2019) Challenging the conventional wisdom on active management: a review of the past 20 years of academic literature on actively managed mutual funds. Financ Anal J 75:8–35

Csaszar FA (2012) Organizational structure as a determinant of performance: evidence from mutual funds. Strateg Manag J 33:611–632

Cuthbertson K, Nitzsche D, O'Sullivan N (2016) A review of behavioural and management effects in mutual fund performance. Int Rev Financ Anal 44:162–176

Dahlquist M, Ødegaard BA (2018) A review of Norges Bank's active management of the Government Pension Fund Global. Swedish House of Finance Research Paper, 18-7

Ericsson KA, Lehmann AC (1996) Expert and exceptional performance: evidence of maximal adaptation to task constraints. Annu Rev Psychol 47:273–305

Fama EF (1970) Efficient capital markets. J Finance 25:383–417

Fama EF, French KR (2010) Luck versus skill in the cross-section of mutual fund returns. J Finance 65:1915–1947

Gobet F (2016) Understanding expertise: a multi-disciplinary approach. Red Globe Press, London

Grant M, Nilsson F (2023) Intuitive expertise and financial decision-making. Routledge, London, New York

Harvey CR, Liu Y (2022) Luck versus skill in the cross section of mutual fund returns: reexamining the evidence. J Finance 77:1921–1966

Ibert M, Kaniel R, Van Nieuwerburgh S, Vestman R (2018) Are mutual fund managers paid for investment skill? Rev Financ Stud 31:715–772

Jensen MC (1968) The performance of mutual funds in the period 1945-1964. J Finance 23:389–416

Kahneman D, Klein G (2009) Conditions for intuitive expertise: a failure to disagree. Am Psychol 64:515–526

Khorana A, Servaes H, Wedge L (2007) Portfolio manager ownership and fund performance. J Financ Econ 85:179–204

Kosowski R, Timmermann A, Wermers R, White H (2006) Can mutual fund "stars" really pick stocks? New evidence from a bootstrap analysis. J Finance 61:2551–2595

Pástor L, Stambaugh RF, Taylor LA (2015) Scale and skill in active management. J Financ Econ 116:23–45

Pástor L, Stambaugh RF, Taylor LA, Zhu M (2022) Diseconomies of scale in active management: robust evidence. Crit Financ Rev 11:593–611

Shanteau J (1992) Competence in experts: the role of task characteristics. Organ Behav Hum Decis Process 53:252–266

Shanteau J (2015) Why task domains (still) matter for understanding expertise. J Appl Res Mem Cogn 4:169–175

Statistics Sweden (2025). https://www.statistikdatabasen.scb.se/pxweb/sv/ssd/. Accessed 28 May 2025

Swedish Investment Fund Association (2025) Årsrapport: Fondsparandet 2024. https://www.fondbo lagen.se/globalassets/faktaindex/manadsstatistik/arsrapport_2024.pdf. Accessed 14 Feb 2025

Zhu M (2018) Informative fund size, managerial skill, and investor rationality. J Financ Econ 130:114–134

Searching for Expert Fund Managers

Martin Abrahamson⊙ **and Michael Grant**⊙

Abstract Consistently outperforming the market is difficult if not impossible for an individual investor but also for a fund manager. Finance research indicates there are various profound skills in fund management. These include the ability to select stocks, effectively time the market, acquire and utilise (private) information, and maintain a disciplined investment strategy that avoids cognitive biases. These findings are inferred from analysis of data at the level of funds. Consequently, they do not say much about the skills and characteristics of an expert fund manager. For example, what are the abilities and traits of an expert fund manager who is skilled in timing and selecting stocks. Research on expertise shows that developing necessary abilities and skills in a domain requires an extended period of deliberate practice. This involves high-quality experience with feedback, reflection, and progressively increasing challenges. Drawing on literature in expertise and finance, this chapter explores fund manager expertise by interviewing recruiters of fund managers and fund CEOs to understand how they characterise expert fund managers.

Keywords Characteristics · Expertise · Financial management · Fund manager · Recruitment

1 Introduction

Stock market investors often claim that consistently outperforming the market is difficult, if not impossible. Others argue that the very essence of the fund industry is that it can be outperformed, but only by a few fund managers, the experts. The Holy Grail for fund market investors is obviously how to find the expert fund manager. However, for recruiters specialised in the fund industry, this is part of their daily

M. Abrahamson (✉) · M. Grant
Department of Business Studies, Uppsala University, Uppsala, Sweden
e-mail: martin.abrahamson@fek.uu.se

M. Grant
e-mail: michael.grant@fek.uu.se

© The Author(s), under exclusive license to Springer Nature Switzerland AG 2025
F. Nilsson (ed.), *Exploring Fund Management Expertise*, Contributions to Finance and Accounting, https://doi.org/10.1007/978-3-032-08545-0_3

work. In this chapter, we search for expert fund managers through the eyes of specialist recruiters. We explore their views and how they search: the signs, characteristics, typical career-building paths, and necessary experience for developing fund management expertise.

The assumption of this study is that there is expertise in fund management. An expert can in general be described as consistently performing better than average within a domain. Chevalier and Ellison (1999, p. 876) describe fund managers 'as skilled professionals.' From studies on other skilled professionals, e.g., auditors and M&A specialists, Grant and Nilsson (2023) describe an expert as someone who consistently shows superior performance in their profession for a long period of time (see chapter 'Performance and Fund Managers' Expertise' in this volume for an elaborated discussion on performance, including the definition of performance).

This is applicable to fund managers, but there is another component involved. Both the fund performance (compared to an index) and the fund manager are evaluated. The setting for a fund manager is to be evaluated continuously, in both the short and long term in a challenging environment. The market for fund managers is competitive, and consequently there is a high turnover among fund managers (Chevalier and Ellison 1999). Recent results show that a similarly high turnover is persisting in the twenty-first century (see Table 1 in chapter 'Performance and Fund Managers' Expertise' in this volume). Those that succeed are highly rewarded financially (Böhm et al. 2023).

Expertise in fund management essentially concerns active fund management, not passive funds. Active funds generally charge their investors fees that exceed index funds by a large margin. To be considered active, a fund has to deviate from the passive index of the market the fund invests in. Most countries have regulations for active fund management, for example, how much of the fund needs to be traded within a given time period or that the composition of the fund must deviate from the passive index (e.g., active share or tracking error). Hence, active funds are regulated to trade more than a certain minimum threshold and in order to be qualified to charge higher fees than index funds (also called passive funds). A down-side of the trading activity regulations can be that funds might overtrade, which can affect fund performance. Barber and Odean (2000, 2001, 2013) have shown that overtrading is a significant reason for underperformance among investors.

The employment risk shown in the high turnover of the highly competitive fund market affects managerial behaviour in active funds, where poor performance leads to dismissals (Cuthbertson et al. 2016). Cuthbertson et al. (2016, p. 170) also claim that 'herding behaviour is driven by a fear of conspicuous poor performance relative to peers.' For fund managers being evaluated regularly and benchmarked with both peers and passive index funds, we could assume that there is an issue of maintaining a balance between blending in with the herd and standing out in the crowd. Wulfmeyer (2016) shows that fund managers are prone to the disposition effect, that is, selling winners too early and keeping losers too long, and that this increases with the systematic risk level. Hence, we might expect fund managers to be associated with similar behavioural biases as non-professional investors. Nonetheless, lack of diversification is probably less significant for fund managers due to investment rules in the fund (Abrahamson 2016, 2020).

When searching for expertise it is necessary to separate the fund from the fund manager, in order to evaluate the latter. Clare et al. (2022) use manager characteristics (age and university degree) to predict fund performance, rather than using fund data. Hence, they show that the manager is of importance and that there might be a methodological problem using fund data instead of fund manager data, when evaluating fund managers' performance. Cuthbertson et al. (2016, p. 173) highlight the problem of the unit of analysis in the fund industry research. They state that, of the 'vast bulk of the fund performance literature we review, the unit of analysis is the fund rather than the manager.' By focusing on specialist recruiters who hire fund managers, we expect to find sought-after characteristics of fund managers rather than fund characteristics. The focus of this chapter is specialist recruiters' view of fund manager expertise and what they look for when recruiting an expert fund manager (or a promising future expert). Thereby, we contribute to the field with our focus on the individual fund manager, rather than the fund, when we explore fund manager expertise.

The findings of this study show that performance is recognised by fund management recruiters as a more difficult concept than one might think. Fund manager performance includes several aspects, depending on the stakeholder in question (this is elaborated further in chapter 'Performance and Fund Managers' Expertise' in this volume). Recruiters seem to search for individuals with grit, interest in the surrounding society, relations, nerdy almost obsessive interest in the field and an ability to balance herding with self-reliance. It seems like recruiters look for a blend of abilities, interest, education, personality and a sense of deliberate practice when they try to identify experts in the field, in other words, features rather similar to more general expertise characteristics, but applied to the fund industry and specific tasks of fund managers. Furthermore, fund manager experts are expected to be open to and recognise changes in the surrounding environment (the market) and adapt their investment strategy accordingly.

2   Searching for Expert Fund Managers

In this section we discuss a selection of finance studies related to characteristics of expert fund managers. This includes literature on challenging tasks where fund managers need to balance their behaviours and strategies, that is, passive versus active management, and herding versus conviction. Finally, we include a discussion of certain personality traits.

2.1   Characteristics of Fund Managers' Expertise

When recruiters are searching for a fund manager, they look for the best match for their client. According to Chevalier and Ellison (1999), active fund managers are expected to beat the market even after fees are taken from the return. Their results also show that university degrees and SAT-scores are positively related to the fund manager's performance later on in life. Additionally, attending a top-ranked university might assist in building personal networks that are important for future fund managers. Chevalier and Ellison (1999) also show that managers with the highest SAT-scores from universities systematically outperform other fund managers using risk-adjusted returns. Building on the methodology of Chevalier and Ellison (1999), Gallagher (2003) examines, in an Australian setting, portfolio managers' characteristics (such as the prestige of the university degree) in relation to performance and risk. He finds that active funds earn superior risk-adjusted return. Furthermore, his study shows that fund tenure, that is, several years with the same firm, is negatively related to risk.

Several studies show characteristics and skill sets for fund managers affecting performance. Fang and Wang (2015) describe a framework of fund manager characteristics and its effect on fund performance. They divide the skill of the fund manager into stock-picking ability and market-timing skill. Dahlquist et al. (2000) highlight the value added by active fund management when they evaluated funds adjusted for fees, in their study of fund characteristics and performance. Fang and Wang (2015) use gender, age, educational background, overseas experience, work experience, and professional qualification as independent variables to explain the excess risk and return as well as the stock-picking ability and market-timing skill of the fund manager. Their results show that even though their overall model explains most of the variation in the dependent variable(s) only a few of the independent variables are statistically significant. They find that both gender and educational level are significant, showing that female fund managers generally take slightly less risk, as do those with an advanced degree in business or economics. For timing skill and stock-picking ability, only a high academic degree (Master, Ph.D., or MBA) and CFA-certificate is statistically significant; all of them are positively related to stock-picking ability.

2.2   Persistence or Hot Hands

The debate on the value for investors in passive vis-à-vis active funds has been ongoing in the academic community for decades. Carhart (1997) finds no evidence of persistence in fund performance, which supports the idea that it is difficult, not to say impossible, to outperform the market over time. In contrast, Otero-González et al. (2022) state that for bond mutual funds, they find strong evidence of fund performance persistence. Additionally, they argue for the importance of rating agencies as a useful measure for persistent future fund inflow, where funds with higher ratings attract more inflow of capital.

In behavioural finance, one well-known fallacy is *hot hands* (originally from basketball), where previous success is falsely seen as a guarantee for future success. However, Hammouda et al. (2023) examine fund performance in Europe and show significant results for *hot hands*, i.e. that some funds deliver higher performance than others, period after period. They control for investment strategy and use risk-adjusted returns, and these results support the idea of fund management expertise. Hammouda et al. (2023) also show that portfolio turnover is negatively related to performance, showing that a more active fund is penalised in its trading, echoing the results of Barber and Odean (2000), for individuals.

2.3 Herding or Conviction

In a competitive market, one would need to stand out of the crowd in order to be noticed and build a reputation. Herding behaviour in financial terms could be seen as the opposite of standing out in the crowd, where an investor in the financial market would invest like the main stream of the market, that is, would invest like a passive fund or an index. In their review paper, Choijil et al. (2022) show that both the research interest and concern for herding behaviour in the financial markets have increased substantially during the last 30 years.

A herding-behaviour investment strategy might appear to reduce risk and put the investor closer to the passive index. This would make the investor look at least as successful as the average investor. For funds, a herding strategy could imply that the fund manager follows his/her peers, which is not necessarily the same as the passive index. However, the passive investment index will in a sense follow the general investor conviction, since the portfolio of the index follows the market as a whole. According to Jiang and Verardo (2018) funds using a herding strategy underperform their peers by more than 2% per year.

Even though underperforming your peers is not desirable, hiding within the herd, might also be a risk-reducing strategy. Casavecchia (2016) shows that fund managers who use a herding strategy have less capital redeemed by investors when they under-perform, compared with funds not following the herd. This could be counter to intuitive investor behaviour, since a fund manager who follows the herd is less likely to outperform than a fund manager with conviction to invest against the herd. In contrast to Casavecchia (2016), Liang et al. (2020) show that fund managers with strong conviction have more inflow when they outperform, but have less outflow when they underperform, compared to managers with more herding strategies. Jin et al. (2020) show similar results, with an inverse U-shape between conviction and subsequent performance, suggesting that a 'balanced' level of conviction, not too low or too high, delivers the best performance. Hence, the study shows that investors award fund managers with high conviction when they outperform but not necessarily when they underperform.

For individual investors, Barber and Odean (2000, 2001, 2013) show that over-trading is a significant reason for underperformance, with overconfidence being one explanation. Palomino and Sadrieh (2011) study the effect of investor overconfi-dence in investment decisions in financial institutions. They show that overconfident fund managers trade lower quantities than an ideal rational investor. In contrast, they also show that overconfident fund managers tend to overinvest in information acquisitions and, when they do, they overinvest in larger quantities compared to the rational investor. Thereby, they argue that overconfident fund managers either under- or over-invest rather than invest fully rationally.

Glebkin and Kuong (2023) argue that when large investors (large funds) do not trade based on asset fundamentals, they trade more aggressively and the price becomes less informative. Hence, the market efficiency is reduced. Together with investors with other investment strategies than asset fundamentals, this would cause asset prices to deviate from their fundamental values, causing even more over-trading. Glebkin and Kuong (2023, p. 1) suggest that '[T]his trading complementarity can engender three unconventional results: (i) increased competition among large investors makes all investors worse off, (ii) more precise private information reduces price informativeness, creating complementarities in information acquisition, and (iii) multiple equilibria emerge. Our results have implications for competition and transparency policies in financial markets.'

Jin et al. (2020) examine the role of conviction in fund management and its relation with the performance of the fund. They show that fund manager conviction—that is, how much the fund portfolio deviates from the benchmark index—increases after a period of both inferior and superior fund performance compared with the benchmark performance. Furthermore, Jin et al. (2020) describe an inverse relationship between conviction and future performance and the risk level of the fund, with high levels of conviction being followed by greater future risk and lower performance of the fund.

2.4   The Fund Manager: An Expert in Transition?

In the past, personality traits for expert fund managers, such as being a good colleague, were considered less important as long as the financial return was high. This is one view that we came across during our study and is in line with ten Brinke et al. (2018, p. 214): 'It is widely assumed that psychopathic personality traits promote success in high-powered, competitive contexts such as financial invest-ment.' However, in reality it shows the contrary, and in their study ten Brinke et al. (2018, p. 214) show that for hedge fund managers, 'greater psychopathic tenden-cies produced lower absolute returns than their less psychopathic peers.' They also show that 'managers with more narcissistic traits produced decreased risk-adjusted returns.' Holmén et al. (2023) use an experiment to study characteristics of finance professionals. They found that finance professionals—in their sample consisting of analysts, advisors, traders, brokers and fund managers—had higher levels of psychopathy, narcissism and Machiavellianism than the general population. Their results also suggest that finance professionals are less trustworthy and more selfish compared with the general population. Still, when Holmén et al. (2023) control for socio-economic background, the differences between the groups are less significant. This raises the question of whether recruiters are aware of these tendencies among candidates, and if so, how they should deal with it. Is it something to be preferred or avoided?

2.5   Key Insights from Literature

Taken together, previous research uses measurable characteristics, e.g., degree, SAT-scores, university reputation, age and gender. The studies examine how these characteristics affect fund manager performance. Connected to these measurable variables, there seems to be a rather standardised view of career building. This might be beneficial for developing expertise rather than being key indicators of an expert fund manager. Furthermore, studies suggest that even for expert fund managers there are difficulties in dealing with investment biases. There is also evidence of a tension between using herding behaviour as an investment strategy and building performance and reputation, especially since the work environment for fund managers is highly competitive and continually evaluated. Finally, a possible transition in skill set is highlighted, where there might be a tendency for recruiters to search for other, softer skills.

3   Finding Expert Fund Managers

To explore the expertise of fund managers empirically, we interviewed specialist recruiters. Our aim was to examine how they evaluate and find experts in fund management. This included what characteristics they look for and what expertise they associate with fund management. Each recruiter had extensive experience, having worked as recruiters for more than 20 years, with both domestic and international assignments. The Appendix describes the method used. The respondents are identified by number after each quote.

3.1   The Expert Fund Manager's Career

From the recruiters we seek a general path that shows how a fund manager starts building a career. As Gallagher (2003) suggests, a prestigious university degree is one important characteristic. This is supported by Fang and Wang (2015), who suggest that in particular an educational background in the form of an MBA or Chartered Financial Analyst positively affect future performance of the fund manager. However, education is only a starting point for becoming an expert. In line with this, one of the interviewees provided a more detailed description of how a typical fund manager with a 'solid academic background' develops into an expert, in the following quotes below.

> Well, a solid academic background, getting involved pretty early, maybe during your studies or through internships, getting to work on the inside, maybe first as an analyst in various forms, really analysing companies. And if you get the trust to be responsible for a number of companies early in your career, you grow with that too because you're interacting with senior stakeholders, which is good. You're in contact with portfolio managers, so you deliver, and

they are your clients, and there are many who cover certain companies, but it also becomes important that you can handle it and, relative to your competitors, the client notices who stands out. But then I think it could be good if, contrary to expectations, you don't have a master's degree, that maybe you take a CFA certification along the way, maybe prefer that if you have a bachelor's degree, that you take it rather than an MBA, because the latter seems more management oriented. So, I think it's good to work for a while, and then I think you get more out of a CFA if you take it a little later, we like to see that. (5)

A solid educational background and relevant industry experience were requirements and sorting criteria in a first stage of recruitment. This agrees with previous studies which show that a strong economic education from a reputable university is common for fund managers (e.g., Chevalier and Ellison 1999; Fang and Wang 2015). Recruiters describe that some fund firms can also prefer a specific background when choosing interns. This will test the suitability for some skill sets of the applicants for their future careers. As respondent 5 continues the quote, speaking of early career jobs.

Also, which brands you have worked for, we find that quite exciting because where you get early responsibility, where you might get to work the first few years, because there are others who have so many people that there are some who are more senior than you are, you can see differences in places where you get to take on a fairly large responsibility early and grow in that way. [...], that you also understand governance, and it's important that there is order and structure rather than just selling your funds. Also, how things have gone and what your role in it was, if you were an assistant portfolio manager to a star, that doesn't mean you're a fantastic portfolio manager, because it was the other one, but what role you had. The more you can show what you've done and that it has gone well, maybe not just in a market that has gone well but also in a market that may have been a little more challenging, those are things we also talk about. (5)

However, interviewees also mentioned that experience from other industries could be important for developing fund manager expertise. As illustrated below, another recruiter emphasised the ability for fund managers to balance financial models with intuition and their perception of society, including adapting their fund management strategies to changes in the environment.

Having the right formal competences and a suitable academic education, this expertise is hard. I still find that those who are persistent and skilled over time, they have the ability to use both quantitative methods, their intuition, they are usually very interested in society, they often have a philosophy and a model that they adhere to. They are not so easily influenced; of course, they are influenced, but they question what happens based on their worldview. (1)

3.2 Persistence of Fund Managers

The recruiters searched for fund managers with experience of active trading, not too close to index trading. Furthermore, working within different contexts and in multiple organisations was seen as valuable experience.

We also think it's good that you've seen a few different environments. [...] I think you have more to offer a new employer if you've seen more, but also that, maybe you've had it a little too easy sitting in the same place and staying close to the index for many years, and then maybe it's good if you're a little above the index, but it can be good to have shown it in other environments as well. (5)

To show that you have been active is seldom enough, rather fund managers have to show performance in several environments. Considering Jin et al. (2020), where investors follow the high-conviction managers and increase the inflow when they outperform. To hire a high-conviction fund manager with a solid investor base is a way to attract new investors. Being able to show that the conviction has been tested in several environments demonstrates a higher resilience and could be considered an asset to presumptive employers. The recruiters used references to a wide extent. Personal knowledge of both the referent and the candidate was used, but for junior fund managers the recruiters were more prone to utilise tests, as discussed below.

> If you're recruiting someone who has worked as a Swedish equity manager for ten years with okay or good results, you rarely conduct any knowledge tests, and you hardly even do any aptitude tests either. You feel like, no, but this is it. We rely heavily on references for people. I think that's important, both the references the person provides themselves but also that we speak with—since we've been doing this for so long—it's rare, at least within certain niches like this one, for a person to show up whom we've never heard of or don't know someone who has worked with them before. So, I would say that performance is some sort of hard fact. As a client, you might say something like, 'We can't hire someone who has a one or a two in [Rating agency] because we can't sell that product, it's not possible.' (1)

With this statement, we sense the heavy weight of references and the importance of previous relationships including ability to work together with others. However, the interviewee also addresses the threshold of previous performance. Furthermore, one well-known secret in finance is that there are few or no guarantees for future performance based on past performance (i.e., hot hands fallacy). However, according to Chevalier and Ellison (1999) previous performance is used among investors to select assets and it affects their expectations for future performance.

> We look a lot towards the future, trying to assess whether the candidate can foresee what's around the corner. We try to evaluate how this person thinks about future threats, opportunities, ESG, whatever it may be, strategies around such things. (4)

This indicates that even though the recruiters and their clients obviously are aware of the well-known story of performance prevalence, there appears to be a value to the threshold on past performance, and that the past performance cannot be too low regardless of previous references of the manager characteristics.

3.3   Expert Fund Manager Characteristics

When it comes to what characteristics, recruiters look for in an expert fund manager, previous research mentions the value of educational level and SAT-scores (Chevalier and Ellison 1999), while others use gender, age, overseas experience, work experience, and professional qualification (Fang and Wang 2015). To add to those categories, we asked the specialist recruiters to explain some general characteristics. An example of this is quoted below.

> We speak with informal references, maybe from a previous workplace, and ask about how this person performed and personality aspects. Our evaluation is based on our four criteria [setting strategy, executing for results, leading teams, relationship and influences] that's what our assessment is based on. Is this a person who can see around the corner and understand where asset management is heading? And, you know, if we look at active management, there are a lot of trends in that area. Can we discuss these trends? And you get a sense of the person's intellect, that is part of our assessment. (4)

Staying on top of trends and anticipating new trends and market swings are also useful skills or characteristics to have in this area of expertise. How this is articulated and argued seems to be important to recruiters. From studies of other industries, passion and grit are mentioned as characteristics often connected to expertise (Grant and Nilsson 2023). Hence, it can be expected that this also would be found in the fund management industry.

> I would say there are all kinds of variations in this [finding the expert fund manager]. But as I said, this expertise is difficult to see. I still find that those who are persistent and skilled over time and have the ability to use both quantitative methods and their intuition. They are usually very interested in society, often have a philosophy and a model they stick to. They aren't easily influenced, of course, they are influenced—but they question what's happening based on their own view of the world. [...] I mean, like this passion for what they're doing and this broad interest in society that I believe successful managers actually have. Being curious, and really good at both adopting new things, seeing what's coming, but also the idea of 'kill your darlings' and not getting too attached to your holdings. I think skilled managers are good at renewing their portfolios when the market and conditions change. (1)

Apart from the interest and knowledge of the fund and its holdings, being open, curious and in connection with society seem to be important for expertise of fund managers. A fund manager's understanding of how the fund and its investments are affected by macro trends and conditions in society appear to add value to the fund. This suggests that it could affect the performance of the fund, even though it is not seen ex-ante in the performance, at least not as measured financial return.

> The important thing is that you are a person who is structured, has an investment philosophy and a process, and so on, which perhaps aligns with the way this fund is managed. (1)

The ability to stick to the investment strategy you have developed, but also to balance that with adapting your portfolio to changes in market conditions also seems crucial for expertise in the fund industry.

> Usually, you don't get very far if you're not presentable and well-groomed, but questions about ethics and morals can come up later—how you behave, how you've treated colleagues, if you're a man, how you've treated women, or if you have a particular view that doesn't sit well with others, then it's a no-go. You can be excluded, no matter how skilled you are. Then there are also personal qualities that fit the situation you're in, which often becomes the deciding factor. So, if you're not ready for a major transformation journey, and perhaps that type of person has a more traditional profile, you might lean toward something more conventional for steady growth in a calm environment, which can be decisive. (5)

Taken together, we find evidence that performance measured as past financial returns are important. In addition, some personal characteristics are also sought after. How fund managers have performed in the relationship with previous co-workers but also during various market conditions seem valued. The recruiters appear to seek characteristics beyond financial returns and argue that some behaviours would not be accepted regardless of past returns.

3.4   The Importance of Performance and Failures

The fund managers are regularly evaluated, which affects them, their strategy and the fund's customers. Something not often mentioned in previous studies of fund managers is how expertise is developed. Research shows that deliberate practice is vital in developing expertise. This means repetition, feedback, feedforward, reflection and a gradually increasing level of challenge. Consequently, admitting, allowing and of course learning from mistakes are essential for acquiring expertise, as proven in other professions, and should be similar for fund managers. Hence, reflecting on failures and the ability to reason on how periods of low performance is dealt with, is important, when searching for expert fund managers.

> It's happened more than once that a manager [tells the recruiter] has run into trouble, espe-
> cially if you can get under their skin a bit regarding [questions about] tough periods, when
> things really went against them, to see that they didn't stop functioning as a person. I don't
> envy people managing funds that drop by 40–50 percent. But it's always interesting to see
> how they handle it compared to how they might have handled 2020 and 2021 when those
> same funds went up by 50–60 percent. [...] But to separate different things from each other
> and be open and communicative about it, like now it's tough and now it's going well and so
> on, without letting it affect you too much. (1)

> We look more at the importance of having failed at some point. And what did they learn from
> this? To gain that knowledge about the candidate, what did they learn when things went well,
> but also when things went bad? Because everyone who's managed money or is a manager
> has experienced that, and it's important for us to see how they talk about those issues and
> how they discuss the negative side of management. When things go wrong, what happens?
> What do they do? What is their strategy around it? That's something we try to dig into. [...]
> It's more talking about how someone handles adversity. How do they handle certain things?
> We try to gain an understanding of that. I think those aspects are really important. (4)

As with examining expertise in other fields, the recruiters are keen on knowing how the fund managers react to failure. The fund industry often has long investment horizons and therefore a high degree of forecasting (where the concept of foresight may be used as a tool, see chapter 'Individual Foresight and Fund Management Expertise' in this volume). This means at the same time dealing with stochastic elements together with an information overload and a vast number of actors who want to affect decisions. One specific source of failures for fund managers is their investment strategy, and another is how they handle underperformance especially during a market shift. The recruiters wanted to get the personal reactions but more importantly catch how knowledge was developed and discussed, in the actual situation and market environment. The fund manager's role is also important for assessing the performance during the failure, as this might explain whether the underperformance is due to the fund manager or has a more structural cause.

3.5 Herding or Conviction

Within a field that is known for having a stochastic element, as theory and the literature tell us, it is hard to consistently outperform the market (or your peers). Fund managers are expected to perform better than the individual investor in their stock market investments on a risk-adjusted basis. Generally, we expect this is due to the information on the market being less evenly distributed than perfectly symmetric. This contrasts to the efficient market hypothesis which typically assumes symmetric information for all market participants. We expect fund manager experts to be immune, or at least less prone, to investment biases. This includes common biases such as disposition effect, anchoring, home bias, under- or overreaction to stock movements, and under- or overtrading. The information advantage that fund managers presumably possess and the resistance to bias should provide fund managers consistent advantage over time, which is something to consider when explaining outperformance. However, the information advantage seems harder to maintain in the information era, with big data and AI able to handle vast amounts of information in an instant. Biases would still separate experts from 'novices' if fund manager experts were resistant to biases. A bias can be an emotional attachment to a certain company, as illustrated in the following quote.

> I also believe that fund managers, just like us individuals, can fall in love with a company, thinking, 'This is such a great company, they're the best in the world,' but you're the only one who cares about what they're doing. (1)

The above example suggests that we can expect fund managers to be aware of biases, but not immune. This only makes fund managers human. Experience of biases is shared by novices as well as experts, thus providing another explanation to the struggle expert fund managers have in consistently trying to beat the market.

> That's where I think leadership in asset management comes into play. You say you're going to be long-term, but at the same time, these people are evaluated on a daily basis. And how does that affect them? It's not just that the market is behaving irrationally (laughs), but as a manager, you can also lose confidence if people start questioning what you're doing, despite explaining, - 'Yes, but I'm following this strategy, we agreed on this. That was yesterday, we agreed on that then, but now things have gone badly, so we don't agree on it anymore, and so on. [...]' And if things start going badly, it's easy to waver in your conviction. (1)

The interviewees described that fund managers have a clear overarching investment strategy for the fund. The fund manager has one-to-one meetings with major clients to explain the strategy, in several cases even each specific investment of the fund. Obviously, when handling other people's money, there is a need for trust in the fund manager from the client/investor. There are also expectations of what the fund manager should do and how the investment should perform.

> But when things go badly, then everything is questioned, even though the person who is under-performing might have a much more well-thought-out investment process and a philosophy that holds up over time, while the one who is doing really well short-term… two years later, that person might crash and burn, and it will be a big mess. So, it's a… it's a special world in that sense. (1)

Even with a previously proven, well-functioning investment strategy, the stochastic elements of the financial markets will affect fund performance. Hence, the fund manager–client relationship is under constant pressure of uncertainty and adapting the strategy without changing it (too much).

3.6   Fund Managers: Expertise in Transition?

'Being a decent person and a good colleague, I think, is becoming more and more important.' (1). This quote illustrates how a specialist recruiter describes changing demands of characteristics that an expert fund manager of today should have. The recruiters speak of a shift in focus from solely financial performance to something beyond that. Being in line with the society, building teams of your co-workers and being a good colleague seems to be more important than before, in short illustrated by this quote. The fund manager still needs to be good at investing and upholding a decent financial performance of the fund. Hence, in addition there are several other aspects that fund managers also have to excel in.

> If you're narrowing it down on any search today, it's very much around EQ and it's very much around the softer skills. You know most of the time you can assume that someone is there [to recruit], if they have had the right relevance and experience. They have worked in the industry for many years. You can assume that they are a very good practitioner within that industry and therefore what we are typically looking for now, that more clients are looking for, it is much more client focused. Plus, if we went back say five years or so looking at the product and how can we build the product, how can we grow that product piece today is very much around the client focus, the customer focus, the softer pieces around that, so having individuals who are much more multinational. So, understanding of different cultures, maybe worked overseas, or worked with different jurisdictions. Obviously D&I [diversity and inclusion] is a key part I would say 40% of our short list should be diverse and I will say the purpose of social responsibility is key today as well. It is high on the agenda. It's always that somebody who is much more forward thinking, innovative, someone who has a change mindset. And aside from what I've just mentioned, the governance piece is key as well. (9)

> It's a changed mindset, it takes one who loves the challenge of taking on development, building teams, growing teams, building a succession beneath them as well. It's a very different person to the one that you saw 10 years ago. And I was actually talking to [CEO of financial firm] about it and, I said to her, what is it that gets you out of the bed in the morning? She said that years ago, it was just about making money. Now it's about making a difference. (9)

Studies have problematised and changed the methods of performance measures (e.g., Barras et al. 2022; see also chapter 'Performance and Fund Managers' Expertise' in this volume). However, softer skills have not been highlighted by research in fund management, and we have not seen it measured in the fund rankings so far. Hence, in coming years we might see a shift in the underlying data and criteria from rating agencies. In recent years we have seen a rapid growth of robotics or AI-traded funds. Thus, we could also expect an interest and demand for harder skills like tech, programming and AI.

> I mean, take these quant funds for instance, where decisions are more made by computers, removing the emotional aspect of owning companies or thinking something is fantastic, or whatever it may be—it's just cold facts that guide the decisions. I'm not saying it results in better management, but some want to eliminate the human factor as much as possible. Then, of course, it's humans who program these algorithms, but that's another story. So… no, but I think skilled managers succeed in, as much as possible, viewing the world as it is. (1)

There are changes in the context of fund management due to tech innovations, with growing investments in non-actively managed funds, for example, index fund, ETFs and robotics or AI traded funds (see also chapter 'Artificial Intelligence in Discretionary Fund Management' in this volume, which focus on AI and fund managers). Building expertise in new areas takes time, even though some spill-over skills might increase the speed of adapting to new tasks or developing domains.

> [...] much more focus on sustainability issues. What experience do they have of sustainability in different dimensions, in these roles? In sustainable investments, there are people clearly responsible for that, but there aren't many with long experience in it. Some have the title, but when you look at their CVs, you see they've stepped into the roles, but they may neither have the relevant education nor extensive experience, yet they are titled responsible for sustainable investments. (5)

> I think going back a few years, it was very much selling a product or you were managing your fund. It's much more sort of collegiate now. [...] So, you still need the expertise, and you still need to be able to manage money and still need to invest it wisely and you still need to be doing all of that. But I think if you're managing your customer, you know your customer better. [...] Everyone is becoming more of a specialist now. I mean if you domestically had this conversation five years ago, we have just had to order and name you the best five [fund managers]. Now I can still do the same, but they are the best, in sustainability, others the best in equities. That's changed. (9)

Taken together, the recruiters tell stories of changes in the fund industry, with softer skills and more complex measures of evaluating. This would also call for new more complex ranking criteria with performance measures beyond financial return of the fund. The demand for knowledge of sustainability seems evident (see chapter 'Integrating ESG Information in Active Fund Management' in this volume, which focuses on ESG in fund management). There is also more demand for being a team player than before. Moreover, the accountability might be affected by the change to teamwork, since there is not one sole fund manager to be held accountable (see chapter 'Analysing Fund Managers' Accountability' in this volume, where accountability of fund managers is discussed and problematised).

4 Conclusions

Specialist recruiters searching for fund management expertise seem to be proof in themselves that expertise exists, and that some fund managers perform better than others. According to these recruiters, fund managers often have a similar career path, with a base in substantial and relevant academic education, typically having achieved high grades from reputable universities. Moreover, recruiters search for candidates who have had responsibility early in their career, individuals who survive as well as perform despite high turnover and on average short longevity of fund managers. The stochastic nature of the stock market means that it is inevitable that fund managers will sometimes make mistakes and fail. Consequently, being able to reflect on and learn from their shortcomings or failures was essential. Furthermore, expert fund managers should be interested in society at large and have a nerdy, almost obsessive interest in their assets under management. Taken together these findings suggest that developing fund management expertise have strong similarities with those in other financial domains. In other words, expertise is developed through feedback, reflection, and gradually increasing challenges over several years, also highlighting the importance of having grit, being strongly motivated and showing persistence (Grant and Nilsson 2023).

Another balancing act we found is to handle the competition in the industry, with continuous performance evaluations, vis-à-vis an index and peers, and be different enough to outperform these, and, at the same time, not to take more risk than the market allows at the time. This suggests that the fund manager needs to have a conviction and stick to it yet be ready to adapt to changing market conditions, which connects to the adaptability of an expert as defined by Ward et al. (2018, p. 42[1]):

> Timely changes in understanding, plans, goals, and methods in response to either an altered situation or updated assessment of the ability to meet new demands, that permit successful efforts to achieve intent [...], or successful efforts to realise alternative statements of intent that are not inconsistent with the initial statement but more likely to achieve beneficial results under changed circumstances. (Ward et al. 2018, p. 42)

Another finding is the significance of the fund manager's ability to describe and reason about the investment strategy, which could be seen as the fund manager's 'contract' with the investor. One way of limiting the risk of substantially underperforming your peers involves a herding strategy or at least a herding behaviour. It is plausible that fund managers try to avoid herding and other investor biases. But we can also find reasons for them to use this as a risk-reducing mechanism, even though it on average lowers their performance (Jiang and Verardo 2018). In contrast to herding an investment strategy built solely on self-reliance could be a risk. It would put the fund manager in a difficult situation when the market is not in the favour of the fund manager's strategy. The fund manager needs to convince the investors, and at the same time there is a risk of self-doubt. In summary, we argue that a trademark

---

[1] In the article the second part of the quote is in italics, highlighting an extension of the previous definition of adaptability.

of fund management expertise is to balance self-reliance with adaptability to new market conditions.

The recruiters painted a picture of searching for other types of fund managers than a few years or decade ago, with more emphasis on softer skills, sustainability, and governance. They seek not only the next fund manager with the highest stock market returns of the fund, rather fund managers who prevail in several other areas. The recruiters search for management skills, to join or lead a team, and applicants that show that they can be a good colleague. These results are in line with studies that emphasise other values in addition to financial return, as signs of fund management skills and expertise (Barras et al. 2022; ten Brinke et al. 2018). Our contribution to the literature on fund manager expertise comes from a focus on the fund manager (rather than the fund), supporting Clare et al. (2022) and Cuthbertson et al. (2016) in their notes that most previous studies tend to evaluate the fund rather than the fund manager (when evaluating fund manager expertise). We also contribute through adding the recruiters view of fund manager expertise. We highlight what characteristics or signs the recruiters look for when they need an expert fund manager, e.g., grit, clear investment strategy, adaptability, investment failures (and how you deal with them), longevity and performance in different market sentiments. We also note that softer skills, sustainability and collegiality are sought after, especially in recent years. Hence, we show that individual characteristics include more than previous studies tend to use, e.g., age and university degree. Even though we can't offer a simple solution or one sole indicator for investors to seek for, when selecting their fund (and fund manager), we still believe that we offer some insights. For practitioners within the industry, our results might serve as a sign of shift in what recruiters seek. For investors this might serve as call for the necessity to discuss the values in fund manager performance and to understand the complex role and tasks of fund managers.

This study has several limitations. First, considering its explorative nature and limited number of interviews, the findings should be interpreted with caution. Second, the aim was to explore fund manager expertise through the eyes of specialist recruiters. The recruiters were indeed experienced in the fund industry. However, some of them currently recruit not only fund managers, but also fund CEOs, as seen in some of the quotes where fund CEOs are mentioned. Third, the results presented in this chapter are far from conclusive, and the design is limited to exploring the area with assistance of a few experienced specialist recruiters. Still, we hope to generate a greater interest in understanding the characteristics of expert fund managers. As detailed in chapter 'Does Expertise Matter? Concluding Reflections' in this volume, we highlight several promising directions for future investigation.

Acknowledgements The authors acknowledge financial support from the *Jan Wallander and Tom Hedelius Foundation* and the *Tore Browaldh Foundation* (*P22-0239*). We thank the editor and our fellow authors of the book for valuable comments. We are also thankful for the support of the *Ingmar Bergman Foundation*, which allowed us to focus on our thinking and writing in the magical environment of the home of the late Ingmar Bergman.

References

Abrahamson M (2016) Rookies to the stock market: a portrait of new shareholders. Res Int Bus Finance 38:565–576

Abrahamson M (2020) Shareholders and cherry-picking IPOs: studies on shareholders, initial public offerings and firm ownership structure. Doctoral theses no. 203, Department of Business Studies, Uppsala University, pp 1–58

Barber BM, Odean T (2000) Trading is hazardous to your health: the common stock investments performance of individual investors. J Finance 55:773–806

Barber BM, Odean T (2001) Boys will be boys. Gender, overconfidence and common stock investments. Q J Econ 116:261–292

Barber BM, Odean T (2013) The behavior of individual investors. In: Constantinides GM, Harris MM, Stulz RM (eds) Handbook of the economics of finance, vol 2, Part B. Elsevier, pp 1533–1570

Barras L, Gagliardini P, Scaillet O (2022) Skill, scale and value creation in the mutual fund industry. J Finance 77:601–638

Böhm MJ, Metzger D, Strömberg P (2023) Since you're so rich, you must be really smart': talent, rent sharing, and the finance wage premium. Rev Econ Stud 90:2215–2260

Carhart M (1997) On persistence in mutual fund performance. J Finance 52:57–82

Casavecchia L (2016) Fund managers' herding and the sensitivity of fund flows to past performance. Int Rev Financ Anal 47:205–221

Chevalier J, Ellison G (1999) Are some mutual fund managers better than others? Cross-sectional patterns in behavior and performance. J Finance 54:875–899

Choijil E, Espinosa Méndez, Wong W-K, Vieito JP, Batmunkh M-U (2022) Thirty years of herd behavior in financial markets: a bibliometric analysis. Res Int Bus Finance 59:101506

Clare A, Sherman M, O'Sullivan N, Gao J, Zhu S (2022) Manager characteristics: predicting fund performance. Int Rev Financ Anal 80:1–11

Cuthbertson K, Nitzsche D, O'Sullivan N (2016) A review of behavioural and management effects in mutual fund performance. Int Rev Financ Anal 44:162–176

Dahlquist M, Engström S, Söderlind P (2000) Performance and characteristics of Swedish mutual funds. J Financ Quant Anal 35:409–423

Fang Y, Wang H (2015) Fund manager characteristics and performance. Invest Anal J 44:102–116

Gallagher DR (2003) Investment manager characteristics, strategy, top management changes and fund performance. Account Finance 43:283–309

Glebkin S, Kuong JC-F (2023) When large traders create noise. J Financ Econ 150:1–41

Grant M, Nilsson F (2023) Intuitive expertise and financial decision-making. Routledge, Abingdon, New York

Hammouda A, Saed A, Vidal M, Vidal-Garcia J (2023) On the short-term persistence of mutual fund performance in Europe. Res Int Bus Finance 65:101963

Holmén M, Holzmeister F, Kirchler M, Stefan M, Wengström E (2023) Economic preferences and personality traits among finance professionals and the general population. Econ J 133:2949–2977

Jiang H, Verardo M (2018) Does herding behavior reveal skill? An analysis of mutual fund performance. J Finance 73:2229–2269

Jin L, Taffler R, Esraghi A, Tosun OK (2020) Fund manager conviction and investment performance. Int Rev Financ Anal 71:1–15

Liang J, Taffler R, Eshraghi A, Tosun OK (2020) Fund manager conviction and investment performance. Int Rev Financ Anal 71:101550

Otero-González L, Leite P, Durán-Santomil P, Domingues R (2022) Morningstar star ratings and the performance, risk and flows of European bond mutual funds. Int Rev Econ Financ 82:479–496

Palomino F, Sadrieh A (2011) Overconfidence and delegated portfolio management. J Financ Intermed 20:159–177

ten Brinke L, Kish A, Keltner D (2018) Hedge fund managers with psychopathic tendencies make for worse investors. Personal Soc Psychol Bull 44:214–223

Ward P, Gore J, Hutton R, Conway GE, Hoffman RR (2018) Adaptive skills as the conditio sine qua non of expertise. J Appl Res Mem Cogn 7:35–50
Wulfmeyer S (2016) Irrational mutual fund managers: explaining differences in their behavior. J Behav Finance 17:99–123

Judgments and Decisions by Expert Fund Managers

Martin Abrahamson⊙ and Michael Grant⊙

Abstract This chapter explores how expert fund managers exercise judgment and make decisions, that is, the decision-making process. The study draws on explorative interviews with fund managers and other actors in the fund industry together with insights from previous studies on the decision-making processes of financial experts. The findings identify three areas. First, they indicate that intuition and heuristics are vital in expert fund managers' judgments and decisions, and hence that fund managers' decision-making consists of qualitative and quantitative assessments using intuition and analysis. This contrasts with a view of decision-making using sophisticated models for optimal asset allocation and detailed valuations of companies, and where the use of intuition and heuristics leads to erroneous decisions. Second, the study indicates a salient role of investment strategy for communicating with investors and highlights the high uncertainty of the environment in which fund managers' decision-making is taking place. Third, the study consequently suggests that the environment is prone to emotions and therefore that strategies for managing these are essential for effective decision-making. This also pertains to the ability to be decisive in spite of a sense of high uncertainty, to avoid decision paralysis for fear of making the wrong decision.

Keywords Expertise · Fund manager · Decision-making · Intuition · Heuristics

M. Abrahamson (✉) · M. Grant
Department of Business Studies, Uppsala University, Uppsala, Sweden
e-mail: martin.abrahamson@fek.uu.se

M. Grant
e-mail: michael.grant@fek.uu.se

© The Author(s), under exclusive license to Springer Nature Switzerland AG 2025   47
F. Nilsson (ed.), *Exploring Fund Management Expertise*, Contributions to Finance and
Accounting, https://doi.org/10.1007/978-3-032-08545-0_4

1   Introduction

Judgments and decisions about what stocks to buy, sell or hold are vital, if not the essence of an equity fund manager's tasks.[1] To be characterised as an expert fund manager, the individual's judgments and decisions presumably need to lead to superior performance over a long period of time (see chapter 'Performance and Fund Managers' Expertise' in this volume for an elaborated definition). However, there is a significant lack of knowledge when it comes to the performance of individual expert fund managers, as the majority of research and understanding of fund management performance is based on quantitative studies at the fund level, rather than the individual level (Clare et al. 2022). This pertains not only to the characteristics of expert fund managers but also how expert fund managers reach judgments and make decisions, that is, the decision-making process. In this chapter we investigate this through exploratory interviews and by drawing on insights from prior studies on the decision-making processes of financial experts.

Previous research on financial decision-making suggest that experts rely on varying combinations of intuitive and analytical processes, drawing on their deep and long experience in the domain, e.g., auditing, mergers and acquisitions (Backman et al. 2024; Grant and Nilsson 2020). It appears that financial decision-making depends less on models and more on the combination of intuition and expertise, so called intuitive expertise (Grant and Nilsson 2023). Moreover, cognitive research suggests that heuristics are used for reaching effective judgments in complex financial settings (Gigerenzer and Gaissmaier 2011). In contrast to this, fund management is typically portrayed as being immersed in analytical models and tools. Effective judgments based on intuitive expertise can hardly be discerned in the literature, where the perspective rather is that intuition and heuristics should be avoided as they lead to behavioural biases (Hirshleifer 2015). The context of fund management can be seen, as in research on financial decision-making, as involving a high degree of uncertainty, prone to triggering emotions. However, even if this suggests that fund managers' judgments and decisions regarding their fund portfolios evince similarities with what we know from other studies of financial decision-making: there is a dearth of knowledge about fund managers' decision-making.

To explore how fund managers make judgments and decisions, we interviewed five highly experienced persons both within and outside funds. The interviews were adapted to the specific category of the interviewee (e.g., fund managers and recruiters), but underlying the interviewees was a quest to capture how the interviewee perceived expert fund managers' decision-making. In this way we obtained

---

[1] Judgment can be described as 'the capacity to recognize relationships, draw conclusions from evidence, and make critical evaluations of events and people' (APA 2025), and decision as a choice 'between two or more alternatives' (APA 2025). Decision-making is similarly to financial decision-making seen as a process consisting of judgments and decisions leading up to the commitment to buy, sell or hold a stock (Grant and Nilsson 2023). In practice it can be difficult to make a distinction between judgments and decisions. Hence, in this chapter we focus on decision-making from the perspective of judgmental tasks and do not make a distinction between judgments and decisions.

multiple perspectives on fund managers judgments and decisions. For a detailed description see the Appendix.

The findings of this study highlight three areas. First, they suggest that intuition and heuristics are vital in expert fund managers' judgments and decisions, creating a picture of fund managers' decision-making as consisting of qualitative and quantitative assessments using intuition and analysis. This contrasts with a view of decision-making based on sophisticated models for optimal asset allocation and detailed valuations of companies, with intuition and heuristics seen as leading to erroneous decisions (Hirshleifer 2015). Second, the study indicates a salient role of investment strategy for communicating with investors and supports the view that the fund manager's decision-making is in an environment characterised by high or even extreme uncertainty. Third, the study suggests that the environment is prone to emotions, which therefore makes it essential to have strategies for managing these feelings in effective decision-making. This also pertains to the capacity to be decisive in spite of the face of high uncertainty and thereby avoid decision paralysis stemming from fear of making the wrong decision. Consequently, managing emotions also concern the ability to make decisions while being aware that some of them will lead to poor results.

2   Literature Review

A common cognitive perspective used when studying judgments and decisions is the dual process hypothesis, which describes two ways of thinking, one *fast* and one *slow* (Kahneman 2011).[2] Evans and Stanovich (2013) call them Type 1 and Type 2 processes. Type 1 processes are fast and intuitive, and Type 2 processes are slow and require deliberate thinking.[3] Kahneman and Tversky who can be seen as founders of the heuristics and biases (HB) paradigm examined when intuitive judgments and decisions, that is Type 1 processes, lead to systematic errors in judgments and decisions in contrast to analytical solutions. HB research is one of the cornerstones of behavioural finance and has brought valuable knowledge of the role of individuals' cognitive biases in financial judgments and decisions (Hirshleifer 2015). However, when it comes to intuition of experts and their use of Type 1 processes that lead to successful outcomes, there is a paucity of, if any, studies in the finance field. Notwithstanding, there are several field studies of experts' use of intuition and analysis in financial decision-making leading to successful outcomes (for an overview see Grant and Nilsson 2023). At the same time, when it comes to fund managers use of dual processes, there is a dearth of knowledge.

---

[2] This section builds on Grant and Nilsson (2023) although it adds fast and frugal heuristics (e.g., Gigerenzer and Gaissmaier 2011) and emotions (e.g., Fenton-O'Creevy et al. 2012; Lerner et al. 2015).

[3] Some researchers question the sharp distinction between Type 1 and Type 2 processes and suggest that these rather should be seen as two endpoints joined by a continuum (De Neys 2023).

The program of fast and frugal heuristics uses a cognitive model different from the HB paradigm and does not rely on the dual process hypothesis. The program studies another type of heuristics than HB researchers do, that is, heuristics leading to efficient decisions (Gigerenzer and Gaissmaier 2011). Heuristics are described as 'a strategy that ignores part of the information, with the goal of making decisions more quickly, frugally, and/or accurately than more complex methods.' (Ibid., p. 454). This research program has identified and analysed several types of heuristics which reach more accurate results than complex analytical methods. This includes a study on portfolio strategy suggesting that a model allocating stocks to a portfolio based on the equal weighting of heuristics can perform better that an allocation based on optimal asset-allocation models.

A theme related to judgments and decisions using Type 1 processes is emotions. Previous studies have often been associated with poor and biased outcomes, i.e., stock market anomalies, or irrational decisions. Yet research in neuroscience shows that the emotional system is required for effective decision-making (Bechara et al. 1997). Bechara et al. (1997) simply separate emotions from the feeling of emotions. Emotions are necessary for rational decision-making even when they are not consciously felt and can only be measured in bodily reactions. Studies show that feeling of emotions like being angry or happy can influence decision-making negatively, but that there are several strategies to manage this (Lerner et al. 2015). Moreover, studies of traders suggest that experts learn how to regulate emotions (Fenton-O'Creevy et al. 2012).

2.1 Dual Process Hypothesis

The dual process hypothesis suggests that we have two ways of making judgments and decisions, namely, Type 1 processes, which are fast and intuitive, and Type 2 processes, which are slow and analytical.

The HB program shows how people make systematic errors, biases, in judgments and decisions compared to an 'analytically rational solution' when using intuitive processes (Type 1 processes). The method used is typically experiment based, inducing fast intuitive answers to statistical and logical problems with unambiguous analytical solutions. Hence, if time is provided, these should preferably be solved by using an analytical process (Type 2 processes). However, HB researchers argue that people in general are cognitive misers, i.e., that a person 'seeks out quick, adequate solutions to problems rather than slow, careful ones' (APA 2025). Still, in a professional setting with experts, this is typically different, as time is provided to use both intuitive and analytical processes, and expertise can be applied. Consequently, field studies in financial decision-making show that expert professionals use both intuitive and analytical processes interactively (Grant and Nilsson 2023). When it comes to experts' use of intuitive processes—that is intuitive expertise—Daniel Kahneman, one of the founders of the HB program, describes 'intuitive thinking and decision making as generally skilled and successful' (Kahneman 2003, p. 697).

However, intuitive expertise depends on certain conditions which Kahneman and Klein discuss in their seminal article from 2009. In this study, even though we are interested in fund experts' use of intuition, we do not rule out investor biases, such as herding, as discussed in chapter 'Searching for Expert Fund Managers' in this volume, or overconfidence.

The conditions Kahneman and Klein (2009) describe are that the domain and its tasks are favourable for expertise, and the intuition is based on expertise. Hence, the domain needs to be suitable for expertise, meaning that the person can learn the rules of the environment. For example, chess is a domain highly favourable for expertise, whereas long-term economic and political forecasting is typically affected by unexpected events or sudden changes and is thus not favourable for expertise (Kay and King 2020; Taleb 2007). Like long-term economic forecasting, the domain of fund management has generally been viewed as a domain that does not lend itself to expertise owing to its stochastic nature. However, several studies show that expertise can be found in the domain, not least before fees paid to the fund (Cremers et al. 2019; for an in-depth discussion on fund managers' performance and expertise see chapter 'Performance and Fund Managers' Expertise' in this volume).

Based on an in-depth examination of current knowledge in intuition and expertise, including a review of extant field studies in financial decision-making, Grant and Nilsson (2023) add and modify the conditions for intuitive expertise described by Kahneman and Klein (2009). First, the efficient use of intuitive expertise is dependent on the character of the task (Dane et al. 2012). This can be seen along a continuous range from judgmental tasks to intellective tasks. Judgmental tasks are ambiguous and lack 'objective criterion or demonstrable solution' (Laughlin 1980, p. 128). Examples of these are investments in mergers and acquisitions, and start-ups. For these types of tasks, intuitive expertise, Type 1 processes, lead to better solutions than analytical processes.[4] Intellective tasks 'involve a definitive objective criterion of success, within the definitions, rules, operational, and relationships of a particular conceptual system' (Laughlin 1980, p. 128). Hence for tasks where an analytical solution is preferable, Type 2 processes are efficient vis-à-vis Type 1. The statistical and logical questions used in the HB program typically belong to this category of Type 2 processes. Fund management, like mergers and acquisitions and start-ups, displays a high level of ambiguity where there is not one right or wrong answer on which stocks to buy, sell or hold. This suggests that judgments and decisions based on intuitive expertise can be effective in fund management.

Second, Kahneman views Type 1 processes as the default mode and that people typically stay with these and do not use Type 2 processes even if they are more efficient. In contrast to this, field studies show that in real-life settings, like financial decision-making, Type 1 and Type 2 processes are used interactively and in parallel, such as to test the outcome of financial models or to analytically test an intuitive judgment (Grant and Nilsson 2023). Decision-making in fund management, like other financial decision-making, involves a multitude of judgments and decisions over an

---

[4] For a more detailed discussion and overview of research on this, see chapter 4 'Intuitive expertise,'., in Grant and Nilsson (2023).

extensive period of time. Consequently, it seems reasonable that fund managers also use intuitive and analytical processes interactively and in parallel.

Third, Grant and Nilsson add further insights into expertise, how it is developed and the need to continuously learn to maintain expertise. To become an expert requires high quality or so-called deliberate practice, over a long period of time. In financial decision-making, studies of top executives and board members, suggest 10–20 years is needed to acquire and develop expertise. This requires repetition, feedback, reflection and gradual improvement. It is also about being challenged and developing an adaptability to adjust to new situations (Ward et al. 2018). Moreover, an expert needs to continuously keep up with new knowledge and tools (see chapter 'Artificial Intelligence in Discretionary Fund Management' in this volume for a discussion of tools for fund managers like Big Data and AI). This should be similar for an expert fund manager, who also needs experience over a long period of time to include learning from challenging volatile periods in the stock market to develop adaptability.

2.2 Heuristics

Gigerenzer and colleagues show how fast and frugal heuristics lead to efficient judgments and decisions (Gigerenzer and Gaissmaier 2011).[5] As this program reveals successful use of heuristics, it can be seen as similar to studies of intuitive expertise and a special case of intuitive expertise (Sadler-Smith 2023). However, the heuristics program does not rely on dual processes and uses a different methodology than intuition research. The heuristics program identifies different types of heuristics and shows formally with mathematics or by computer simulation why these are superior to more complex strategies, arguing that heuristics have an ecological rationality matching the structures of the environment (Gigerenzer and Gaissmaier 2011). Thus, their method is different from that used in intuition research, in which experts' use of intuitive expertise is typically inferred based on interview studies and supported by findings from psychological experiments.

There is a dearth of studies of heuristics related to finance, not least fund management. Thus, not surprisingly Gigerenzer calls for finance researchers to examine the use of heuristics, arguing that it is one important tool in the financial toolbox (Gigerenzer 2018). In addition, the use of complex modelling is appropriate in situations with risk 'In situations of uncertainty where the future state space is not known, fast and frugal heuristics are likely to succeed.' (Ibid., p. 116). As judgments and decisions by fund managers involve uncertainty, heuristics could play an important role. This is further elaborated in a paper by Forbes et al. (2015), supporting the call for further research of heuristics in fund management. Two studies directly relating to this are Ortmann et al. (2008), and DeMiguel et al. (2009). Ortmann et al. (2008)

---

[5] In this subsection fast and frugal heuristics is used interchangeably with heuristics. Hence, heuristics in this subsection has a different meaning from that used by HB researchers. For a detailed discussion of HB heuristics and fast and frugal heuristics in finance see Forbes et al. (2015).

tested the recognition heuristic in the stock market, that is, chose stocks in the relevant markets that are highly recognised. The study covered the German and the US markets using laypeople taken from the street and graduate students in finance, whom they classified as experts. The results point in the direction that the recognition heuristic possibly can yield better performance than an index. However, more thorough and robust studies are needed to understand if recognition heuristics are used and, if so, when they can be effective. A more rigorous study by DeMiguel et al. (2009) tested what they call the naïve model, consisting of allocating stocks to a portfolio based on equal weighting, 1/N. This corresponds to what heuristic researchers call the equal-weighting principle (Gigerenzer and Gaissmaier 2011). DeMiguel et al. compared the performance of the equal-weighting portfolio with 14 other asset allocation models. The result shows that 1/N performed better in all cases.

In addition to the ecological perspective, Bingham and Eisenhardt (2011) add heuristics that individuals have learned through experience, what they call 'simple rule' heuristic. Hence, in contrast to fast and frugal heuristics (Gigerenzer and Gaissmaier 2011) these heuristics are developed by individuals' learning from process experience. Still, they concern judgments and decisions in situations of high uncertainty, typically leading to successful outcomes. Hence, they relate to expertise, as Bingham and Eisenhardt (2011) demonstrate. In a strategic context with high uncertainty, they illustrate what experts have learned—that is parts of the knowledge that expertise consists of—by identifying specific simple rules of thumb. Moreover, the context of fund management and the strategy of technology-based ventures which Bingham and Eisenhardt (2011) studied can both be characterised as having high uncertainty and as concerning the future. Consequently, studying the use of 'simple rule' heuristics in fund management could also be fruitful.

2.3 Emotions

Emotions and decision-making is a large field in psychology and neuroscience (Lerner et al. 2015). This subsection selectively draws on findings by Damasio and colleagues (Bechara et al. 1997; Damasio et al. 1991; Damasio 1994) and studies by Fenton-O'Creevy and colleagues on traders and emotions (for an overview see Vohra and Fenton-O'Creevy 2014).

Emotions are particularly related to the use of Type 1 processes. Damasio and colleagues distinguish between emotions and feelings. Emotions relate to specific neural systems and the somatic (bodily) state, whereas feelings are perceptions of the emotional states. By studying patients with damage to the emotional system, it is shown that emotions (unconscious emotions not manifested in a feeling) are necessary for rational decision-making (Bechara et al. 1997). At the same time, however, positive or negative feelings of emotions, for example anger or happiness, can affect judgment and decisions leading to biased decision-making (Lerner et al. 2015). Studies also show different strategies in managing emotions such as: delaying the decision; sleeping on it; reappraisal; increased awareness of how emotions can affect decision-making; and design of the decision-making process to avoid biases (Ibid.).

Fenton-O'Creevy and colleagues have made several studies of traders' decision-making and in particular their use of intuition and the role of emotions. In essence the studies are largely based on interview data encompassing 118 professional traders and an experiment-based study measuring heart rate variability as a proxy for emotions. The trading environment is 'a fast-paced decision environment with significant cognitive and emotional demands. Traders make judgments about risk and potential return under time pressure with potentially major financial consequences for the bank (and via bonus structures) for themselves.' (Fenton-O'Creevy et al. 2012, p. 227). Hence, it is in many aspects similar to the situation of fund managers, albeit fund managers' decision-making has a much longer time frame. A main finding is that experts—that is more successful traders—seem to regulate emotions better than less experienced traders and consequently they, most likely, have learned to regulate emotions in decision-making. Examples of strategies identified are reappraisal (framing of losses and profits) and increased awareness.

2.4   Key Insights from the Literature

As mentioned, there is a dearth of studies of how expert fund managers make judgments and decisions. However, drawing on literature on other financial decision-making, we can hypothesise that intuitive expertise plays a vital role and that expert fund managers use intuition and analysis in their judgments and decisions. The reasons are that, as is the case with other financial decision-making by experts, the task of deciding which stocks to buy, sell or hold, is judgmental and thus benign for the use of intuitive expertise. Moreover, expert fund managers' decision-making is typically a process with a multitude of judgments and decisions over a longer period of time. This suggests the use of both intuitive and analytical processes. Finally, to develop expertise a fund manager most likely requires a long-period of time with deliberate practice including learning from challenging volatile periods to develop adaptability.

The literature suggests that the use of heuristics by fund managers is an interesting avenue to explore as the environment for a fund manager is characterised by high uncertainty. Gigerenzer and colleagues have shown how fast and frugal heuristics are benign to use in situations of uncertainty, leading to efficient judgments and decisions (Gigerenzer and Gaissmaier 2011). They argue that heuristics are ecologically rational, thus adapted to the environment, and lead to effective decision-making. Still, in the finance literature the use of heuristics has been overlooked, with a few exceptions, one being DeMiguel et al. (2009). They show how the use of equal weighting, a heuristic, in portfolio allocation yields a better performance than sophisticated financial asset allocation models. Furthermore, the literature indicates that the use of 'simple rule' heuristics based on individuals learning from experience (Bingham and Eisenhardt 2011) can also be expected in fund management.

The literature shows that emotions are tied to and can affect decision-making, in particular when it comes to intuitive judgments and decisions. It also shows how different strategies can be used for managing emotions. Moreover, studies on traders suggest that dealing with emotions seems to be an ability of successful traders. While the environment of fund managers is similar to that of traders in many aspects, we can expect that expert fund managers use different strategies to manage emotions in their judgments and decisions.

3   Results

This section presents findings from our interviews. First, we describe the use of analysis and intuitive expertise followed by the use of heuristics. Then we discuss the high uncertainty of the environment, feelings of emotions, and strategies used to manage these.

3.1   *The Use of Analysis and Intuitive Expertise*

Like other studies of financial decision-making, the findings indicate that intuitive expertise plays a vital role along with analytical processes. One of the interviewees characterised it as being a craft, which one can see as being opposed to more auto-mated algorithmic processes, with little consideration to qualitative aspects. In line with the view of a craft, interviewees portrayed judgments and decisions in fund management as a holistic assessment, not at too detailed a level.

> It's a craft to be a fund manager, but it doesn't really happen at the screen. (7)

> In other words, you have to learn to ask the right questions and focus on the big picture instead of getting caught up in the details. (6)

Interviewees described the importance of focusing on the companies, their environ-ment, including assessment of the management of the companies. This seemed to be more important than the models or what one interviewee described as the technical parts. Hence, this suggests that judgments of the qualitative aspects of companies are critical, judgments which typically are commensurate with and make use of intuitive expertise.

> A fund manager must form an idea of whether a company's management is good or bad, and what drives them. I mean, it always goes another step further, and also evaluate the people there. Again, I believe that the technical aspects [excel models etc.] are not always the most important. (7)

> If you're an equity manager, you should focus on the companies and the environment in which they operate, not exactly buying... at the best time during the week or month, that's not what determines long-term success. But there are many, or not many, but at least some who, I think, spend too much time believing that trading must be perfect. (7)

In line with the quote above, one of the interviewees described that some analysts focusing on details and analysis actually had a poor feeling or understanding for stocks and the stock market and hence had not developed expertise in this area. In contrast to these where those with *fingerspitzengefühl*, or intuitive expertise.

> I've met so many analysts over the years; some are incredibly meticulous—you can tell they're really good with details and such—but they have no sense for the stock market. And then there are others whose presentations might be a bit sloppy, yet they have an amazing feel for stocks and the stock market. So sometimes you wonder, what is it that sets these people apart? It's not so much about theoretical competence but rather some sort of intuitive flair that's really hard to pinpoint. (6)

In the interviews we could identify typical characteristics of the development of intuitive expertise such as learning by doing, learning from mistakes, and the importance of having experience and learning from shifts in the market. Furthermore, one of the interviewees, a CEO of a fund management company, expressed that he searched for 'nerds' who reflect a deep interest and perseverance.

> I think I would rather work with people who have been more involved at the nitty-gritty level and have built their own process—developing something that actually works. I mean, those who have established their own investment process for the product they've worked with for a number of years, I find that much more interesting. Because the people who go for such jobs are also the nerds. (7)

> Always being willing to make a comeback when needed, and learning from mistakes. (7)

> And that's also a skill—to be able to sense which way the wind is blowing and... sometimes you have to. I mean, I've seen many bubbles over the years. 2000 was an extreme bubble. (6)

Several of the interviews suggested that expert fund managers have different cognitive styles. Some were more structured than others, some more quantitatively oriented, while others were more intuitive and qualitatively orientated.

> Some are more structured than others, more methodical, more quantitatively oriented, whereas others are more relationship-driven, a bit more intuitive, more inclined to talk with company management. I mean, we have fund managers who manage active funds who have practically never spoken with either the sell-side or anyone else—they're almost entirely quantitative, believing that there's no point in talking with a company's management because we focus more on key figures. Because I mean, if a CEO says that things are looking really good, well, what does that mean? Nothing. It might mean something in that it's good he's positive, but what CEO isn't positive about his own business? And some don't want to be influenced by that; for them, it's all about the hard facts. (1)

> And some had many meetings with external analysts, while others had not so many—it really depended on the individual. Some want a lot of input, while others prefer to work with the numbers themselves, so it's quite personal. (6)

Some of the interviewees emphasised the importance of being curious and developing an ability to see what they expressed as, 'what's around the corner' or being a step ahead. Yet, another interviewee described the risk of using intuition when there is a fundamental shift in the markets.

Can the person see what's around the corner? (4)

He was quite curious by nature. [...] One could say he was a bit ahead of his time, a step ahead. [...] And he had that in abundance, so he possessed the ability to see what's around the corner as well. (6)

Understanding that something will be big in the long run – essentially, being able to look around the corner and grasp a trend. (6)

Equally, intuition can let them down; I think that's why our performance rates fall at a moment when there is a paradigm shift in the markets, where fundamentally the ground changes beneath their feet and they see something new for the first time. (3)

3.2 The Use of Heuristics

The interview with the fund manager provided several examples of strategies and execution, that is buy, sell, or hold judgments and decisions, which seemed to be based on rules of thumb or heuristics rather than sophisticated models for optimal asset allocation or valuation of separate companies.

An example of the use of heuristics in strategy was to have a fairly concentrated portfolio of high-quality companies instead of trying to over-perform an index by adjusting weights of some of the companies in the portfolio. Furthermore, the simple effect of compounded returns was something which was mentioned.

Now [company X] has dropped—whatever it was—by 80–90 percent. How smart is that when it had such a heavy weight? How smart is it, then, to have a slight underweight in a stock that makes up thirty percent of the index if you think it's expensive and believe you've done something good? You know, 30 percent goes down 90 percent, and you have 28 percent that goes down 90 percent, and then you get an outperformance. So, you really have to think about that—it's not really how you should manage money. (6)

Generally, I believe what is somewhat underestimated in our industry is the power of compounding. If you own a company that increases its earnings by 15–20 percent per year, it becomes massive—it turns into an incredible journey after ten years. (6)

Another example of a heuristic related to the strategy and in line with the discussion above, was the rule that superior or high performance is not about trading. As described below, the fund should focus on having the right companies and avoid the bad companies.

Generally speaking, I don't believe you can trade your way to performance; a fund should focus on having the right size, the right companies, and the right exposure—significant exposure to the companies that perform well while really trying to avoid the poorly performing companies. So, trading only makes a small difference; it's not a major factor. (6)

A heuristic in the execution phase was to discuss with and use input from a network of trusted people for different industries. Another input was analyst reports. The fund manager provided a detailed description of how he assessed the company and its share price based on the report. It was apparent that he relied on some key operational and valuation ratios, and forecasts. Adding to this was the underlying narrative explanation provided in the report. Hence, suggestively, fund managers used several heuristics in the form of key ratios rather than immersing themselves in the detailed analysis. In addition, the narrative describing the development of the company was used.

> It's not that easy to keep track of all those things, so it's probably best if you have a friend in the field—someone like, 'Yes, [xx], he's good with forestry,' so I call him; and we know that [yy] is good with tech and telecom, so I call him if that's what you need. So, you have your favourites. (6)

> I still think it's pretty nice to be able to sit at your computer, log in to a broker's website, click on a company, pull up some key figures, look at some forecasts, and make your own assessments—see how it feels, and so on. [...] So if you ask me how I did it, I rarely read a thirty-page analysis; I just went in, checked out the key figures, the forecasts, how they looked, examined how they reasoned about the valuation and what they thought was a reasonable value and why, and so on. Then you process that internally. (6)

Furthermore, as described below, people working in the funds tried to find characteristics of good companies. Seemingly this could be interpreted as they were looking for heuristics to use. One of these was quality of the management of the company.

> We worked a lot on trying to discuss what characterises good companies, what exactly we're looking for. It was like, management is often very important, but oh so difficult to assess from day one. (6)

Two other heuristics related to execution related to price earnings ratios and relative valuations. The fund manager described that he had learned over time that a low-price earnings ratio is not a criterion for a good investment. Rather a company should sometimes justifiably have a low-price earnings ratio. Another learning which could be seen as a heuristic was to not buy, or be cautious, on using relative valuations.

> But it's one of those key lessons I've learned: okay, low P/E ratios, fine, but sometimes they are actually worth low P/E ratios. I mean, [an example of a company with a low P/E ratio] doesn't make any shareholder happy. (6)

> And back then it was all very hyped up; the market had gone up 65 percent in 1999 and Ericsson was probably valued at eighty times earnings [...] because Cisco was at ninety times earnings. So, you have to be a bit questioning sometimes and think [...] what is it that indicates that choosing to invest in Cisco is the right decision? (6)

3.3   High Uncertainty and Emotions

Several of the interviewees emphasised the high uncertainty and fast shifts of the stock market leading to poor and good performance, which everyone in the fund industry is aware of. Still, like one of the interviewees described it 'you live with, you are your performance' (1). Consequently, it is an environment benign to triggering emotions.

> But I still want to assert that everyone in this industry is aware that performance goes up and down. (1)

> You know that performance will vary over time, and periodically all fund managers will have tough times because the market is like its own monster that keeps moving around. (1)

The interviews discerned different strategies to manage emotions. Awareness of this and the use of analytical reasoning to manage the situation was one example. One interviewee described awareness as part of their philosophy of having their investments 60% right and 40% wrong.

> Some years are just sour years—you just have to grit your teeth. Of course, you try to figure out whether you're structurally off for the long term or if this is just a temporary blip, because some years are cyclical and some are defensive years. But we still tried to hang on, though sometimes you have to think, 'No, now we're on the wrong track.' (6)

Furthermore, we observed that a well-thought-out investment strategy could help manage emotional responses. This could create a boundary for the cognitive processes of buying and selling stocks, as it is something to stick to and rely on when making judgments and decisions, also in turbulent times. Hence, in this way it seemed to mitigate some of the feelings of emotions, especially in times of poor outcomes.

> That you, as a fund manager, still have a proven investment process, that you are structured, that you know why you invest in certain companies and why you don't. You have an investment process that you can fall back on, especially perhaps when things are as chaotic as they are now. (1)

> So, it becomes important that you have such an [investment process/strategy] and that you are systematic, and that, to the extent possible when things are fluctuating so much, you can somehow set aside the emotional swings and focus on what work you actually need to do—so that you don't end up, one day, up among the clouds and the next day wanting to jump in front of a train. That's not good, because I think it's hard if you haven't experienced it yourself to understand how these things affect you mentally. (1)

Interviewees provided examples of the importance of being able to avoid decision paralysis in spite of the high or extreme uncertainty. There appeared to be a lot of ambiguities also in evaluating whether an investment decision was right or not. Furthermore, as described in chapter 'Performance and Fund Managers' Expertise' in this volume, the longevity of fund managers is short, and after 5 years fewer than half of the fund managers remained. This can, suggestively, be related to the difficult environment fund managers operate within.

> You mustn't be shot-shy either, as they say in handball. A goalkeeper mustn't be afraid of shots—if he is, he just closes his eyes when they all come in. So, you have to dare to make decisions, and sometimes we invested in companies that we felt, 'No, this is wrong...' And what happens then? Unfortunately, if you enter at the wrong level, you exit at the wrong level—but again, you only know the final outcome much later. It might have been the right decision after all, even though the stock fell... rather than saying, 'No, let's wait until it bounces back,' which might never happen, and then you're stuck. So, there are a lot of tough decisions you have to make all the time. (6)

> Decisiveness is extremely important. [...] And decisions can be good or bad, but you have to dare to take risks and know how to reduce risk. [...] As I said, resilience—to be willing to make a comeback whenever needed and learn from mistakes. (7)

4 Conclusions

Based on the interviews and drawing on current knowledge of financial decision-making, this study explores three areas related to how fund managers make judgments and decisions. The results suggest that the use of intuition and heuristics, together with analysis, is vital in fund managers' decision-making. This contrasts with the commonly held behavioural perspective of fund management that intuition and heuristics lead to erroneous decisions (Hirshleifer 2015). Further, it highlights that an investment strategy is essential for communicating with investors and supporting fund managers' decision-making in times of high uncertainty. Investment strategy remains an understudied field with significant opportunities for additional research. Finally, the study proposes that the highly uncertain environment in which fund managers operate can trigger emotions but can also make fund managers indecisive. Nonetheless, expert fund managers appear to have strategies to manage this. At the same time, how they do this and what strategies they use remain to be explored.

The interviews suggest that expert fund managers, in line with previous research in financial decision-making (Grant and Nilsson 2023), use both analysis and intuitive expertise in forming judgments and decisions. Accordingly, they indicate that fund management is not primarily about the use of models and quantitative analysis but that qualitative analysis of, for example, company management has an important role, a task that can be characterised as judgmental and suitable for intuitive expertise. This aligns with one of few qualitative studies on fund management (Barker et al. 2012), which demonstrates how meetings between companies and fund management contribute valuable information to fund managers' decision-making. Moreover, even though it seems reasonable to assume that all expert fund managers use analysis and intuitive expertise, the interviews indicate that there are different cognitive styles, some seem more prone to analysis and others to intuitive decision-making. This can be compared to similar findings from early-stage investments which also are characterised by high uncertainty (Huang 2018). Furthermore, the interviews suggest that expert fund managers have the ability to 'see what's around the corner,' i.e., having a kind of foresight and ability to adapt to new situations. This relates closely to the concepts of adaptive expertise (Ward et al. 2018) and foresight, as discussed in chapter 'Individual Foresight and Fund Management Expertise' in this volume. Arguably, these concepts are essential as fund managers' decision-making involves judgments about the future development of companies and their share prices in a highly uncertain environment.

The study indicates the use of heuristics, rules of thumb, by fund managers—based on learnings from experience (Bingham and Eisenhardt 2011). These seemed to consist of rules applied in strategy and execution, i.e., judgments and decisions with a long-term view of the portfolio and a short-term view of what stocks to buy, sell or hold. An example of the former was number of companies in the portfolio. Execution concerned, for example, key financial ratios but also input from a network of trusted people. Gigerenzer (2018) argues that complex modelling should be used in situations of risk, whereas in situations of high uncertainty, like in fund management, 'heuristics are likely to succeed' (Ibid., p. 18). Moreover, Bingham and Eisenhardt (2011) complement Gigerenzer's ecological perspective by adding additional rules of thumb that individuals have learned through experience. In a strategic context with high uncertainty, they demonstrate how identifying specific simple rules of thumb can illustrate what experts have learned. Hence, the role of heuristics in judgments and decisions merits deeper exploration. For example, the number and weighting of companies in the portfolio could be examined from the perspective of the equal-weighting principle (DeMiguel et al. 2009; Gigerenzer and Gaissmaier 2011). Moreover, the question of which heuristics expert fund managers use and how they use them in their decision-making is a topic in itself. This could include a comparison between expert fund managers and those who are less proficient.

The findings of what role the investment strategy plays for the fund manager concerned both communication with investors and guidance in times of high uncertainty. The investment strategy is also discussed in chapters 'Performance and Fund Managers' Expertise' and 'Searching for Expert Fund Managers' in this volume, with respect to performance and characteristics of expert fund managers. This attests to the importance of an investment strategy; however, we have little knowledge of what an investment strategy is and how it can be characterised. In finance studies strategies are mentioned in terms of, for example, long-short strategy, socially responsible strategy, and fixed allocation to benchmark (Cremers et al. 2019). Still this only scratches the surface and fails to provide a deeper understanding of investment strategies. Cremers et al. (2019), in their review of the past 20 years' literature on active fund management, adhere to this. They write: 'Even less information is available about the investment processes used by active managers to identify new opportunities and monitor their current positions. We are aware of no research that even summarizes those processes.' (Ibid., p. 23).

Another finding suggests that the environment plays a vital role in how fund managers act and that it can trigger emotional responses. The environment can be characterised as having high or even extreme uncertainty. Nevertheless, fund managers continually need to make judgments and decisions, so it was not a surprise that emotions and ways to handle emotions were described in the interviews. Examples were to rely on and stick to an investment strategy and invest in companies which they believed they could reasonably predict. There were also examples of the importance of not letting emotions lead to decision paralysis. Thus, being able to be decisive in highly uncertain environments seemed to be an important criterion for expertise. Studies of emotions in neuroscience and psychology show a strong linkage between emotions and decision-making (Lerner et al. 2015; Phelps et al. 2014). Lerner et al. (2015) describes different strategies in managing emotions in order to make efficient decisions such as: delaying the decision; sleeping on it; reappraisal; being more aware of how emotions can affect decision-making; and designing the decision-making process to avoid biases. Our findings on the reliance on an investment strategy seem to fit into the awareness and design of the decision-making process. Even though this is only a scant example, it points to the potential benefits of further examining how strategies in managing emotions affects fund managers' decision-making. This is further accentuated by the studies of Fenton-O'Creevy et al. (2012), which suggest that expert traders have learned to manage emotions better than less successful ones have.

To summarise, even though this is an explorative study, arguably, by moving from studies at the fund level to the level of the individual fund manager, it contributes to our knowledge on fund managers' decision-making. It shows that expert fund managers' use qualitative and quantitative assessments based on intuition and analysis. This is in line with financial decision-making in other domains (Grant and Nilsson 2023) and complements the knowledge presented in the few studies examining the individual fund manager (e.g., Barker et al. 2012; Vohra and Fenton-O'Creevy 2014). Moreover, the findings on the use of heuristics provides a contrasting perspective to the typical behavioural finance literature (Hirshleifer 2015) by showing, in line with Gigerenzer (2018), how the use of heuristics can lead to effective decision-making in fund management. Furthermore, the findings indicate that managing emotions plays a prominent role in how expert fund managers' make judgments and decisions, in line with studies of traders (Fenton-O'Creevy et al. 2012). However, taken together, and as detailed in chapter 'Does Expertise Matter? Concluding Reflections' in this volume, the most important contribution is that the study opens several avenues for future research, which each can contribute with important pieces to the puzzle of understanding judgments and decisions made by expert fund managers. Examples of these are the adaptability of expert fund managers, the use of heuristics, characteristics of investment strategies and fund managers' strategies to manage emotions.

For practitioners, the findings suggests that the use of intuitive expertise and heuristics, under certain conditions, can be vital in judgments and decisions. Arguably, this is a capability which can be trained and developed (Sadler-Smith 2023; see also chapter 'Individual Foresight and Fund Management Expertise' in this volume). Furthermore, the study points to the importance of having strategies to manage emotions.

This is an explorative study based on a limited number of interviews hence the findings should be interpreted with considerable caution. Obviously, as outlined above, more detailed and extensive studies need to be carried out in order to test the findings of this study. Moreover, as the perspective is at the level of the individual fund manager the role of, for example, the fund organisation in individual fund managers' decision-making has yet to be examined. Regardless, we hope this study increases the interest in understanding how judgments and decisions about what stocks to buy, sell or hold are made by expert fund managers.

Acknowledgements The authors acknowledge financial support from the *Jan Wallander and Tom Hedelius Foundation* and the *Tore Browaldh Foundation* (*project: P22-0239*). We are thankful for valuable comments from the editor and our fellow authors of the book. We are also thankful for the support of the *Ingmar Bergman Foundation*, which allowed us to focus on our thinking and writing in the magical environment of the home of the late Ingmar Bergman.

References

APA (2025). https://dictionary.apa.org/. Accessed 25 Apr 2025

Backman J, Grant M, Nilsson F (2024) Expertise in financial auditing. In: Marton J, Nilsson F, Öhman P (eds) Auditing transformation: regulation, digitalisation and sustainability. Routledge, London, New York, pp 338–359

Barker R, Hendry J, Roberts J, Sanderson P (2012) Can company-fund manager meetings convey informational benefits? Exploring the rationalisation of equity investment decision making by UK fund managers. Account Organ Soc 37:207–222

Bechara A, Damasio H, Tranel D, Damasio AR (1997) Deciding advantageously before knowing the advantageous strategy. Science 275:1293–1295

Bingham CB, Eisenhardt KM (2011) Rational heuristics: the 'simple rules' that strategists learn from process experience. Strateg Manag J 32:1437–1464

Clare A, Sherman M, O'Sullivan N, Gao J, Zhu S (2022) Manager characteristics: predicting fund performance. Int Rev Financ Anal 80:102049

Cremers KM, Fulkerson JA, Riley TB (2019) Challenging the conventional wisdom on active management: a review of the past 20 years of academic literature on actively managed mutual funds. Financ Anal J 75:8–35

Damasio AR (1994) Descartes' error: emotion, reason, and the human brain. Grosset/Putnam, New York

Damasio AR, Tranel D, Damasio HC (1991) Somatic markers and the guidance of behaviour: theory and preliminary testing. In: Levin HM, Eisenberg HM, Benton AL (eds) Frontal lobe function and dysfunction. Oxford University Press, Oxford, pp 217–229

Dane E, Rockmann KW, Pratt MG (2012) When should I trust my gut? Linking domain expertise to intuitive decision-making effectiveness. Organ Behav Hum Decis Process 119:187–194

De Neys W (2023) Advancing theorizing about fast-and-slow thinking. Behav Brain Sci 46:e111, 1–71

DeMiguel V, Garlappi L, Uppal R (2009) Optimal versus naive diversification: how inefficient is the 1/N portfolio strategy? Rev Financ Stud 22:1915–1953

Evans JSB, Stanovich KE (2013) Dual-process theories of higher cognition: advancing the debate. Perspect Psychol Sci 8:223–241

Fenton-O'Creevy M, Lins JT, Vohra S, Richards DW, Davies G, Schaaff K (2012) Emotion regulation and trader expertise: heart rate variability on the trading floor. J Neurosci Psychol Econ 5:227–237

Forbes W, Hudson R, Skerratt L, Soufian M (2015) Which heuristics can aid financial-decision-making? Int Rev Financ Anal 42:199–210

Gigerenzer G (2018) The heuristics revolution: rethinking the role of uncertainty in finance. In: Viale R, Mousavi S, Alemanni B, Filotto U (eds) The behavioural finance revolution. Edward Elgar Publishing, Cheltenham, pp 115–134

Gigerenzer G, Gaissmaier W (2011) Heuristic decision making. Annu Rev Psychol 62:451–482

Grant M, Nilsson F (2020) The production of strategic and financial rationales in capital investments: judgments based on intuitive expertise. Br Account Rev 52:100861

Grant M, Nilsson F (2023) Intuitive expertise and financial decision-making. Routledge, London, New York

Hirshleifer D (2015) Behavioral finance. Annu Rev Financ Econ 7:133–159

Huang L (2018) The role of investor gut feel in managing complexity and extreme risk. Acad Manag J 61:1821–1847

Kahneman D (2003) A perspective on judgment and choice: mapping bounded rationality. Am Psychol 58:697–720

Kahneman D (2011) Thinking, fast and slow. Farrar, Straus and Giroux, New York

Kahneman D, Klein G (2009) Conditions for intuitive expertise: a failure to disagree. Am Psychol 64:515–526

Kay J, King M (2020) Radical uncertainty: decision-making for an unknowable future. Norton & Company Inc., New York

Laughlin PR (1980) Social combination processes of cooperative problem-solving groups on verbal intellective tasks. In: Fishbein M (ed) Progress in social psychology, vol 1. Lawrence Erlbaum Associates, Hillsdale, pp 127–155

Lerner JS, Li Y, Valdesolo P, Kassam KS (2015) Emotion and decision making. Annu Rev Psychol 66:799–823

Ortmann A, Gigerenzer G, Borges B, Goldstein DG (2008) The recognition heuristic: a fast and frugal way to investment choice? In: Plott CR, Smith VL (eds) Handbook of experimental economics results, vol 1. North Holland, Amsterdam, pp 993–1003

Phelps EA, Lempert KM, Sokol-Hessner P (2014) Emotion and decision making: multiple modulatory neural circuits. Annu Rev Neurosci 37:263–287

Sadler-Smith E (2023) Intuition in business. Oxford University Press, Oxford

Taleb NN (2007) The black swan: the impact of the highly improbable. Random House, New York

Vohra S, Fenton-O'Creevy M (2014) Intuition, expertise and emotion in the decision making of investment bank traders. In: Sinclair M (ed) Handbook of research methods on intuition. Edward Elgar Publishing, Cheltenham, pp 88–98

Ward P, Gore J, Hutton R, Conway GE, Hoffman RR (2018) Adaptive skill as the conditio sine qua non of expertise. J Appl Res Mem Cogn 7:35–50

Individual Foresight and Fund Management Expertise

Melissa Innes⊕ **and Sajid Anwar**⊕

Abstract Expertise is commonly understood to comprise two key elements, domain expertise and adaptability. In the context of fund management, corporate knowledge and industry experience are critical for achieving positive investor outcomes. However, expertise becomes especially valuable when applied to non-routine, changing or unexpected scenarios. In such cases, fund managers could benefit from Individual Foresight (IF), the ability to imagine future scenarios by drawing on past experiences, planning future actions, and assessing these actions to determine future success. Importantly, IF is not developed in isolation. While it draws on a fund manager's personal knowledge, experience and intuition, it also requires engagement with collaborative learning, reflection, and both formal and informal social networks. Cognitive strategies such as future-thinking further enhance this capability. By examining the unique skills and processes involved in IF, traditional competencies such as stock selection, prior analyst experience, group decision-making and market timing, can be better understood and integrated into future fund management development initiatives. This chapter explores how fostering IF can enhance adaptability and decision-making in dynamic investment environments.

Keywords Collaborative learning · Emotional intelligence · Fund management · Future-thinking · Individual foresight

1 Introduction

...if this had been a brand new team, we would have really struggled to identify those options so quickly...corporate knowledge was invaluable...as much as corporate entities love having people come in – and bring in fresh ideas...it's also important to retain that

M. Innes (✉) · S. Anwar
School of Business and Creative Industries, University of the Sunshine Coast, Sippy Downs, QLD, Australia
e-mail: minnes1@usc.edu.au

corporate knowledge…we rely on the collective wisdom of the group.[1] (Howard, Executive Manager, Planning)

Knowledge plays a significant role in foresight used in organisations. Howard's reflection describing his team's response to a critical incident highlights valuable insights gained through the foresight of team members. It demonstrates the value of corporate-specific knowledge gained through employee tenure. Through fostering a culture of foresight, Howard's organisation is harnessing the knowledge and experience of its employees, capturing and sharing these insights to support innovative outcomes and prevent similar incidents escalating in the future. In fund management, future-thinking is central to the everyday work of fund managers and their teams— thus, understanding how organisations can nurture this foresightful culture becomes even more important. So, we ask the question: *How can fostering individual foresight through organisational learning mechanisms assist in developing fund management expertise?*

We live in an era where work is undertaken at a furious pace. Employees in the finance industry increasingly face uncertainty resulting from changing work parameters and influenced by dramatic environmental factors associated with geopolitical tensions, post-pandemic work redesign, and changing investor preferences for portfolios that prioritise Environmental, Social, and Governance (ESG) factors. While the finance sector has long been a dynamic work environment, changes have been exacerbated by the rise of sophisticated technologies that facilitate a level of connectivity, operational efficiency and artificial intelligence that blends the physical and digital realms of people's work. Interest in the 'adaption and diffusion of technology in the financial services' (Tao et al. 2021, p. 1) is evidenced by the rise of fintech companies seizing opportunities through AI and other automated technologies that increase efficiency and provide greater accessibility. Consequently, traditional financial institutions are seeking innovations and alternative strategies to remain competitive.

Despite the frenetic nature of change in the finance sector, researchers continue to explore the value of fund managers in investment firms. Fund managers draw on extensive industry knowledge and experience when utilising skills and traits such as emotional intelligence (the ability to self-manage one's emotions and manage interpersonal relationships) and trust (Verma et al. 2024), or intuitive decision-making (Wu 2022) (or see chapter 'Judgments and Decisions by Expert Fund Managers,' in this volume). They utilise their communication and judgement skills to build networks for the valuable flow of information essential for investor and fund manager confidence (Barker et al. 2012). And despite the advantages technology offers in managing big data (see chapter 'Artificial Intelligence in Discretionary Fund Management,' in this volume), researchers continue to highlight the necessary role of human

---

[1] Findings presented throughout this chapter originate from a larger qualitative study exploring the lived experience of Individual Foresight (IF) in organisations (Innes 2023). Data was collected from a sample which comprised 12 interviews with employees from an organisation within the Finance & Insurance Industry, and 15 interviews with employees from an organisation within the Utilities Industry, both organisations located in Australia.

intervention in data analysis and decision-making (Meyer 2024). Similar to analytical, decision-making, judgement and other useful skills, investigating the role of foresight in fund management expertise offers novel insights for fund managers to consider at both the individual and collaborative levels in organisations.

Individual Foresight (IF) is defined as:

> The ability of humans to imagine future scenarios by drawing on past experiences, planning future actions, and assessing these actions to determine future success. (Innes 2024, p. 2)

Drawing on a larger exploratory study (see Appendix) focused on the lived experience of employees engaging with IF in organisations (Innes 2023, 2024) this chapter introduces a framework of IF and considers its potential relevance to expertise in fund management. The application of the IF model to fund management is premised on the future-oriented nature of decision-making in this domain. However, the transferability of the model may be subject to critique, particularly in terms of its contextual relevance and theoretical alignment with fund management practices. For this reason, the authors have sought input from an expert in fund management (see Appendix), who provides additional commentary throughout the discussion.

The original study engaged an interpretive phenomenological analysis (IPA), which revealed several individual-level contributors to foresight including knowledge and experience, intuition, and individual skills and dispositions such as risk-tolerance, emotional intelligence, and the ability to assess and prioritise information. Employees utilise these skills and attributes when experiencing foresight to arrive at a decision, action and/or inputs to organisational policies and procedures. The resulting IF Framework (see Fig. 1, Sect. 2) features contextual factors such as organisational culture, supervisory style, and the levels of trust, autonomy and reward, among others, that emerge as significant in influencing employees' experience of foresight in their organisations and presents several pertinent opportunities for the development of fund management expertise. Outcomes of the original study, informed by data from the insurance and utilities industries, inform this chapter's conceptual application of IF to fund management through applying an IF Framework which comprises four elements: The Person, The Process, The Outcomes and The Context.

First, we introduce IF and the framework that underpins the conceptual argument presented in this chapter—that IF is a valuable capability to be utilised to develop expert fund managers. Second, we introduce the micro-foundations of foresight at the individual-level, asking *How can individual-level IF contributors be utilised by fund managers to develop fund management expertise and contribute to an organisation's foresightfulness?* Complementing the work of Grant and Abrahamson (see chapter 'Judgments and Decisions by Expert Fund Managers,' in this volume), we present a foresight-focused exploration of the role that a person's industry knowledge and skills, propensity for intuitive decision-making, and use of emotional intelligence plays in positioning IF as a valuable fund manager capability. Third, we examine IF development strategies for fund managers before presenting implications for future research in fund management expertise.

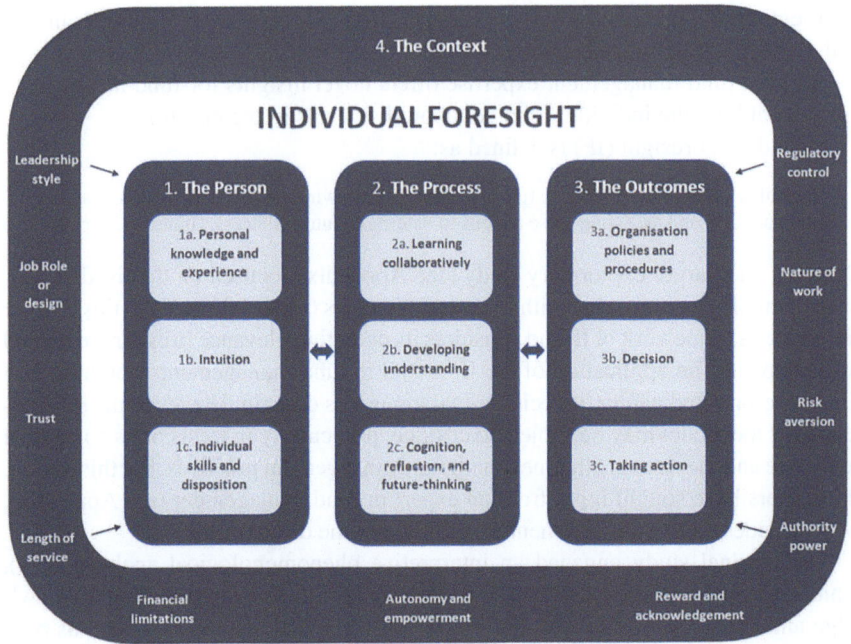

Fig. 1 Individual foresight framework (Innes 2024)

2 The IF Framework and Fund Management Expertise

Drawn from the foresight study underpinning this chapter, the IF Framework (Fig. 1) is operationalised here for firms seeking to foster foresight in fund managers.

Aligning IF with expertise allows the application of elements of IF to fund managers' work. This section details strategies that fund managers could harness to develop and foster IF potential. Examining the experience of foresight in organisations for employees across two industries, finance and insurance, and utilities, reveals that IF comprises four major elements: The Person, The Process, The Outcomes, and The Context. Each of these elements is defined, highlighting potential opportunities for fund management experts to harness foresight to offer enhanced benefits to the investor. By working through the IF framework elements presented in Fig. 1, this chapter seeks to explore opportunities for IF to be applied to fund manager work, and the development of expertise.

2.1   Individual Foresight: The Person

When considering the unique attributes of individuals that contribute to IF ability, three key contributors emerge: Personal knowledge and experience, intuition, and individual skills and disposition.

2.1.1   Personal Knowledge and Experience

Firstly, personal knowledge and experience is key to facilitating foresight in individuals. The unique ability for humans to mentally travel into the past (remembering) or future (imagining) enables them to draw on their experience and future-thinking skills to ascertain the best course of action in their current work. Participant Alan describes the role of experience in determining if proposed changes at work might lead to improved outcomes:

> …it's trying to predict before making a change – the outcome of that change, so that you can try and proactively learn from your past mistakes, rather than making those same mistakes over and over again. (Alan, Senior Manager, Operational Strategy)

The value of experience for financial experts was underlined by Grant and Nilsson (2023) who observed the effectiveness of 'long experience' of operating managers and key staff in merger and acquisition expertise. They found that corporate or industry-specific knowledge attained in the merger and acquisition context resulted in a level of expertise effective in identifying suitable targets (Grant and Nilsson 2023). Aligned with IF, this learning for fund managers could stem from either personal past relevant experience, or learning through others (e.g., story-telling or group reflection). Evidence of the benefits of expertise were observed in how efficiently longer-term employees were able to act on, report and/or prevent incidents due to existing knowledge and expertise related to their organisation (Innes 2023). Further, valuable knowledge and skills for fund managers was highlighted by our expert in fund management who reflected on the success of fund manager work:

> …[fund managers'] understanding about our industry and the skills they've created over time within finance, investing, or funds management is super important. With fund managers it's equally or almost equally as important to understand the industry in which they're analysing. So, they can't just be a funds management expert and not know anything about infrastructure if they're an infrastructure stock picker. (2025, personal communication)

This insight highlights the value of the first person-level IF attribute—personal knowledge and experience. It is interesting to note the comment about industry-specific knowledge being considered important for fund managers, which could be particularly pertinent when considering the role of intuition in their decision-making.

2.1.2 Intuition

The second way in which aspects unique to The Person contribute to IF is explained through an individual's tendency to draw on intuition in decision-making. Influenced by personal knowledge and experience, the role of intuition as a key contributor to decision-making in organisations has been previously established (Hodgkinson and Sadler-Smith 2018). When describing the use of intuition at work, participants described physical symptoms that informed or influenced how they were feeling and the consequent actions or decisions they took. For fund managers, the proposition by Grant and Nilsson (2023) that intuitive expertise, valuable for financial decision-making, involves two types of intuitive processes also applies when considering the development of IF for fund management expertise. As discussed in chapter 'Judgments and Decisions by Expert Fund Managers,' in this volume, these two broad categories that describe a more intuitive or analytical form of decision-making shed light on the value of intuitive decision-making in this context.

Type 1 (intuitive) and Type 2 (reflective) decision-making were observed in participant responses related to foresight. One participant with extensive corporate-specific knowledge and experience described their decision-making as follows:

> …there is this intuitive thinking that occurs early, where you rapidly sort of jot down everything that you think could work … but when it's such high stakes, you can't rely on intuition to make the final decision, you have to have some facts or evidence base … you have to understand the risk … in the knowledge gap. (Howard, Executive Manager, Planning)

Evident in this recount was Howard's self-description of his early cognitions during a serious incident accruing 'rapidly' in the early stages of the event. This observation supports 'experience based' or Type 1 intuitive decision-making, where the participant's 'sensory intuition' was possibly triggered by the risk identification and more 'rational thought' about the cognition process he was experiencing (Sinclair et al. 2009, pp. 400–401). Howard also reverts to Type 2 decision-making in terms of the reflective process undertaken to reduce the 'risk' of the intuitive decision. Grant and Nilsson (2023) summarise experiences such as those described by Howard as intuitive expertise—where experts demonstrate a dual-process approach to decision-making, involving both intuitive and reflective cognitive processing. Interestingly, our expert in fund management described the potency of intuitive decision-making from 'traditional rock star portfolio managers,' acknowledging the value of an increasingly quantitative approach to analysis:

> …the intuitive guys who really backed their conviction, really made everybody a lot of money… their portfolios got too big and mathematically they start to underperform because they're too big to be nimble… the human biases probably got a little bit ahead of themselves, and the overconfidence, and anchoring and loss avoidance… and so the performance charts, you know, not so good next year, which is why some will [now] lean right towards process. (2025, personal communication)

An important aspect of The Person element of IF, understanding the value and potential pitfalls of intuitive decision-making for fund management experts, and how intuitive decision-making skills can be developed and utilised at opportune times in the right context, should be considered a priority.

2.1.3 Individual Skills and Disposition

The third and final aspect of The Person element of IF encompasses several skills and attributes of employees that contribute to their IF approach including their ability to assess or prioritise a situation; their emotional intelligence, confidence, and length of service; their emphasis on self-development; their level of risk-aversiveness, passion about a cause, desire to avoid mistakes or challenge solutions; and their propensity for early intervention of certain situations/incidents. While this component of The Person element of IF captures multiple aspects that impact an individual's propensity for foresight, only those more widely discussed among participants of the foresight study will be included here.

When discussing their experience with IF, one of the contributing factors is an employee's ability to assess and prioritise a situation. The decision-making advantages stemming from this ability can be identified in the following description:

> I looked at my mapping and everything ... it only takes 10 seconds or 5 to 10 seconds. It just brings me back a little bit. But yeah, it's hard to do because everything's going at once but actually doing that creates better decision-making and helps you prioritise what's important. (Ronnie, Manager, Maintenance)

Fund managers ability to assess and select successful portfolios for their investors is clearly important. Paired with other foresight elements such as future-thinking a skilled fund manager should be able to utilise IF when researching and networking to establish promising opportunities in the market.

Emotional intelligence, specifically the ability to self-manage, be self-aware, control emotions influencing foresight ability, and understand any personal knowledge limitations or expertise—all emerged as important aspects of an employee's IF. Of significance to fund managers is one utility employee's description of how his foresight ability 'fall[s] away' when he is in a 'heightened emotional state.' This is worth noting in terms of the necessity for fund managers to manage stress and demonstrate resilience during their work. For example, fear could lead to panic selling, while overconfidence could result in important oversights leading to investor losses. As discussed earlier, fund managers need to consider their own emotional stability and professionalism when meeting or managing key stakeholders, as exemplified by a financial institution employee attempting to share her IF insights with others:

> ... a bunch of different emotions really ... I was trying to manage – was keeping cool, calm, and collected ... trying to manage those feelings ... thinking about articulating this clearly and instinctually to ... intelligent people who maybe don't have the information but have the capacity to understand the information. (Janelle, Senior Manager, Legal)

Another significant observation about employees using their IF, is the role of confidence. Most relevant to fund managers is task confidence. Bonnie demonstrated how this can make a difference to a situation where multiple stakeholders are involved, 'My response to that straightaway would be right, stop the job...Other people won't have that same confidence and will probably just maybe hang around and try and help with the situation....' Applying this insight to fund managers' task confidence highlights a balancing act. Some level of confidence is necessary to back their own decisions—especially in situations of uncertainty. However, overconfidence, as mentioned, could lead to an overestimate of their judgement and possible oversight of important environmental factors that might influence their portfolio (see chapter 'Integrating ESG Information in Active Fund Management,' in this volume). Social confidence is also important in terms of fund managers communicating their investment insights and strategies with investors or other relevant stakeholders.

Another interesting disposition related to IF is the length of time an employee had been part of the business. This was shown to impact either positively or negatively on how they utilised IF. Corporate-specific knowledge is valued in certain situations where foresight could be beneficial. One participant of the foresight study referred to newer incumbents as not having '…drank the Kool Aid…they don't really have the same pattern recognition that we have…you're able to have a different level of experience and a different perception on things [when you've been with the organisation longer].' However, being with an organisation too long could be detrimental to IF outcomes, as highlighted by Ronnie:

> …over a period of time – they don't have to use foresight – because their job is to go from A to B…do this, do that…they haven't used foresight because they haven't had any need to use it. (Ronnie, Manager, Maintenance)

For fund managers utilising IF, a self-awareness about the tendency for patterned behaviours to develop over time would be critical to ensuring new information or insights are not overlooked. As our expert in fund management described, '…the portfolio manager is really the head of a think tank and not a stock picker at all. In fact, he wants to have all of his human biases removed.' (2025, personal communication). Whilst some may debate the value of biases to fund manager performance, awareness by fund managers in situations of long service or lengthy industry experience could overcome tendency for biased decision-making around portfolio investments.

There are certainly benefits though to extensive experience in fund management with accumulated experience linked to fund manager skill and overall performance and performance persistence (when a fund continues to perform well over a period of time) (Clare et al. 2022). Perhaps considered beneficial to any professional position, and therefore relevant for fund managers too, is the need to prioritise self-development. When reflecting about how they had developed their IF ability, foresight study participants spoke of the value of seeking feedback, experiencing adversity in their younger years, and being able to approach others when they don't have the answers. Learning from experience was also deemed an important way to develop IF: 'Learn from every interaction and how to get better – and to actually care to be better.' Given the volatile nature of the financial world fund managers should consider self-development and life-long learning an important aspect of their career.

Risk-taking is another key aspect of IF skills and disposition, particularly relevant to fund manager decision-making. Study participants emphasised the importance of feeling supported, rather than punished, when sharing IF insights in the workplace. However, for fund managers, risk-taking requires a different lens. It varies based on incentivisation structures. For instance, Ma and Tang (2019) found that portfolio manager ownership reduces both intra-year and across-year risk-taking—an important contrast to other approaches that may encourage greater risk-taking. Self-awareness regarding risk-taking during IF is essential for fund managers to strike a balance between risk tolerance and avoidance when making portfolio decisions (see chapter 'Integrating ESG Information in Active Fund Management,' in this volume). This underscores the critical role of fund management organisations in fostering healthy risk-taking strategies.

Finally, within The Person element of foresight, employees demonstrate varying tendencies to act early based on their IF abilities. Acting swiftly on IF outcomes often stems from capabilities and the anticipation of consequences associated with action—or inaction. While future-thinking is discussed in detail later, it is introduced here as an individual disposition, highlighting the need for fund managers to develop both future-thinking skills and the confidence to make timely, effective investment decisions. Notably, fund managers often rely on qualitative approaches when navigating these decisions, including leveraging social networks and meetings (Coleman 2015).

2.2 Individual Foresight: The Process

The foresight study revealed three key elements exist that help understand the process of IF in organisations: Learning collaboratively, developing understanding, and cognition, reflection and future-thinking practices (Innes 2023). Each of these elements are explored in relation to their potential influence on fund manager expertise and fostering a supportive culture for fund management.

2.2.1 Learning Collaboratively

Collaborative learning in organisations as part of the IF process was a surprising and useful insight about how employees experience IF. Although unexpected, the role of collaborative learning in IF, and the implications for fostering and developing foresight in organisations through understanding organisational learning as a principle, is promising for any fund management firms seeking to foster IF.

When describing their experience with IF, employees often referred to a process of team-based reflection in the work environment which either contributes to the development of team members' foresight or offers an opportunity to capture IF within a team. Group reflection opportunities can be fostered by supervisors, as exemplified below:

> [you] go out on site with those guys…and what I personally do is go… we've got this job here today – what do you think is the best action? …what can you tell me on how we can do this job? If you don't ask those questions …they don't think about that information. (Alan, Senior Manager, Operational Strategy)

When asked about the role of collaborative learning in fund management teams and if employees were encouraged to share knowledge our expert in fund management confirmed:

> Unquestionably… I mean it's [portfolio management] built that way, right? So, you just keep building on the understanding of the investment team… these 30 people, some of them are a bit more junior, some of them super senior portfolio managers… [they] have an investment committee… they come to the table with the research… and they vote on whether or not they all agree with the analysis of the juniors… and they [the juniors] question the portfolio managers. Everybody's questioning each other, even outside their specialty. Because they're all finance people. And if they're not – they [the juniors] probably aspire to be portfolio managers and they're you know, keen to have a good idea recognised. If they can catch somebody on something that would have been a mistake… the more valuable you are to your team… that's a critical part of our process. (2025, personal communication)

As similarly described above in company-fund manager meetings, foresight study participants described reaching out to colleagues, their network, or their teams in their own process of developing understanding. Foresight learning tends to be a two-way process—where the employee seeks input from other into their own IF, but then is willing to contribute foresight to others' IF through an information exchange process. Participant Alistair explains:

> …it's a way of setting yourself up for success…to have a network of people that you know…if you're sort of seeking a bit of support or advice to resolve a particular issue…it's also good when it works back the other way and they feel comfortable to be able to contact me. (Alistair, Manager, Operations)

Strategies of working collaboratively or developing others in a fund management firm may not at first seem appealing given the sensitive nature of information held by fund managers. However, essential to IF are the networks, both professional and social, that employees utilise to develop their foresight or share their foresight with trusted others. Liang et al. (2022) found that fund managers connected with alumni networks tend to achieve higher returns and have information advantages. These valued networks are likely to contribute to the knowledge and understanding of fund managers, a valuable process in IF.

2.2.2 Developing Understanding

Several strategies emerged to reflect how those involved in a process of IF developed understanding about their situation. Multiple problem-solving techniques (from whiteboard reflections to 'taking five'), the use of scenarios, visualisation, using technology and more were described by participants. A strong theme was the process of reflection:

> I go into a little bit of a mental check on these types of things … then I very quickly go in towards the solutions…. (Sarah, Manager, Compliance)

Others preferred more formal methods to record and process information, particularly in a team setting:

> ... we'll use our foresight to identify things ... and we'll start to put that process and document that into a formal checklist or something like that. And then we'll update that by using myself and my collective teams' foresight to improve on that ... we'll probably use it again in the future. (Hugh, Manager, Operations)

While this discussion about developing understanding is necessarily limited (see Innes 2023 for a broader discussion on use of scenarios, planning, visualisation and more for problem solving), of interest is how fund managers draw on multiple qualitative methods to gather data to inform decision-making, for example formal groups to discuss global economic data, company-fund manager meetings and research to determine internal conditions of firms, and often judgements and intuition that guide asset allocations and stock selection (Coleman 2015). These methods highlight the importance of understanding The Person elements of IF and the value of certain attributes in facilitating such qualitative methods i.e., intuitive decision-making, emotional intelligence, confidence etc.

2.2.3 Cognition, Reflection, and Future-Thinking

Beyond the opportunities to learn collaboratively and develop understanding through the IF process, employees explore unique and important ways to think about and solve problems. Different types of cognition processes were observed in IF participants including (among others) reflection, intuition, visioning, chunking and critical thinking. For fund managers seeking insights and/or affirmation of their understanding—emotional intelligence and judgment play a big role when working through a problem with stakeholders. Further, associated with future-thinking, scenarios can be a useful approach when working through information and anticipating future opportunities or risks. Foresight study participant Geoffrey explains,

> I'm projecting my thought process forward, I'll – I guess in a very short period of time in my head sort of seconds not minutes, I just developed over time the ability to almost like picture a scenario. (Geoffrey, Manager, Operations)

Despite the useful role of intuition in decision-making, working in high-risk scenarios fund managers may choose to assess whether intuitive decision-making is the best form of cognition.

> ... there is this intuitive thinking that occurs early, where you rapidly sort of jot down everything that you think could work ... but when it's such high stakes, you can't rely on intuition to make the final decision, you have to have some facts or evidence base ... you have to understand the risk ... in the knowledge gap. (Howard, Executive Manager, Planning)

Participant Howard's cognition process aligns with 'experience based' intuition, while his 'sensory intuition'—which involves affect—possibly triggered risk identification and a more 'rational thought' about his cognitions (Sinclair et al. 2009, pp. 400–401). Understanding the difference in these types of cognitions could prove crucial for fund management outcomes—a process in which reflective practices would be useful.

Reflection emerged frequently as a way participants gained insights, considered priorities, and thought about the future consequences of their actions:

> … so, I'll just step away from the situation and go to somewhere where I can be by myself and just run through those thought processes. (Alistair, Manager, Operations)

Arguably, the uniqueness of a fund manager's knowledge and experience can contribute valuable insights through reflective practice. By remembering past experiences when considering future outcomes, lessons learned in addition to new innovations emerge. Further, group reflection offers a mechanism to share knowledge and gain insights from multiple perspectives—as evidenced when fund managers hold group meetings with other investors or traders.

Of note, participants described temporal differences in their reflective practices—raising important questions about the design of fund management work to allow for reflective practice. Participant Rachel emphasised the value of moving away from her work to:

> … digest it … that's when the foresight…you know, I rummage around with it. (Rachel, Team Member, Technician)

Allowing time for reflective practice and future-thinking results in valuable insights and innovation and shouldn't be underestimated by fund management firms.

When considering future-thinking in fund management work one might determine that all fund managers require the ability to think about the future and, in fact, often consider implications of decisions for the future—in every aspect of their daily work. In terms of IF, future-thinking is positioned as an ability or propensity of employees in their work. For some fund managers, future-thinking is a crucial aspect of analysis—and often undertaken through means of quantitative data analysis utilising AI tools or scenario planning strategies. Our expert in fund management revealed that quantitative portfolio managers act as the 'think tank' for a system that will analyse data based on the design the portfolio managers instigate, answering questions like, 'what are the best questions we can ask all the data… all of the companies in the world… to identify stocks that are likely to perform better than stocks that are likely to underperform…' (2025, personal communication).

From the foresight study, future-thinking revealed a surprising insight regarding *what* employees think about, when they think about the future. Employees are concerned with one of two things when they think about the future of their actions or decisions—implications for people, or implications for the organisation. This highlights the importance of a positive company culture on employee decision-making and emphasises how crucial it is to align fund manager values with values of the firm. A safe culture was also a consideration by foresight participants and highlights the importance of employee actions on outcomes for the firm:

> … if I had gone oh no…I'm really scared to talk about this because this isn't the culture here to talk about these things and learn from them, then we'd be in a position where we're reporting … about a breach of privacy. (Sarah, Manager, Compliance)

Although a summarised explanation of cognition, reflection and future-thinking in foresight, fund managers should consider these insights and the value of reflective moments and future-thinking that can lead to positive outcomes for investment or portfolio decisions. For a broader discussion of cognitions, reflection and future-thinking in IF refer to the original study—Innes (2023).

2.3   Individual Foresight: The Outcomes

The IF study underpinning this chapter focused on individual experiences with foresight, rather than specific outcomes. However, participants described three types of outcomes in relation to their experience with IF: Policies and procedures; decisions; and taking action—all of which offer advantages to fund management firms. Policies and procedures are shaped by IF. Firms should seek alignment between policies and the foresightful behaviours and decision-making they wish to encourage. This requires fostering a culture of openness, risk tolerance, and innovation. IF insights from fund managers can prompt policy improvements, ensuring employee foresight is valued and providing guidance for those with less-developed IF skills.

A fund manager's decisions are influenced by their knowledge, skills and experience. Daily decision-making draws on unique perspectives and the specific contexts in which they operate. Collaborative processes like networking, meetings, and group reflection, enhance decision outcomes by integrating collective intuition, emotional intelligence, and cognitive skills. When fund managers have time to reflect on future outcomes and apply IF insights, they can better anticipate market shifts, optimise portfolios, and drive innovation and efficiency. However, fund managers will only act on new IF insights if they feel safe, supported and empowered to do so. Encouraging appropriate risk-taking builds confidence across all experience levels. Employees in the foresight study reported fearing repercussions for challenging the status quo or voicing intuitive concerns. Firms will need to cultivate a culture that supports foresight and psychological safety to overcome these pitfalls.

2.4   Individual Foresight: The Context

This chapter has so far examined the microfoundations of foresight, emphasising individual strategies like collaborative learning, reflective practices, and future-oriented work approaches. However, culture and leadership are equally critical. A notable finding from the IF study was the powerful influence of supervisory relationships in fostering foresight within firms.

While our focus has been on the IF of fund managers, fund or portfolio managers themselves also play an important role in fostering a foresightful culture in firms. Participants in the IF study frequently mentioned their managers or supervisors, often highlighting negative experiences where they felt their foresight was neither recognised nor rewarded as part of their contributions. Participant Howard describes:

> ... there was this foreman ... he was the classic micromanager [he'd say] 'look, there's the front fence, park your brain there, come in, do what I tell you to do, and you can pick up your brain on the way out.' (Howard, Executive Manager, Planning)

When organisations promote experienced staff into supervisory roles without providing adequate leadership development, it can undermine employee autonomy and empowerment, limiting their capacity to contribute foresight to the firm. Instead, firms should cultivate a culture that supports foresight capabilities. Leaders can encourage IF behaviour by adopting an open, approachable, and trustworthy style in their fund managers. People and culture practices should promote appropriate risk-taking, reward foresightful actions, and nurture IF outcomes to build foresight competence. Despite the competitive nature of fund management, collaborative learning methods like mentoring and group reflection can offer valuable insights and innovation. Sharing ideas and tacit knowledge enhances IF development, benefiting even those focused on personal expertise. Fund managers working with analysts and junior staff should foster a safe, trusting environment that encourages knowledge sharing, creativity, and innovation, as trust is crucial for developing foresight capacity.

Several participants of the IF study talked about the role of trust when collaborating within their network to share information and/or seek feedback they consider important in their own IF development:

> I'll sense check that with someone else that I know ... and trust ... and then I'll do it with someone who's influential as well so I can even get a better understanding of the situation. (John, Manager, Operations)

Where there is mistrust or a perceived lack of job security, employees tend to withhold information to wield expert power (Serenko and Bontis 2016), as described by one participant:

> ... blokes ... that have been here a long time ... don't like to share that information because they feel ... if I tell somebody – I'll lose my job .... (Edward, Team Leader, Maintenance)

As an alternative, fund managers can recognise the unique value and insights that others offer. Through fostering a foresight culture, the tacit knowledge that would otherwise go unshared becomes a powerful source of development for a firm's junior fund managers—essentially providing a competitive edge over other fund management firms. Experienced fund managers, through adopting a mentoring role, could benefit from developing others who contribute their foresight to situations, but will also develop their own foresight capacity through learning collaboratively from other perspectives. Section 3 explores key themes from the literature that specifically relate to how individual-level contributors of IF could be specifically utilised by fund managers.

3   Micro-Foundations of Foresight for Fund Managers

Positioning IF's value to organisational-level outcomes requires an understanding that corporate or strategic-level foresight involves firms undertaking such practices as environmental scanning and scenario planning to anticipate uncertainty (Slaughter 1997). Considered in the context of financial markets, those involved in all areas of the firm need to understand their role in contributing to a firm's foresight capacity. Thus, by asking the question *How can fostering individual foresight through organisational learning mechanisms assist in developing fund management expertise?* we must first consider how foresight ability can be harnessed at the individual level by fund managers to help combat the dynamic elements of their landscape. Section 2 introduced the reader to the IF Framework and presented examples from the IF Framework that demonstrate the value of a micro focus on the phenomenon of foresight and its relevance for fund managers. Key themes identified in the literature—also found within the IF Framework—and their importance to fund manager expertise, are now explored. These include the value of collaborative learning (through essential networking mechanisms), future-thinking, and (among other skills) emotional intelligence.

3.1   IF for Fund Managers: Learning Collaboratively Through Networking

Geopolitical uncertainty triggered by Russia's invasion of Ukraine in early 2022, on the back of the Covid-19 global pandemic, saw inflation surge around the globe (Gourinches 2025). These incidents create uncertainty and volatility in financial markets, with a flow-on effect of sometimes sharp market corrections and a change in investor attitudes. Further, the impact of integrative technology such as AI-powered tools for portfolio construction and risk management (see chapter 'Artificial Intelligence in Discretionary Fund Management,' in this volume) to address increasing volumes of data and rates of change at a global level, can impact positively in areas of enhanced operational efficiency and customer experience (Byrum 2022). These efficiencies support fund managers pursuing impactful and vital tasks associated with networking and information-gathering required to assess and build confidence in portfolio decisions. Professional and social networks are important to IF, as evidenced through the vital role company-fund manager meetings play in developing fund manager expertise (Barker et al. 2012). Fund managers acknowledge these meetings as information gathering and confidence-building for investment decisions, and as Barker et al. (2012) highlight, they enable more accurate interpretation of strategic themes unfolding in organisations.

Grant et al.'s (2022) findings support the value of networks in developing expertise—claiming they are an essential component and capability of experts involved in pre-merger acquisitions. Given the similar nature of investment decisions made by fund managers, and the role networks play in contributing to foresight (Innes 2023), fund managers should embrace efficiencies that will facilitate greater networking capacity.

3.2 IF for Fund Managers: Future-Thinking

An essential element of IF, the ability to 'future-think' has been established as a main function of fund managers (Kacperczyk et al. 2016). The importance of future-thinking to fund managers was highlighted by a fund manager recruiter in chapter 'Searching for Expert Fund Managers,' in this volume:

> We look a lot towards the future, trying to see what's around the corner. We try to evaluate how this person thinks about future threats, opportunities, ESG, whatever it may be, strategies around such things. (4) (Grant and Abrahamson, chapter 'Searching for Expert Fund Managers' in this volume)

Future-thinking requires personal experience and memories. The IF Framework and associated IF study this chapter draws on, stemmed from a gap in our understanding of how individuals experience and contribute to corporate foresight. Early proponents positioned foresight as a human ability and highlighted the value of foresight for strategic or higher-level decision-making (Chia 2004). Benefits of foresight for leaders and visionaries in avoiding future pitfalls through undertaking activities like scenario planning (Chia 2004), improved knowledge creation, diffusion and absorption and social capital and networking and highlighted the opportunity for firms to develop foresight within their workforce. Thus, greater focus on individual skills associated with foresight was required. Reflecting on the IF definition and its reference to drawing on past experiences to imagine future scenarios, we can seek to understand the value of IF cognitions for fund managers. For example, earlier exploration of foresight in the psychology literature through the work of Suddendorf (2017), defined episodic foresight in humans as 'the ability to imagine future scenarios and organise action accordingly' (p. 191). Terms such as *mental time travel into the future* (Suddendorf and Corballis 1997), *episodic future thinking* (Atance and O'Neill 2001), and *episodic simulation of future events* (Schacter et al. 2007) have been used to describe similar phenomena. Each of the definitions involve semantic (facts, etc.) and episodic (personal experience) memory systems vital in the process of foresight.

Although there have been some advances of foresight research in both the fields of business and psychology (in business the emphasis has been on corporate foresight), the benefits of merging these two disciplines to examine foresight in a business context has been limited. Psychologist researchers take a positivist approach to laboratory-style experiments that explain when foresight is developed in humans and which memory systems are involved (Atance 2015). Futurist researchers engage in mostly conceptual debate about cognitive, analytical, and future-thinking skills and their value to corporate foresight.

At the heart of foresight research, is that humans are influenced by unique experiences and often tacit knowledge they acquire in their personal and work lives. Further, adverse situations impact humans in ways that expand their resilience. This resilience offers strength in terms of the 'passion for and perseverance toward especially long-term goals' (Duckworth and Gross 2014, p. 319). Grant and Nilsson (2023) utilise Duckworth and Gross' (2014) term to describe this propensity as 'grit,' arguing its importance in obtaining expertise through the intense pursuit of practicing and learning skills within a domain area of expertise. Related to the pursuit of learning and upskilling, knowledge and expertise held by employees—in this case—fund managers, is key to the IF process.

Importantly, work-specific knowledge is needed for the function of 'remembering' in IF. Innes (2023) determined that longer-term corporate knowledge features as an important aspect of IF in employees—which supports Suddendorf and Corballis' (1997) mental time travel process of remembering (drawing on episodic memory or experiences) in order to 'imagine' or mentally travel through time to visualise actions and adjust current actions and decision-making accordingly. In the field of fund management, this skill offers potential advantages—but should also be a caution to fund managers. Emotions that drive investment decisions (such as intuition stemming from past experience) could result in biases in decision-making (Verma et al. 2024)—pointing to another essential IF element to combat this—emotional intelligence.

3.3   IF for Fund Managers: Emotional Intelligence

While emotional intelligence is bundled under the descriptor 'Individual skills and disposition' in the IF Framework, it is central to the function of communication for the role of fund managers. For example, Tuckett and Taffler (2012 in Verma et al. 2024) propose that extensive expertise obtained by fund managers means they can console and direct investors when markets are volatile. Further, fund managers describe the critical nature of judgements made of company leaders during company-fund manager meetings. In these meetings tacit knowledge and leader sentiments are interpreted by fund managers (requiring emotional intelligence) to establish confidence in their strategy (Barker et al. 2012) (see chapter 'Judgments and Decisions by Expert Fund Managers,' in this volume, for an extended discussion around the role of emotions in decision-making for fund managers). In conversation, our expert in fund management raised the dilemma of 'super genius' fund managers who may not possess social awareness as a component of emotional intelligence—sometimes prioritising misleading facts and figures over 'listening' (2025, personal communication). Section 4 explores several opportunities for fund managers seeking to develop their IF.

4   Development Opportunities for Fund Managers

Several opportunities exist for fund managers seeking to develop IF in the pursuit of fund management expertise. Employees working in highly regulated sectors often cultivate future-thinking skills out of necessity, driven by reporting mechanisms and regulatory controls that require them to anticipate the impact of decisions across their work. For others, future-thinking may be an inherent propensity, exhibited in varying ways. The IF study revealed that employees experience future-thinking under different conditions and apply it through different approaches. For instance, some employees rapidly assess the potential outcomes of their decisions in the moment (e.g., during a meeting), while others engage in a more extended, deliberate evaluation process, influenced by concerns for people or the business before acting on their foresight (for a broader discussion on the temporal nature of IF and the role of sensemaking in these differences, see Innes 2023). For fund managers, future thinking infiltrates all aspects of their work making it a crucial capability for success.

This chapter has explored the possibilities for fund managers to develop their IF through building in reflective time in their work to allow for reflective practice and future-thinking. Developing and practicing skills like visioning, assessing and prioritising tasks are important features of their work, developing understanding around when intuitive decision-making might be useful, and exploring opportunities to develop emotional intelligence will all contribute to fund manager expertise. While there are formal courses that can develop some of these skills, seeking opportunities to collaborate, draw on networks and mentor others will all contribute to IF capacity.

Support from leadership in fostering a foresight culture is equally important. Allowing people time to reflect during poignant moments in their work will result in enhanced IF through the opportunity to future-think, reflect, learn collaboratively and develop understanding to achieve foresightful decisions that result in improved outcomes for clients and the firm. Encouraging People and Culture to support mentoring and group reflection mechanisms, and to develop strategies to reward and/or acknowledge decisions and insights from fund managers and their teams that encompass IF insights, will foster foresight capacity across the firm.

While we are only beginning to understand the value of IF to firms, research indicates that employees who think about the future implications of their work, build strong formal and informal social networks, and foster or partake in an open culture of trust, empowerment and healthy risk-taking, are more likely to engage in collaborative learning opportunities resulting in innovative outcomes for firms (Innes 2024). Fund managers who develop IF expertise are better equipped to navigate uncertainty, identify emergent opportunities, and enhance both their personal performance and the firm's long-term success. In our fast-paced, dynamic and increasingly data- and technology-driven society, it is encouraging to know that unique aspects of human behaviour and cognition are to be valued and embraced for future firm success.

5 Conclusions

This chapter explores individual-level contributors to IF, and organisational processes that foster IF behaviours and practices. Using illustrative examples supported by expert commentary, it presents a unique opportunity for fund managers and fund management firms to embrace IF in their pursuit of fund management expertise and competitive advantage. Fund managers have been partaking in foresightful activities for decades: Assessing and prioritising risks and opportunities; researching and analysing data for portfolios; networking to gather tacit information valuable to decision-making and more. Foresight is a prevalent feature of fund manager work. However, the IF Framework provides a structure for fund managers at all levels to seek opportunities to extend IF capacity in their work to enhance performance.

The framework posits that focused efforts on personal development associated with a fund manager's individual knowledge, skills and experience can foster advanced skills in intuitive decision-making, emotional intelligence, and future-thinking. Combined with a considered approach to collaborative learning opportunities, where tacit knowledge of fund managers and their associates can be shared in the pursuit of building foresight capacity in the firm, outcomes from the IF study indicate that IF contributes to knowledge capabilities of a firm leading to valued learning and innovation outcomes (Innes 2024).

IF behaviours and how IF manifests in employees or firms is not something easily measured and defined. While there are facets of foresight we do understand in terms of human knowledge and experience leading to memory system function and recollection for remembering and imagining (Suddendorf and Corballis 1997), other measures such as the influence of IF on organisation or fund manager performance will prove more challenging. However, measuring a single or higher-order organisational performance measure fails to capture the intention of IF and the IF framework. Measuring elements of IF such as the outcomes of collaborative knowledge-sharing practices of experienced fund managers, or the use of intuition in IF decisions, or the effectiveness of social networks in addressing fund managers knowledge gaps—is more feasible and valuable to firms. More formalised measurement scales for IF are needed. The IF study underpinning this chapter provided qualitative insights to identify key dimensions on which the IF framework is founded, however, it is now necessary to validate these dimensions through future quantitative research. This chapter explored the opportunities for IF fund managers and firms to engage with the IF Framework in pursuit of fostering a foresight culture and foresight as a core competence. As research in IF progresses, fund managers can seek to master relevant IF elements to build foresight capacity in their teams and pursue their own paths as expert fund managers.

Acknowledgements The authors gratefully acknowledge the valuable comments from the editor and co-authors of the book, as well as the anonymous commentary received during the preparation of this chapter.

References

Atance CM (2015) Young children's thinking about the future. Child Dev Perspect 9(3):178–182

Atance CM, O'Neill DK (2001) Episodic future thinking. Trends Cogn Sci 5(12):533–539

Barker R, Hendry J, Roberts J, Sanderson P (2012) Can company-fund manager meetings convey informational benefits? Exploring the rationalisation of equity investment decision-making by UK fund managers. Acc Organ Soc 37(4):207–222

Bevan MT (2014) A method of phenomenological interviewing. Qual Health Res 24(1):136–144

Byrum J (2022) AI in financial portfolio management: practical considerations and use cases. In: Babich V, Birge J, Hilary G (eds) Innovative technology at the interface of finance and operations, vol I. Springer, New York, pp 249–270

Chia R (2004) Re-educating attention: what is foresight and how is it cultivated. In: Tsoukas H, Shepherd J (eds) Managing the future: foresight in the knowledge economy. Blackwell Publishing, Hoboken, pp 21–37

Clare A, Sherman M, O'Sullivan N, Gao J, Zhu S (2022) Manager characteristics: predicting fund performance. Int Rev Financ Anal 80:102049

Coleman L (2015) Facing up to fund managers: an exploratory field study of how institutional investors make decisions. Qual Res Financ Mark 7(2):111–135

Duckworth A, Gross JJ (2014) Self-control and grit: related but separable determinants of success. Curr Dir Psychol Sci 23(5):319–325

Gourinches PO (2025) As one cycle ends, another begins amid growing divergence. IMF blog. https://www.imf.org/en/Blogs/Articles/2025/01/17/as-one-cycle-ends-another-begins-amid-growing-divergence. Accessed 17 Jan 2025

Grant M, Nilsson F (2023) Intuitive expertise and financial decision-making. Routledge, Abingdon, New York

Grant M, Nilsson F, Nordvall AC (2022) Pre-merger acquisition capabilities: a study of two successful serial acquirers. Eur Manag J 40(6):932–942

Hodgkinson GP, Sadler-Smith E (2018) The dynamics of intuition and analysis in managerial and organizational decision-making. Acad Manag Perspect 32(4):473–492

Innes M (2023) Exploring the lived experience of individual foresight in organisations. Doctoral dissertation, University of the Sunshine Coast, Queensland

Innes ML (2024) Exploring individual foresight: implications for organizational learning and innovation in firms. J Innov Knowl 9(4):100604

Kacperczyk M, Van Nieuwerburgh S, Veldkamp L (2016) A rational theory of mutual funds' attention allocation. Econometrica 84(2):571–626

Liang Q, Liao J, Ling L (2022) Social interactions and mutual fund portfolios: the role of alumni networks in China. China Financ Rev Int 12(3):433–450

Ma L, Tang Y (2019) Portfolio manager ownership and mutual fund risk taking. Manag Sci 65(12):5518–5534

Meyer J (2024) Doing artificial intelligence (AI): algorithmic decision support as a human activity. Decision 11(4):481–492

Rennie DL (2000) Grounded theory methodology as methodical hermeneutics: reconciling realism and relativism. Theory Psychol 10(4):481–502

Schacter DL, Addis DR, Buckner RL (2007) Remembering the past to imagine the future: the prospective brain. Nat Rev Neurosci 8(9):657–661

Serenko A, Bontis N (2016) Understanding counterproductive knowledge behavior: antecedents and consequences of intra-organizational knowledge hiding. J Knowl Manag 20(6):1199–1224

Sinclair M, Sadler-Smith E, Hodgkinson GP (2009) The role of intuition in strategic decision-making. In: Costanzo, LA, MacKay, RB (eds) Handbook of research on strategy and foresight. Edward Elgar Publishing, Cheltenham, pp. 393–417

Slaughter R (1997) Developing and applying strategic foresight. ABN Rep 5(10):13–27

Smith J, Flowers P, Larkin M (2009) Interpretative phenomenological analysis: theory, method and research. Sage, London

Suddendorf T (2017) The emergence of episodic foresight and its consequences. Child Dev Perspect 11(3):191–195

Suddendorf T, Corballis M (1997) Mental time travel and the evolution of the human mind. Genet Soc Gen Psychol Monogr 123(2):133–168

Tao R, Su C-W, Xiao Y, Dai K, Khali F (2021) Robo advisors, algorithmic trading and investment management: wonders of fourth industrial revolution in financial markets. Technol Forecast Soc Change 163:120421

Verma S, Rao P, Kumar S (2024) Is investing inherently emotionally arousing process? Fund manager perspective. Qual Res Financ Mark 16(2):380–400

Wu H (2022) Intuition in investment decision-making across cultures. J Behav Financ 23(1):106–122

Artificial Intelligence in Discretionary Fund Management

Haojun Hu ⓘ

Abstract This chapter examines the evolving implementation of artificial intelligence (AI) in discretionary fund management. Drawing on interviews with fund industry experts, a recent survey, and existing literature, the study concludes that the development of AI augments rather than replaces professional judgment. AI's role remains primarily as a specialised tool in expanding data access, enhancing data processing, and supporting idea generation. The chapter highlights that experience-based expertise is difficult for machines to mimic and that professional judgment is needed to distinguish useful signals. They provide discretionary managers with a distinct competitive edge, especially in choppy markets. This need for a 'human in the loop' emphasises the complementary relationship between advanced technical skills and business domain knowledge. Generally, discretionary fund management is depicted as a data-driven, technology-assisted, and human-centric discipline.

Keywords AI · Data abundance · Fund managers' expertise · Human–AI collaboration · Investment decision making

1 Introduction

> 25 years ago, the typical fund manager would be trained in finance or economics from the business school. I think today, to an overwhelming extent, we hire engineers as newcomers in this profession. […] I think this really points to a different technological skill set that is needed. And, AI is just that sort of prolongation of that. (A)

One of the interviewed asset managers with over 25 years of experience highlighted the evolving skill set required for fund managers over time. Andrew Ng, the founder of Coursera and DeepLearning.AI, stated, 'what will happen is not that AI will replace people, but I think people that use AI will replace other people that don't' (Ossola 2024). They both emphasise the potential importance and significance of integrating

H. Hu (✉)
Department of Business Studies, Uppsala University, Uppsala, Sweden
e-mail: haojun.hu@fek.uu.se

human expertise with machine intelligence. However, the practical implementation of the 'human + machine' assumption in fund management is unclear. It raises two questions: to what extent is artificial intelligence (AI) actually implemented into fund managers' investment processes, and how fund managers perceive the interplay between AI and their expertise.

According to Mercer (2024)'s Global Investment Manager Survey, 'current use of AI across investment strategies and research stretches far beyond the traditional "quant" cohort. 91% of managers are currently (54%) or planning to (37%) use AI within their investment strategy or asset-class research.' This survey highlights that AI is primarily used to augment existing capabilities by expanding data sets, enhancing analysis, and supporting idea generation. Notably, 'more than half of AI-integrated investment teams report that AI analysis informs rather than determines final investment decisions.' Around 20% state that AI can propose investment decisions, which can be overridden by human teams. Rather than fully replacing fund managers or making final investment decisions through complete automation, it is currently best positioned as a specialised support tool for specific tasks that enhance productivity and efficiency throughout the investment process.

The continued presence of human managers in AI-powered funds and regulatory requirements (Regulation (EU) 2024/1689 (EC) 2024) for human oversight in governance and risk management in financial services emphasises the critical role of human involvement in the implementation of these technologies. While the potential capabilities of AI are becoming increasingly clear in terms of what it could be and do, its actual future role—what it will be—is still unknown. Given the requirement for continued human involvement, it is unclear how AI is implemented in practice since it could differ from what it is capable of doing.

Fund managers play key roles in shaping how AI is implemented in fund management. While fund managers influence the usage of AI, the technology can, in turn, reshape human decision-making processes and professional behaviours. Therefore, it is essential to understand how fund managers work with AI and how their expertise interacts with AI. Quantitative managers,[1] who rely on model-based strategies (Abis 2020; Dugast and Foucault 2025), already depend on systematic and data-driven models, making diversified data sources and AI natural extensions rather than transformational tools. Therefore, studying discretionary managers who rely more heavily on their own judgments and human expertise (Abis 2020; Dugast and Foucault 2025) provides deeper insights into these two questions.

According to semi-structured interviews with nine discretionary professionals in the fund industry, the study concludes that discretionary managers typically see the core investment process as involving three tasks: exclusion, where they filter sectors

---

[1] Discretionary analysis, in essence, is the human-driven qualitative analysis approach, relying heavily on the intuition, experience, and judgment of investors. This method involves a more subjective examination of data, where managers use their judgment to interpret information to estimate the value of a stock by analysing various internal and external factors. In contrast, the quantitative analysis approach utilises quantitative tools to mine, process, and analyse data to discover new predictors (Abis 2020; Dugast and Foucault 2025). This method relies more on statistical, mathematical, and computer models, as well as fixed rules.

or companies based on compliance requirements; integration, which involves portfolio construction; and trade execution. They have a clear view of their decision-making processes, which rely heavily on professional judgment and experience-based expertise to interpret and distil complex information (see also chapter 'Judgments and Decisions by Expert Fund Managers' in this volume). According to the interviewees, AI in this context refers to the implementation of advanced technologies that enable timely access to diverse raw data, sophisticated data analysis capabilities, and automated execution tools—such as platforms that facilitate cross-trading. They generally view AI as supportive tools that provide the information involving data overhead functions—the background tasks used to make raw data more digestible for humans. They include quantitative data collection, handling, and processing. They also see AI as useful in generating reports, serving as assistants during internal meetings, and offering additional insights that help facilitate communication with investment targets. In practice, AI used as a summariser is now more widely implemented, helping managers efficiently distil large volumes of information into actionable insights. However, AI as a recommender—which offers explicit trading recommendations—is used more cautiously and to a lesser extent.[2]

AI is not systematically implemented in fund managers' investment processes due to challenges such as signal noise that could disperse human attention and the limited ability to anticipate future uncertainties that lack sufficient data, such as sustainability data (see chapter 'Integrating ESG Information in Active Fund Management' in this volume). Guided by the interview responses related to the interplay between human expertise and AI, this study indicates the need for a 'human in the loop.' Rather than replacing professional judgment, rooted in business domain knowledge developed through years of experience and exercised through intuition, AI emphasises its importance. Advanced technical skills serve as a valuable complement rather than a substitute. Overall, discretionary fund management is characterised as data-driven, technology-assisted, and human-centric.

This chapter is organised as follows: Section 2 reviews the selected relevant literature and introduces two research questions derived from the literature. Section 3 describes the evidence from the interviews regarding AI in investment decision-making. Section 4 provides discussions of the findings, and Section 5 concludes with limitations and future research ideas. The research design of this chapter is detailed in the appendix.

---

[2] In this context, the terms Summariser AI and Recommender AI are used by the author to distinguish between two specific applications of AI: the former refers to AI as an assistant in summarising raw data, while the latter denotes AI that acts as a decision-maker by providing specific investment recommendations. For more details, see Nazari and Mahdavi (2019) on text summarisation, and Zhang et al. (2021) on recommender AI.

2 Literature Review

With the growing volume of data generated from business processes, individual activities, and sensors (Kolanovic and Smith 2019), AI techniques have the potential to provide real-time insights, uncover economic fundamentals, and aid investment decisions. Previous studies converge on the predictability of various data sources and AI algorithms (Aziz et al. 2022). However, when these predictive signals become widely recognised, adopted, and chased by market participants, the effectiveness of these signals diminishes. Then, the competition remains in chasing novel and useful data, adopting the latest technologies, and applying the most advanced models. It is often associated with quantitative strategies in fund management. However, for discretionary and hybrid funds that rely more on fund managers' professional judgment and expertise, it remains unclear what AI means to those fund managers and to what extent AI is implemented in their decision-making processes. Additionally, since it is not the tools themselves but the effective implementation of these tools that matters, it is essential to understand how fund managers, serving as implementers and decision-makers, work with AI and how their expertise interacts with it.

2.1 To What Extent Is AI Implemented in Fund Managers' Investment Processes?

AI algorithms, such as machine learning (ML), are valuable tools for analysing complex and large-scale data. This data-analysis capability has four main applications in finance: price forecasting, financial market analysis, risk forecasting, and uncovering new financial perspectives, as identified in Aziz et al. (2022)'s literature review.

AI enables the use of diverse datasets that could not be efficiently analysed using traditional methods. This is particularly relevant in the era of big data (BD), characterised by the large quantities of data generated (volume), the speed at which data is produced and processed (velocity), and the diverse types and sources of data available (variety) (Laney 2001). Scholars find that alternative data sources that are apart from the data generated from business processes contain novel and valuable information about economic indicators, corporate fundamentals, and stock pricing. For example, consumer and employee behaviour data, such as mobile device activity (Froot et al. 2017), online product reviews (Huang 2018), and crowdsourced employer ratings (Green et al. 2019), is beneficial to the predictability of the company's sales, earnings, and profitability. Digital footprint, like Google search volumes, can predict key economic indicators such as automobile sales, unemployment claims, travel planning, and consumer confidence (Choi and Varian 2012). Sentiment data, such as Twitter comments, also has predictive power on firm fundamentals. This power may be attributed to the 'wisdom of crowds.' Tang (2018) argues that the sentiment conveyed in Twitter comments is often dominated by expert opinions. Additionally,

Umar (2022) uses a field experiment with Seeking Alpha, a financial news and investment research platform, and shows that textual complexity influences investor attention to news and market outcomes (lowering announcement turnover and volatility). While the usefulness of previous data sources is largely from the predictability of market sentiment, some other data sources provide more objective insights, such as satellite imagery of weather conditions (Mukherjee et al. 2021) as an alternative to government data and parking lot traffic, which provide real-time, external indicators of firm activity (Bonelli and Foucault 2023).

Among these studies, Bonelli and Foucault (2023) explore satellite imagery of parking lot traffic data in the context of active fund management. They find that such data reduces information acquisition costs, allowing sophisticated investors to develop profitable trading strategies. However, it diminishes the relative stock-picking ability of active fund managers, as the availability of alternative data makes the stock prices of covered companies more transparent. In general, while existing research highlights the potential of these data sources, their practical application by fund managers remains uncertain. What can hinder the application of AI is whether professional fund managers actively implement these diverse data sources into their investment processes.

While AI can support fund managers in making investment decisions, it can also be used by fund investors to identify and select outperforming funds. Li and Rossi (2020) and DeMiguel et al. (2023) demonstrate that non-linear ML methods, such as boosted regression trees, gradient boosting, and random forests, outperform traditional linear models in selecting portfolios of funds by using fund holdings and stock characteristics. Wu et al. (2021) find that deep learning is particularly effective in predicting future hedge fund returns based on historical return characteristics. Kaniel et al. (2023) use neural networks to predict mutual fund alpha using a broad set of predictors, including stock and fund characteristics, along with macroeconomic variables.

The possible use of AI algorithms in fund selection may create a feedback effect, influencing fund managers to prioritise the indicators that these algorithms emphasise. Cao et al. (2023) examine the feedback effect while in corporate disclosure, finding that the growing prevalence of AI readership incentivises firms to make their filings more machine-friendly and neutral in tone. They show that increased machine readership reduces negative sentiment, particularly with high benefits or low costs of sentiment management. This finding has potential implications for fund management, where managers must publicly disclose information and attract investors. Consequently, they may also respond to AI-driven fund-selection models, potentially influencing investor preferences.

Moreover, the proliferation of BD and real-time analytics has also enabled faster trading activities, minimising delays in information gathering and trade execution across platforms (Biais et al. 2015). They could ensure the need for fund managers to have time-proper, value-driven trading practices. Given these capabilities, AI has the potential to automate the investment process. However, Mercer (2024)'s survey indicates that this potential has not yet been realised in practice. Then, to what extent is AI actually implemented into fund managers' investment processes, and how do they perceive the usefulness of AI?

2.2 How Does AI Interact with Fund Managers' Expertise?

One might expect funds to rely more on alternative data and advanced techniques to make their portfolios less susceptible to human managers' limitations in processing information; e.g., Chen and Ren (2022) observe the reduced behavioural biases in studying AI-powered mutual funds. However, compared with discretionary funds, quantitative funds may exhibit more correlated trades (Khandani and Lo 2011) and be less adaptable to changing market conditions (Miguel and Chen 2021). Dugast and Foucault (2025) characterise quant funds as 'data miners' and discretionary funds as 'experts.' 'Experts have fixed ability to generate trading signals of a given precision about a risky asset, while data miners obtain trading signals through a search process to discover the best (i.e., highest-precision) trading signals' (Ibid., p. 244). When faced with data abundance, 'data miners' tend to search less intensively for high-precision signals, as the availability of abundant data increases the precision of the best predictors. This behaviour often leads to more dispersed performance outcomes and a reduction in capital inflows. The authors also find that while data abundance enhances price informativeness, it can lower average asset manager performance.

Fund managers' expertise is crucial in navigating these dynamics. Skilled investors efficiently allocate their attention to understanding both idiosyncratic shocks (stock-picking ability) and aggregate shocks (market-timing ability), reflecting their expertise. Kacperczyk et al. (2016) develop an attention allocation model based on the business cycle. It shows that 'fund managers optimally choose to process information about aggregate shocks in recessions and idiosyncratic shocks in booms' (Ibid., p. 572). Abis (2020) expands this research and concludes that discretionary managers are more flexible and focus more on stocks for which relatively little information can be learned. This approach allows them to reduce their information-processing disadvantage relative to quants.

As data becomes increasingly abundant and AI enables the extraction of more timely signals, awareness of attention constraints becomes even more important. Dessaint et al. (2024), using financial analysts as the case, argue that much alternative data is short-term-oriented, often shifting analysts' focus to immediate information, at the expense of long-term perspectives. It also reflects a misalignment problem in the AI agency (see agency problem discussed in chapter 'Analysing Fund Managers' Accountability' in this volume), where short-term AI-optimised objectives may conflict with long-term strategies. Humans' ability to analyse the information, integrate it into a cohesive strategy, and make timely decisions is constrained by how much attention they can allocate to different data points without becoming overwhelmed or distracted. Fund managers' expertise is essential for efficiently allocating attention in chasing good performance despite technological advances.

Cao et al. (2024) propose that 'From Man vs. Machine to Man + Machine' by adding analyst forecasts into machine learning models. They argue that humans have the advantage in institutional knowledge, e.g., involving intangible assets and financial distress. AI can outperform when information is transparent but voluminous. Therefore, the optimal approach lies in leveraging the complementary strengths of both humans and machines. It will not only generate incremental value but also substantially reduce errors. However, how does AI interplay with fund managers' expertise in practice?

3   Findings

> We use AI not as a peer asset or portfolio manager but more like a team of interns whom we send out into the space to dig through data for us. For us, AI really is about efficiency in the work that we have always done. (G)

Interviewees' reflections are reality-based, focusing on whether and how AI is used in their work. Based on their reflections, this section firstly describes the extent to which discretionary fund managers utilise AI in their investment process, including exclusion, integration, and trade execution. Secondly, it focuses on how fund managers perceive the interplay between AI and their expertise, progressing from what they consider essential in fund management to how they perceive their own expertise and, ultimately, how they envision the interplay between human and machine.

3.1   AI as a Supportive Tool

Rather than being used directly as a decision-making tool, AI is more commonly employed as a productivity-enhancing tool without directly influencing final decisions, as interviewee F pointed out.

> It [AI] is really like a productivity tool at this point. (F)

According to the interviewees, the core investment tasks include exclusion, integration, and trade execution, which involve filtering out securities to ensure compliance, constructing portfolios, and executing trades, respectively. Data overhead functions are the background tasks used to make raw data more digestible for humans. Including quantitative data collection, handling, and processing, they are regarded as supporting functions that could assist their decision-making. But interviewees do not really treat those functions as the core stage in the human decision-making process. Rather, they generally treat the information generated after this process as inputs to be considered, relying on their personal judgment to interpret and incorporate it into decision-making. In addition, discretionary managers actively acquire information through direct engagement with invested targets and discussions with colleagues.

Some interviewees acknowledged the potential usefulness of AI in providing supplementary insights that help guide these conversations. AI writing tools, like ChatGPT, are also seen as useful in supporting tasks such as drafting reports.

3.1.1   Exclusion

Firstly, exclusion serves as the preliminary step in investment activities, aiming at filtering out securities that do not align with the investment strategy, regulations, or policy constraints. It is also a critical phase for ensuring compliance by providing data-driven solutions. Especially during this stage, the analytical process of quantitative data is important. BD could be helpful in this step by enabling accurate mapping between invested assets and the fund's strategic objectives.

> Our models ensure that exclusions are accurately mapped to specific issues. Big data is essential in verifying that securities and funds are correctly aligned. (B)

AI, although not widely implemented at present, holds potential for future applications in automating market screening to ensure compliance requirements.

> AI may help us screen the market for targets and identify companies that fulfil certain criteria. (C)

According to interviewee B, AI is likely to be a beneficial productivity tool in analytics in supporting the 'overhead functions of data, including data collection, data handling, and data processing.' Interviewee C similarly described applying AI to specific analytical tasks.

> I expect us to use AI tools mainly for specific analytical aspects of our operations, rather than in decision-making. (C)

3.1.2   Integration

Secondly, integration is the core stage where fund managers focus on portfolio construction, which could be treated as the real investment decision-making stage. At this stage, fund managers have a relatively small pool of companies to analyse. They consider their interactions and prior experience with these companies to be more efficient sources of information for decision-making. They place significant emphasis on qualitative insights gained through this active engagement. The ability to interpret conversations was also highlighted as a critical human skill. Some interviewees expressed scepticism about whether more and timely data and data analysis could enhance such judgment.

> You read and you feel how the CEO talks and what the owners say about the company. It's not the figures. That's more important. So, I'm not sure if an artificial intelligence-driven data model with 1 billion data points will do anything better. (H)

> We did not work so much with [alternative/big] data at all. We only work with sales gross, profit margin, and PE ratio, and look at the balance sheet. So, you will not go bankrupt if the business goes down. We try to make things simple so we could put our time into meeting the management. And we sat all days talking about the company, how is this going. We read that article. Does this have something to do with the company? We went for lunch and listened to that company, and then we talked about that for an hour. (E)

Interviewee D described this process as one that involves a greater degree of subjectivity.

> It's rather, not at our level, but at the level maybe of the advisors that are assisting us in the analysis and due diligence. I think at our level, it's rather decision-making and subjective decisions, so to say. And it's rather like a level below that it might be developed for the use of AI. (D)

Therefore, it is hard to automate using AI.

> The human element is actually talking to the people running the companies we are investing in, talking to clients and customers. Those can be elements. I think that's very, very hard to automate to any large degree. (B)

However, the interviewee also acknowledged the potential of AI to assist by providing additional data support or context for managers to guide conversations and engagement strategies effectively. The information from AI could be viewed as a valuable 'source of knowledge' (A).

> AI systems could form part of the inputs for other strategies by generating ideas for fundamental research or providing support. (B)

Additionally, apart from the interaction with the invested target, AI could also facilitate the interaction with their colleagues by facilitating a quicker and more efficient understanding of their holdings.

> A colleague fed data coming from our sources and online tools into AI, asking it to produce 300-word summaries about each company. He prepared summaries for 20 companies in just one day. The next day, we had a very productive meeting, and we went through all of them. It was incredibly efficient and helped us refocus on understanding our holdings. (G)

3.1.3 Trade Execution

Thirdly, AI, referred to here as portfolio management systems, proves potential usefulness in 'simplified portfolio construction, simplified trading' for interviewee B. This implementation allows for internal balancing of flows as needed when managers operate across different trading systems.

> Portfolio management systems also depend on both big data and [advanced techniques] in order to take big data, and also process it, and have a continuous flow between different systems internally as well. (B)

3.2   AI as a Complement to Human Expertise

> The progression towards more and more technical skills, I think that we will see a return
> to more, more soft skills now, since the capability of this AI system will give the ability to
> more people from more backgrounds to actually do more technical work. (B)

In response of the citation at the beginning of this chapter from interviewee A,
another respondent from the same company noted that with technology becoming
more advanced, there is a growing opportunity to shift the focus back to soft skills,
such as interpersonal skills and professional judgment developed through years of
experiences (see also in chapters 'Performance and Fund Managers' Expertise,'
'Searching for Expert Fund Managers,' and 'Judgments and Decisions by Expert
Fund Managers' in this volume), rather than prioritising hard skills like advanced
technical knowledge in AI designing. Discretionary fund managers described their
work as grounded in basically fundamental tasks, focusing on core objectives that
address straightforward questions using basic information aligned with the characteristics and strategies of the funds they manage. They perceived that their competitive edges lie in their professional judgments. And the insights brought by their
experience-based expertise are difficult for machines to mimic. Overall, they view
AI as a complement to their expertise and advanced technical skills as complements
to their business domain knowledge.

3.2.1   Basics Have Not Been Changed

AI has not fundamentally changed the basic way fund managers work. It primarily
provides access to more diverse data and generates signals at a faster speed.

> And there's always some debate on how rigorous the data is. So, what we can do is we can
> look at satellite images and count how many trucks are coming in and out of the factories to
> sort of gauge whether activity is picked up or slowed down and is that consistent with the
> official data. So, this has been around for quite a few years now. But as we get into more data
> processing capabilities and AI, etc., and automating all of these or just giving huge amounts
> of datasets to your AI engine, you're able to generate this sort of analysis and signals at
> a much, much quicker pace. So, it doesn't change what we do. It just means that we have
> maybe quicker or more accurate or more data to look at to sort of make investment decisions.
> So, that's kind of where I feel it's going. It's just basically more tools for us, more data for
> us, and obviously, you know, the speed is a huge thing as well. (F)

Other interviewees also expressed the idea of what the basics are. Firstly, the fund
industry is fundamentally profit-driven. Even if one of the respondents foresaw the
future of using AI as an end-to-end solution, they need to ensure that the performance
is actually good.

> We do not have any AI-driven strategy product for an end-to-end solution. But that might
> change if you have an assessment with their performance in the future, of course. (B)

Secondly, interviewee E mentioned that they make the profit-driven decision based
on some basic indicators such as 'sales gross, profit margin, and PE ratio and look

at the balance sheet.' Another risk manager from an alternative investment fund agreed that AI enhances the ability to process and analyse more data. However, the interviewee emphasised that if a manager already has a deep understanding of the fundamentals and relevant information about an investment target, the additional data may add little value.

> Usually, when it comes to asset management or trading, it involves analysing a lot of data. So, any tool that will improve or facilitate the analysis of a lot of data, like an AI tool, will only improve your ability to cover more data. And you can get signals from there. But even with more improvements, you can just analyse more data than you need to know. But if you have already known things that you can find, less data may be easier. (I)

To make a profit, interviewee E emphasised the importance of maintaining consistency and a long-term perspective in some basic questions they need to ask themselves when making decisions.

> In the long term, they [stock prices] can go up and down quite a lot. But every stock is moving like that because people [company managers] sit there and say we send you a new story about the company. It wasn't in your [manager's] story. As a result, it [stock's price] goes up and down. It's so hard to be long-term [in your] thinking. You get so pushed, perhaps every day, over short news. (E)

Interviewee F also pointed out that they avoid reacting impulsively to news or market movements, preferring a repeatable process in making decisions. In their views, exercising patience and waiting for the right moment to act often yields better results than immediate trading in response to market noise. The timely signals provided by AI add little value, as well as the news in this case.

> Ultimately, you know, having the right process means what you do becomes repeatable. So, knowing where your edge is, like, what am I better at doing than the algos and the systematic type of strategies? What is my market specialty? What is it that I have an edge in? Okay, once I know that, then I need to make sure I can repeat that time and time again. So, I have a process. I know I refined my edge. I know what my process is. And then I've got to make sure I'm in a really good place mentally to execute that. And having a good process really helps around that. (F)

Even though AI can process large and diversified data, providing additional information on these indicators, the quality of the data is still questionable.

> It's still the quality of the information that is the most important, but not the amount [...] It's good to have easy access to lots of data. But the data itself is in no way, by definition, interesting or good. And too much data maybe will confuse you. You have so much information that you don't really know what the real effect is and if the valuation is correct. (H)

3.2.2 Competitive Edge of Professional Judgment

Interviewees emphasised the importance of professional judgment in maintaining a competitive edge, particularly in response to the rapid advancements in technology that allow quantitative managers to achieve greater profitability. One of the interviewees highlighted an intriguing perspective on human bias, viewing it as an advantage that helps generate alpha and compete against quantitative funds. He emphasised that the focus should not be on avoiding human bias but rather on addressing mental bias. To him, human bias differs from emotional bias. He views it more as professional judgment, grounded in personal experience, intuition, and individual perspective.

> I don't try to overcome human bias because that's my edge. That's my alpha. If I overcame that, we would shut down my strategy and pass all the money to the quant team. But I think what you want to overcome is like emotional bias, as you need to be sort of flexible around views. This is the very hard part about very discretionary macro trading. It's self-regulation, emotional regulation, etc. (F)

Besides, in most cases, future uncertainty presents a significant challenge due to the lack of information that can accurately reflect future conditions. While the abundance of data available today may enhance the ability to predict certain risks, it does not address the fundamental issue of uncertainty, which is unknown. As pointed out by interviewee C, 'AI is as good as the information it was fed with.' Without sufficient reliable data to account for these unknowns, AI cannot perform as effectively as expected. Therefore, it is still the personal view of professionals that is important.

> We are talking about something where we don't know what will happen. So, the computer doesn't know either just because it has one million data points. It's not that [better] to interpret the future than your personal view. (H)

3.2.3 Experience-Based Expertise Is Difficult to Mimic

Model-based investment strategies rely heavily on alternative data. However, as many models draw from similar data and signals, they can be easily replicated. This replication reduces their effectiveness, requiring constant updates to retain profitability.

> If it could be replaced by a computer, then the market will be more effective, and you have to adjust your model because it doesn't give you any more profit. That's what I think those firms [hedge funds] do. They find a model that works a little bit. Sooner or later, it will arbitrage the way a bit. Because someone else understands, oh, you can do it in this way, and then the profits from [a hedge fund's] model are not working anymore. And then the engineers and analysts start to find other imperfections in the market. They can use it for one, two, or three months. When that model doesn't work anymore, they start to figure out another. (E)

Interviewees highlighted that machines and humans are not in opposition. Rather, they are increasingly interdependent. Machines can enhance investment processes, but they must learn from human expertise.

> It's not black and white. It's not like you can only have the engineering skills. And, of course, you need to understand how to interpret the information. I do agree that it is an important skill to be able to extract what is critical and pivotal in some sense. But that doesn't have to be a human skill, I guess. I mean, one could say that [it can be] a machine skill as well. Maybe not now, but I could definitely see that this could be done by a machine. A machine that would have to learn, of course, from humans. (A)

The effective use of AI relies not just on its raw power, but on the ability of humans to guide, interpret, and evaluate it. Humans act as editors of the system.

> I think the classic quote from Andrew Ng here is that it's people with AI, not AI itself, that's going to take our jobs. We have to channel that power and kind of play the editor role. One thing that I always found hard to delegate is how you structure your tasks properly so that you can actually delegate them to AI efficiently, ensuring sources are reliable. (G)

As the implementation of AI depends on predefined targets and learning from human insights, with humans still playing a central role on top of everything, it is still the experience-based expertise that is difficult for machines to mimic.

> Some of the information we use in our investment process simply doesn't exist as binary code of ones and zeros, as our investment process builds heavily on personal experience. […] But basically, it's very difficult to train AI based on our past three decades of experience. (C)

Another interviewee emphasised that human adaptability—especially in volatile or complex market conditions—remains a key advantage over systematic strategies. In such environments, intuition and the ability to quickly provide a competitive edge that is hard for machines to replicate.

> I'm probably better at trading a choppy market where we're sort of up, down, up, down, up, down. Systematic accounts will do terribly in that environment. So maybe I'm trading very tactically. Maybe I shorten my time frame from the usual one to two months to, like, intraday or a weekly sort of time frame. So, I can adapt pretty quickly. If I see opportunities, that's kind of my skill set. That would require someone to really tweak a lot of parameters within a model. How do you shift it [the model]? Like, you've got to back-test when do you shift from time frame one to time frame two to time frame three? What are your signals? Then you've got to back-test all these. For me, that's hopefully intuition. (F)

4   Discussion

Building on the proposed research questions and interview findings, this section emphasises that human-in-the-loop remains essential in fund management. Professional judgments—rooted in domain knowledge developed through years of professional experiences and exercised by intuition—continue to be critical, even as AI brings additional requirements in technical knowledge. In this context, AI refers to the use of advanced technologies that enable the processing of larger and more diverse datasets, enhanced data analysis capabilities, and improved trading platforms. Beyond traditional quantitative tools, AI includes broader innovations such as large language models (e.g., ChatGPT) that support decision-making, research, and communication throughout the investment workflow. Fund managers interact with different forms of AI for different purposes, leading to variation and sometimes tension in discussions about the efficiency of AI implementation. While AI can reduce cognitive overload by filtering and summarising information, its ability to generate timely signals and process vast quantities of data may also increase the need for and the arousal of attention. Therefore, it emphasises the importance of professional judgment developed through years of experience in the domain.

4.1 Summariser AI and Recommender AI

According to Kaplan and Haenlein (2019), AI refers to 'a system's capability to interpret external data correctly, to learn from such data, and to use those learnings to achieve specific goals and tasks through flexible adaptation' (Ibid., p. 17). Rather than functioning as fully automated systems, AI in fund management is implemented into workflows to support specialised tasks that enhance human decision-making, primarily in the form of Summariser AI and Recommender AI.

Interviewees, on one hand, acknowledge the improvements in work efficiency brought by AI, but on the other hand, express scepticism about its actual effectiveness. This contradiction stems from differing perceptions of Summariser AI versus Recommender AI. Recommender AI generates explicit, actionable suggestions, such as 'Buy,' 'Sell,' or 'Hold' signals, and proposes an optimal portfolio. It received limited implementation and now requires further testing. However, Summariser AI may already be more implemented into their workflows. Tools like ChatGPT can act as summariser assistants, facilitating knowledge exchange and enabling interactive learning between humans and machines.

The Summariser AI directly addresses information overload, which strains a manager's limited attentional capacity. Pre-processing and condensing vast amounts of data reduces the cognitive load required during the initial information-gathering phase. While managers must still perform the core analytical tasks—weighing evidence, assessing trade-offs, and forming judgments—they can use more digestible informational inputs. This can potentially free cognitive resources for deeper analysis and synthesis. However, interview findings reveal mixed perceptions. While many acknowledge the Summariser AI's proficiency in distilling complex information, some question whether its timely signals reduce cognitive overload or introduce additional noise that distracts attention. From this perspective, managers acknowledge the AI's ability to process information but remain unconvinced about its efficiency in enhancing investment decision-making.

The Recommender AI presents actionable solutions. Discussions about algorithm aversion and the perceived usefulness of AI often revolve around this form, as its recommendations can conflict with human judgment (Dietvorst et al. 2015). When recommendations align with a manager's professional assessment and intuition, they can decrease the cognitive load in processing large volumes of data. But when they diverge, managers must engage in extra scrutiny to distinguish accurate insights from misleading ones, especially since AI-generated signals can be myopic because of the short-term-oriented data (Dessaint et al. 2024). In the context of long-term fund management, maintaining attention on the right signals is essential.

Interviewees pointed out that AI can be systematically implemented if its profitability can be tested rigorously. However, since they had not yet systematically adopted AI, they were not aware that risks may still emerge even after the practical usefulness of AI has been demonstrated. Trust in AI can develop quickly after a few successful recommendations, leading these recommendations to serve as anchors from which managers adjust their decisions. This can shift the manager's role from systematic analysis toward a less demanding evaluation and potential confirmation of the AI's suggestions. While both Summariser and Recommender AI can reduce perceived workload, the latter risks fostering a narrower, more biased search for information, in which managers pay disproportionate attention to data that confirms AI outputs while overlooking disconfirming evidence.

4.2 Human in the Loop and Professional Judgment

As data becomes more up-to-date and machines become more powerful, many quantitative funds can trade more frequently by capitalising on sudden signals from the world (Abis 2020). In response to this, discretionary managers with a longer-term perspective gain a competitive edge through their professional judgments. This advantage stems from their ability to provide unique qualitative insights that machines cannot easily replicate, as well as their human biases (not mental biases). Unlike machines, which struggle to predict human behaviour, discretionary managers can leverage these biases to their advantage. This is particularly true when data on individual fund managers is limited.

Additionally, the inputs on the tools still need human input on training, as the quality and relevance of the input data heavily influence the output. Time adds another critical dimension: when decisions must be made urgently and data cannot be quickly or easily processed by machines, human expertise and domain knowledge are amplified. Professional judgment, built on experience, consistency, and a long-term perspective, is crucial for determining which data is relevant, filtering out market noise, avoiding mental biases, and developing foresight (see chapter 'Individual Foresight and Fund Management Expertise' in this volume) in the face of future uncertainty where data may be unavailable.

As machines have changed the way corporations make public disclosure (Cao et al. 2023), the success of investing potentially needs more human involvement. The human element of discretionary fund management, particularly interpersonal skills, was identified as a critical differentiator in maintaining flow balance and unique information acquisition (Dugast and Foucault 2025). They allow for the gathering of unique qualitative information that cannot be easily captured by data-driven tools. According to interviewees, this ability reflects their value and often adds more value than technical skills alone. It suggests that fund management remains, at its core, a human-centric profession.

5   Conclusions

Overall, the theme of fund management is data-driven, technology-assisted, and human-centric. It means data could be used and different types of technology could appear. However, humans will still be needed, and even be emphasised. Professional judgments are essential for sophisticated investors to maintain the market, apply proper data and tech, and understand the signals, no matter whether they come from machines or not.

This study has several limitations, primarily stemming from its data constraints and scope. Firstly, the research focuses on a limited number of discretionary managers or analysts, which may limit its applicability to other investment management approaches, such as algorithmic trading or quantitative funds, where AI often plays a more prominent role. As regulations mandate that final investment decisions must be made by humans, there is a potential for future studies to explore how varying degrees of reliance on AI influence fund managers' decision-making.

Secondly, this study highlights the two primary forms of AI currently used in fund management: AI as a summariser and a recommender. While it recognises their differences and uses them to concretise how AI is implemented in practice, it does not go in-depth into how each form is applied at the individual manager level or across different funds. As discussed in chapter 'Performance and Fund Managers' Expertise' in this volume regarding the distinctions between individual managers and team management, future research could examine the influence of AI on both individual decision-making and team-level dynamics. Such research could systematically investigate how the use of Summariser AI versus Recommender AI shapes managerial behaviour, changes decision-making processes, and impacts investment outcomes.

Thirdly, insights from interviewees suggest that AI amplifies rather than replaces the importance of human expertise and professional judgment. However, this study primarily focuses on the positive aspects of AI adoption, particularly its role in complementing human expertise. It does not address potential negative consequences, such as the risks associated with misuse or overreliance on AI, nor does it fully examine the tension around whether AI helps alleviate cognitive overload or instead adds noise that exacerbates it. Future research could explore the dynamics of human-AI interaction in greater depth, investigating how proper and improper use of AI may improve or undermine decision-making, introduce new biases, or reshape fund managers' cognitive processes.

Acknowledgements The author acknowledges financial support from the Swedish Research School of Management and IT and Uppsala University. The author is thankful for the valuable comments from the editor and other authors in this book.

References

Abis S (2020) Man vs. machine: quantitative and discretionary equity management. SSRN Electron J. https://doi.org/10.2139/ssrn.3717371
Aziz S, Dowling M, Hammami H, Piepenbrink A (2022) Machine learning in finance: a topic modeling approach. Eur Financ Manag 28:744–770
Biais B, Foucault T, Moinas S (2015) Equilibrium fast trading. J Financ Econ 116:292–313

Bonelli M, Foucault T (2023) Displaced by big data: evidence from active fund managers. SSRN Electron J. https://doi.org/10.2139/ssrn.4527672

Cao S, Jiang W, Yang B, Zhang AL (2023) How to talk when a machine is listening: corporate disclosure in the age of AI. Rev Financ Stud 36:3603–3642

Cao S, Jiang W, Wang J, Yang B (2024) From man vs. machine to man + machine: the art and AI of stock analyses. J Financ Econ 160:103910

Chen R, Ren J (2022) Do AI-powered mutual funds perform better? Finance Res Lett 47:102616

Choi H, Varian H (2012) Predicting the present with Google trends. Econ Rec 88:2–9

DeMiguel V, Gil-Bazo J, Nogales FJ, Santos AAP (2023) Machine learning and fund characteristics help to select mutual funds with positive alpha. J Financ Econ 150:103737

Dessaint O, Foucault T, Fresard L (2024) Does alternative data improve financial forecasting? The horizon effect. J Finance 79:2237–2287

Dietvorst BJ, Simmons JP, Massey C (2015) Algorithm aversion: people erroneously avoid algorithms after seeing them err. J Exp Psychol Gen 144:114–126

Dugast J, Foucault T (2025) Equilibrium data mining and data abundance. J Finance 80:211–258

Froot K, Kang N, Ozik G, Sadka R (2017) What do measures of real-time corporate sales say about earnings surprises and post-announcement returns? J Financ Econ 125:143–162

Green TC, Huang R, Wen Q, Zhou D (2019) Crowdsourced employer reviews and stock returns. J Financ Econ 134:236–251

Huang J (2018) The customer knows best: the investment value of consumer opinions. J Financ Econ 128:164–182

Kacperczyk M, Van Nieuwerburgh S, Veldkamp L (2016) A rational theory of mutual funds' attention allocation. Econometrica 84:571–626

Kaniel R, Lin Z, Pelger M, Van Nieuwerburgh S (2023) Machine-learning the skill of mutual fund managers. J Financ Econ 150:94–138

Kaplan A, Haenlein M (2019) Siri, Siri, in my hand: who's the fairest in the land? On the interpretations, illustrations, and implications of artificial intelligence. Bus Horiz 62:15–25

Khandani AE, Lo AW (2011) What happened to the quants in August 2007? Evidence from factors and transactions data. J Financ Mark 14:1–46

Kolanovic M, Smith R (2019) Big data and AI strategies 2019 alternative data handbook. https://ea-pdf-items.s3-eu-west-1.amazonaws.com/J.P.-Morgan-Alternative-Data-Handbook-2019.pdf. Accessed 10 Jul 2024

Laney D (2001) 3D data management: controlling data volume, velocity and variety. META group research note 6.70

Li B, Rossi AG (2020) Selecting mutual funds from the stocks they hold: a machine learning approach. SSRN Electron J. https://doi.org/10.2139/ssrn.3737667

Mercer (2024) Mercer Investments' AI integration in investment management 2024 global manager survey. https://www.mercer.com/insights/investments/portfolio-strategies/ai-in-investment-management-survey Accessed 27 May 2025

Miguel AF, Chen Y (2021) Do machines beat humans? Evidence from mutual fund performance persistence. Int Rev Financ Anal 78:101913

Mukherjee A, Panayotov G, Shon J (2021) Eye in the sky: private satellites and government macro data. J Financ Econ 141:234–254

Nazari N, Mahdavi MA (2019) A survey on automatic text summarization. J Artif Intell Data Min 7:121–135

Ossola A (2024) How artificial intelligence is changing work. WSJ Tech News Briefing. [Podcast]. https://www.wsj.com/podcasts/tech-news-briefing/how-artificial-intelligence-is-changing-work/45c00bcd-f119-45ff-8fde-3b6cd12749bb?mod=Searchresults_pos3&page=1. Accessed 21 Mar 2025

Regulation (EU) 2024/1689 of the European Parliament and of the Council of 13 June 2024 laying down harmonised rules on artificial intelligence and amending Regulations (EC) No 300/2008, (EU) No 167/2013, (EU) No 168/2013, (EU) 2018/858, (EU) 2018/1139 and (EU) 2019/2144 and Directives 2014/90/EU, (EU) 2016/797 and (EU) 2020/1828 (Artificial Intelligence Act) (text with EEA relevance), OJ L, 2024/1689 (2024). http://data.europa.eu/eli/reg/2024/1689/oj. Accessed 21 Oct 2024

Tang VW (2018) Wisdom of crowds: cross-sectional variation in the informativeness of third-party-generated product information on Twitter. J Account Res 56:989–1034

Umar T (2022) Complexity aversion when Seeking Alpha. J Account Econ 73:101477

Wu W, Chen J, Yang Z(B), Tindall ML (2021) A cross-sectional machine learning approach for hedge fund return prediction and selection. Manag Sci 67:4577–4601

Zhang Q, Lu J, Jin Y (2021) Artificial intelligence in recommender systems. Complex Intell Syst 7:439–457

Integrating ESG Information in Active Fund Management

Katarzyna Cieslak⑩, Inna Neskorodieva⑩, and Fredrik Nilsson⑩

Abstract As sustainability has emerged as a major investment trend in recent years, this chapter explores how fund managers integrate ESG information into active fund management. Drawing from interviews with experts in the fund industry, we find that fund managers employ a range of ESG integration strategies—from disregarding ESG factors or applying negative screening to implementing proprietary screening models. Somewhat surprisingly, the findings indicate that ESG-focused investing remains firmly anchored in the financial value paradigm, with the primary objective of enhancing returns. Key skills in ESG-focused investing include the ability to select and validate financially material ESG information, as well as maintaining an agile investment approach, that is, balancing over- and underreaction to ESG information. Given the complexity and multidimensional nature of ESG information, fund managers rely on a combination of intuition and analysis in order to interpret and act upon it effectively.

Keywords Active fund management · ESG information · ESG investment process · Fund industry · Intuitive expertise

K. Cieslak (✉) · I. Neskorodieva · F. Nilsson
Department of Business Studies, Uppsala University, Uppsala, Sweden
e-mail: katarzyna.cieslak@fek.uu.se

I. Neskorodieva
e-mail: inna.neskorodieva@fek.uu.se

F. Nilsson
e-mail: fredrik.nilsson@fek.uu.se

I. Neskorodieva
Karazin Business School, V.N. Karazin Kharkiv National University, Kharkiv, Ukraine

F. Nilsson (ed.), *Exploring Fund Management Expertise*, Contributions to Finance and Accounting, https://doi.org/10.1007/978-3-032-08545-0_7

1 Introduction

Sustainability has become increasingly central to investment decisions, influencing how fund managers assess risks and opportunities and meet investor demands. By June 2024, global assets under management in sustainable funds, integrating Environmental, Social, and Governance (ESG) factors hit a record of $3.5 trillion, though 2024 inflows declined compared to previous years (Morgan Stanley Institute for Sustainable Investing 2024).

Amid growing interest in ESG, many studies have examined whether ESG-labelled funds outperform traditional ones, yet no clear evidence supports consistent superior returns. Although Morgan Stanley reported modest outperformance in 2024 (Morgan Stanley Institute for Sustainable Investing 2024), research indicates that ESG investments may underperform due to lower risk profiles, but returns depend on shifting investor concerns around ESG (Pástor et al. 2022). While performance is widely studied, to our knowledge, there is no research that explores how fund managers, and most notably experts with superior performance (Grant and Nilsson 2023), integrate ESG information in the investment process. Such insight could clarify when and how ESG investments deliver value. Some argue that ESG is no longer the domain of only 'socially responsible investors' but extends beyond ESG-labelled funds to mainstream fund management (Edmans and Kacperczyk 2022). However, whether this is actually the case and how ESG integration is implemented in practice remain largely unexplored. In our study, we therefore examine how expert fund managers integrate ESG information in active fund management. We apply a broad scope, focusing mostly on non-ESG-labelled funds.

Few studies describe the work of fund managers. Existing research tends to focus more broadly on themes such as the role of emotions in high-pressure work environments (Tuckett and Taffler 2012; Verma et al. 2024), or differences across fund manager types, for example, venture capitalists versus other fund managers (Gompers et al. 2020), without specifically addressing ESG. A recent study by Chen et al. (2024) provides initial evidence that active fund managers selectively integrate financially material ESG information, with more experienced managers being better at identifying relevant ESG sources. However, their analysis is based on portfolio-level trading data and does not capture how ESG considerations are applied in fund managers' work.

As sustainable investing gains traction, investors are faced with a choice between active and passive ESG strategies. Passive approaches using third-party ratings offer low-cost alignment with investor preferences, while active strategies enable more nuanced investment assessment and portfolio formation, potentially enhancing impact and performance (Cremers et al. 2023). Active fund managers are thus likely to rely on information beyond standard ESG ratings. Our study adopts an intuitive expertise perspective, proposing that expert managers draw on both expertise and intuition developed through experience in their active fund management (Grant and Nilsson 2023, p. 4).

Given our limited knowledge and understanding of how ESG influences fund management, this chapter explores *how active fund managers integrate ESG information into the investment process and how intuitive expertise is used in ESG investing.*

2 Literature Review

The literature review is structured around three dimensions: first, we examine motives for integrating ESG information into the investment process; second, we review ESG information that is relevant to the investment process; third, we present research on fund managers' intuitive expertise.

2.1 ESG Integration Motives

One stream of previous investment research explores the motives behind integrating ESG into the investment process. Starks (2023) describes motives as searching for financial *value* versus *values* (non-pecuniary preferences). A few studies suggest that investors are driven by *values* and are thus prepared to trade off returns (e.g., Barber et al. 2021; Bauer et al. 2021; Heeb et al. 2023). However, these studies are often based on surveys or experiments to capture retail investors' sentiments (e.g., Barber et al. 2021; Bauer et al. 2021). Still, a Swedish study finds that 'households with stronger pro-environmental values do not hold greener portfolios' (Anderson and Robinson 2022, p. 1552). Research using actual fund flow data suggests pecuniary preferences dominate, with investors expecting long-term financial gains (Döttling and Kim 2024; Gantchev et al. 2024). For example, Döttling and Kim (2024) document outflows from sustainable funds during economic downturns, such as the COVID-19 crisis, attributed to income shocks. Similarly, Gantchev et al. (2024) find that investors withdraw funds when the underperformance of sustainable investments becomes pronounced.

In sum, research does not provide a unanimous view of investors' willingness to sacrifice returns for making sustainable investments, which highlights the importance of researching how expert fund managers respond to these different investment motives.

2.2 ESG Information Sources

Rating agencies are among the primary sources of ESG information for fund managers, and high ESG ratings combined with low rating uncertainty often serve as strong signals for fund managers (Avramov et al. 2022). However, ESG ratings often provide inconsistent assessments, with greater ESG disclosure leading to divergence in ratings, causing, in turn, frictions in firm valuations (Christensen et al. 2022). Berg et al. (2022) document differences across ESG rating agencies in terms of scope, measurement, and weighting of indicators. These differences stem partly from the 'rater effect'—subjective evaluations where overall company perception shapes the assessment of individual indicators. Agencies also rely on varying data sources, collected at different times using diverse criteria (Ibid., p. 1341). In addition, Yang (2022) argues that ratings are inflated by 'greenwashing' and have limited predictive power for corporate misconduct. In contrast, Serafeim and Yoon (2023) find that ratings can predict ESG-related events, though this ability declines when discrepancies between ratings increase. Raghunandan and Rajgopal (2022) further criticise ESG scores, noting they capture the amount of disclosure and not actual ESG performance. They also find that some self-labelled ESG funds in the US invest in companies with poorer compliance with labour and environmental laws than non-ESG funds, highlighting the challenges of accurately assessing ESG information (Ibid., p. 854). Dechow (2023) calls for companies to report not only financially material information for investors but also broader societal and environmental impacts (impact materiality). Such disclosures are in line with European Sustainability Reporting Standards (ESRS), but they increase complexity of reporting. In sum, while ESG ratings may provide information to support investment decisions and reduce costs (Serafeim and Yoon 2023), the uncertainty around them impacts their usability (Avramov et al. 2022; Berg et al. 2022; Raghunandan and Rajgopal 2022; Yang 2022).

Furthermore, the quality of the top leadership team, characterised by experience, knowledge, and professionalism, can provide crucial corporate information for active fund managers. For example, Iliev and Roth (2023) find that US firms improve their ESG performance when directors gain ESG experience in socially progressive countries. Welch and Yoon (2023) suggest that skilled managers foster a balance and positive working conditions within their firms, which in turn boost economic performance. Meanwhile, Block et al. (2021) through experiments with impact investors, highlight that the authenticity of the founding team is a major factor influencing investors' investment decisions, alongside the societal issues addressed and the financial sustainability of the investment.

Companies may also experience agency conflicts characterised by a misalignment of interests between shareholders and managers regarding the importance of ESG strategies (Gillan et al. 2021). When company managers make public declarations about 'stakeholder values' using popular 'stakeholder language,' it can be a 'red flag' for active fund managers, as this language is frequently employed to distract from missed financial targets (Flugum and Souther 2025). Companies' decisions to start, continue, or halt ESG initiatives also offer valuable insight for active fund managers. For instance, the launch of sustainable initiatives triggers the same investors' reaction as general business initiatives, but stopping them triggers a strong adverse reaction and weakens trust in the company (Garavaglia et al. 2024).

A stream of previous studies links institutional ownership with positive ESG performance effects. For example, Cohen et al. (2023) document that ownership by Carbon Disclosure Project signatories increases carbon emission disclosures, which is associated with subsequent lower emissions. Investment funds typically influence companies through voting (Cohen et al. 2023; Dikolli et al. 2022; Tao et al. 2020), but voting can also be symbolic. For example, Michaely et al. (2024) show funds support proposals already with majority backing while withholding votes on contested ones. This result may suggest that institutional investors select firms based on ESG criteria, rather than actively improving ESG practices within their portfolio firms. Additionally, Cao et al. (2023) argue that sustainable and responsible institutional investors prioritise ESG factors over other fundamentals, contributing to market mispricing.

In sum, active fund managers draw on a wide range of ESG information sources. Given the inconsistent quality and lack of standardisation in ESG ratings (Avramov et al. 2022; Berg et al. 2022; Raghunandan and Rajgopal 2022; Yang 2022), effectively interpreting ESG data may require specialised expertise. It can be assumed that fund managers are compelled to rely on additional information sources to supplement ratings with qualitative corporate insights, such as management's approach to ESG, to form a clearer investment view.

2.3 Intuitive Expertise for ESG Investing

Previous research on ESG investing has primarily focused on investment motives and the types of ESG information available, rather than investigating how this information is integrated into the investment process. Since integrating ESG information may require specialised expertise, we now turn to discussing a concept of intuitive expertise, employed by Grant and Nilsson (2023) in a broader context of financial decision-making (see also chapter 'Judgments and Decisions by Expert Fund Managers' in this volume). The concept of intuitive expertise is defined as the capacity to intuitively 'draw on our domain-specific knowledge in the form of expertise accumulated in the past' (Sinclair 2010, p. 382). Intuitive expertise allows for making swift, accurate decisions in complex situations, partly based on expertise from accumulated knowledge, but without overreliance on analytical reasoning, and complementing it with intuitive judgments based on previous experience (Grant and Nilsson 2023, p. 48). Intuition and expertise interact when financial decisions are made. However, there is no empirical evidence on how fund managers integrate ESG information in the investment process using intuitive expertise compared to traditional investing. A parallel can be drawn with research in the context of venture capital (VC). Providing rare evidence on the practice of active fund management, Gompers et al. (2020) find that VC investors rely less on discounted cash flow models and quantitative metrics than chief financial officers or other private equity investors, due to high uncertainty at early investment stages. Instead, VC investors more often make intuitive judgments regarding the management team leading the investment targets, which is more important than analysing investment timing or business models. In an earlier study of financial analysts, Du Rietz (2014) argues that, given the fragmented nature of

ESG data, interpretation is required to determine what is and what isn't captured and to select valuable information while discarding irrelevant accounts. Exploring how ESG information impacts skill utilisation differently from traditional investing presents a compelling research opportunity.

Both components of intuitive expertise (i.e., intuition and expertise) rely on experiential learning, as they are based on previous experience. Mu and Jiang (2024), in their analysis of investment decisions related to new technologies, observe that experiential learning can have a dual effect: it may enhance technological investment by increasing decision-makers' 'absorptive capacity' or hinder it when it leads to a 'competency trap.' Their empirical findings support the latter, indicating that experiential learning can limit technology investments. While the impact of experiential learning has been explored in different organisational contexts (with concepts of organisational exploitation and exploration based on March (1991) being foundational to the competency trap literature), in our study we instead elucidate experiential learning at the individual level within the context of ESG investing.

Furthermore, literature within fund management distinguishes two major domain-specific skills of fund managers, namely stock picking and market timing (Berk and Van Binsbergen 2015; Bollen and Busse 2001; Kosowski et al. 2006). Stock picking is the process of selecting individual stocks based on fundamental analysis in the case of active fund management, whereas market timing is the ability to buy and sell stocks at the right time to maximise gains and avoid losses. Previous quantitative studies highlighted both these skills without a focus on ESG investing. For example, market timing may be less relevant if investors are driven by non-pecuniary motives of value creation beyond financial value.

In sum, our study contributes to scant research on the practice of active fund managers by investigating how intuitive expertise is used when ESG is integrated in the investment process.

3 Results

The results section reports on findings from exploratory interviews with eight experts in fund management (see the Appendix for details on the interviews). We begin by describing how fund managers integrate ESG information in the investment process and, in the following section, how they use intuitive expertise in ESG investing.

3.1 How ESG Information Is Integrated into the Investment Process

3.1.1 Financial Value Paradigm

As noted in the previous section, there is some evidence that investors accept lower returns when firms engage in corporate social responsibility (Barber et al. 2021; Heeb et al. 2023). However, some of these studies rely on experiments or advanced models with strong assumptions. In contrast, our findings suggest that an ESG focus in investing is primarily driven by financial motives (Gantchev et al. 2024). All our interviewees highlighted the central role of financial materiality in shaping their investment strategies.

Starks (2023) distinguishes between 'financial value' and 'values' as motivations for sustainable finance. The former centres on investors' expectations of improved risk-return prospects, while the latter is based on non-pecuniary intrinsic values. Interviewees uniformly adhere to the financial value investing paradigm, which in turn appears to shape how they integrate ESG information into the investment process. Surprisingly, there was no evidence to suggest that intrinsic values play a role in directing finance toward social and environmental investments unless such investments are linked to the prospect of higher returns or backed by a clear mandate from capital providers. The following quotes underscore the importance of financial returns:

> You know, from our point of view, the investors just purely want an absolute return. They would not be happy to see us give up performance, so that we could incorporate some mandate which is not being disclosed to them. So, given that we don't sort of offer an ESG-friendly fund or a green-focused fund, then it's really just about returns. [...] Of course, we can do trades such as 'green' bonds [...] those products might trade at a premium or a discount to traditional bonds that could potentially open areas where we might have an opportunity to make money [...] But currently, these bonds are less liquid and trade at a premium, so we would likely not do so. (F)

> ESG is important whenever it is a value driver. There are between one and three or four value drivers to evaluate a company. If ESG is not one of them, it doesn't matter. [...] If investors choose a fund that is defined to sacrifice returns for ESG then you can do it. But you can't do it as a fund manager without asking, because return is the base. (H)

> I suppose most managers say it (eds. sustainability) is important, as they need to be politically correct. You never know though when it comes to the real decisions. [...] Sustainability was also in a way important before. Because if you had environmental problems sooner or later you could get a fine. [...] So, there is, of course, a cost and a risk side to that. Of course, you have to take it into consideration as an investor. But if the firm reduces the CO_2 by 12 or 22%, that has no value for an investor. If it doesn't affect the profit of the company, if it takes you seven years instead of three years, if you don't get fined, does it really matter for the valuation? I don't think so. Why should it? (E)

Previous research on fund managers' work indicates that the threat of underperformance is a defining element of their everyday experience (Tuckett and Taffler 2012). Because of short-term performance pressures, managers tend to avoid attributing underperformance to a flawed investment strategy. Instead, they often cite external factors, such as unreliable managers at portfolio firms or an inadequate mandate from investors (Ibid., pp. 63, 67). Our interviewees emphasised that only a clear mandate from capital providers would lead them to deviate from a strict focus on return maximisation (see chapter 'Analysing Fund Managers' Accountability' in this volume for a discussion of fund managers' accountabilities). They argue that narrowing the investment universe by including specific ESG criteria potentially reduces returns:

> In the past, many studies have shown that by excluding certain investments, one sacrifices returns. Looking at it through the lens of linear programming, adding constraints will inherently arrive at a suboptimal solution concerning the objective – return. (G)

> I think the biggest challenge for any ESG-focused fund is liquidity. You know, obviously, the range of products available is more limited. If you look at green bonds, the secondary market for those has significantly lower liquidity than the regular bonds. So, I think these tend to be sort of buy-and-hold investors with a certain mandate to invest in socially responsible products. (F)

The interviewees' perception of sustainable investing within the financial value paradigm aligns with Fama's (2021) critique of stakeholder capitalism as an inefficient solution. Fama (2021) argues that since contracts to distribute wealth among stakeholders are not drafted costlessly, especially when they have the power to influence firm decisions, the optimal strategy for a firm is to maximize shareholder wealth rather than stakeholder wealth. Customer preferences and the willingness of customers to pay a premium for sustainable products should drive corporate behaviour instead. However, our interviewees expressed uncertainty regarding whether customers are currently able to pay more for ESG, a concern similar to their scepticism about investors' willingness to sacrifice returns. The following quote illustrates this point:

> The proof is in the spending. You could look at the store: ecological food, ecological meat, and so on. I think that's quite hard to sell because it's more expensive. People say that they care for the environment and nature, but they don't buy it, as I understand it. (E)

While the quote refers to consumer behaviour, it aligns with findings by Anderson and Robinson (2022) concerning investment behaviour. Given the gap between potential unprofessional investors' stated values and their actual purchasing and investment decisions, it is perhaps unsurprising that professional investors regard financial accountability as a key concern.

The financial value paradigm in investment decisions appears to have a significant effect on how ESG information is integrated into fund management. Our interviews revealed three distinct approaches: (1) a lack of ESG integration into the investment process; (2) integration through negative screening; and (3) integration by evaluating the financial materiality of ESG information through proprietary scoring systems. Notably, the fact that some managers do not integrate ESG—illustrated by comments such as 'In terms of the investment process for us, sustainability is not really something that factors heavily' and 'as a fund we have no mandates such as being ESG compliant; it is not really part of our day-to-day mandate'—contradicts recent claims that ESG has moved beyond the realm of socially responsible investors to become a mainstream practice in fund management (Edmans and Kacperczyk 2022). We discuss the latter two approaches in the following sections.

3.1.2 Negative Screening as an Integration Strategy

Based on our interviews, negative exclusionary screening, i.e., avoiding investments due to negative ESG issues (Krueger et al. 2020), appears to be a standard method for integrating ESG information into the investment process, with all interviewees reporting its use. Previous quantitative studies have documented the prevalence of negative screening among institutional investors (e.g., Bolton and Kacperczyk 2021; Hong and Kacperczyk 2009; Krueger et al. 2020). Although this relatively unsophisticated strategy may eventually be replaced by more refined approaches, it remains pervasive in fund management. Firmly anchored in the financial value paradigm of ESG investing, negative screening is thought to improve risk-return prospects by offsetting the limitations of the investment universe with reduced risks associated with ESG underperformance. The following quotes illustrate this perspective:

> The answer to your first question is that it is like a risk overlay. It is not a sustainability-driven investment process. It is an overlay that seeks to find outliers that need to be excluded. Most of the time we tend to go through the flags that come up. […] Applying constraints theoretically reduces return, but if you're using a strict process, you would probably save yourself from severe losses with ESG as a risk overlay. That may even become more important in the future. Unfortunately, transition risks are already upon us, and physical risks are growing more and more present and will play a bigger role in the future. (G)

> ESG comes into play before we contact the company. We have industries to avoid entirely because of the ESG considerations. […] On top of that, even though we don't have specific criteria in our fund documentation, preventing us from investing in a specific industry, we can still drop the investment if we identify major negative ESG issues that we cannot address quickly after our investment. This has happened in the past. (C)

One reason for the widespread use of negative screening is the low quality of ESG information, as we will explain in the next section, making it challenging to integrate ESG information into the investment process. Consequently, negative screening for excluding stocks rather than picking stocks for inclusion may depend on simplified information, such as ESG ratings from rating agencies. These ratings, being summary sources of information, are arguably more suited for exclusion rather than inclusion in investment decisions, at least according to our interviewees:

> We have, for a very long time, worked with the different ESG rating providers, and what we have found when using these ratings is that they are not at all coherent. You know, different providers will put different emphasis on different factors. They will make different assessments of incidents and how companies have handled those, etc. So, while we do find that these ESG rating providers are excellent gatherers of information, and thereby, you know, good sources of information to us, we tend to rely not on the ESG scores as such. (A)

> The information contained in the ESG rating is so high level that it would be never sufficient for us. The fact whether they have 4.65 or 3.5 stars or whether they are F+, whatever, it's not much information to us. Our ESG due diligence are dozens of pages of detailed reports. (C)

> You have to take all that with a big grain of salt because the rating agencies have not showered themselves in glory in the past, you know. I'd probably be as sceptical of sort of Morningstar ratings as I would be of any other rating agency as kind of something that I'd really put weight on to drive my investment process. I'm very sceptical of that. Oh yeah, sure, it's a starting point, but I'm just saying, like it's a very basic starting point to look at labelling and ratings agencies. (F)

It thus seems like these interviewees use the screening-tool more like a 'starting-point' and indicator of companies that potentially need to undergo a thorough analysis. The limited reliance on ratings outside of negative screening aligns with criticisms in the literature, including discrepancies among rating agencies (Berg et al. 2022; Christensen et al. 2022), inflated ratings (Yang 2022), diminished predictive value when ratings conflict (Serafeim and Yoon 2023), and an overreliance on the number of disclosures (Raghunandan and Rajgopal 2022).

3.1.3 Proprietary Scoring as an Integration Strategy

While all interviewees reported using negative screening to mitigate ESG risks, some also described a more advanced approach to integrating ESG information into investment decisions, namely an internally developed proprietary scoring system. These systems are frameworks designed to capture various dimensions of ESG performance in portfolio firms or potential investments. The quotes below illustrate how these proprietary scoring systems are developed:

> In order to facilitate the integration of ESG information or ESG data into investment decisions and portfolio constructions, we have developed our own scoring model. So, we used information from many different sources, the companies themselves, the ESG rating providers, and other sources as well. And we make our own assessment based on those different data points, on what opportunities, and what risks do these companies face individually when it comes to sustainability. [...] We tend to look at the raw data that mix up to those (eds. rating) scores, so that we can make our own. And that's what we do actually in this scoring model, that we put our own materiality assessment into those raw scores and we can sort of build scores that are more relevant for us. So, you know, the underlying information of the ESG ratings is definitely part of our model, but the scores, the aggregate scores themselves, are not. [...] I would say that we apply, you know, our view on different parameters in that scoring model. (A)

> We have internally developed an ESG guideline for our investment team, which includes a very specific list of all the areas that we have to look at. And it's a document which has a couple of dozen pages which says, okay, in the environmental space, you have to look at this area. And these are the specific topics or questions we need to ask. And for these topics, we need to have an external auditor, mainly for topics like environmental, background checks on individuals, things like that. We rely on external auditors. So, again, our guidelines help us know what to probe in each area. (C)

According to our interviewees, a major challenge in integrating ESG information in active fund management is the low quality of the data, which depends on three aspects: (1) low validity; (2) multidimensionality; and (3) lack of standardisation of ESG data. First, the validity of the information is often in question, not only because of intentional greenwashing (see e.g., Flugum and Souther 2025; Yang 2022), but also due to data scarcity and reliance on estimates. The following quotes illustrate this concern:

> There's also a lot of greenwashing within corporations where products are marketed as green, but upstream processes tell a different story. That's one of the key problems with scope one, two, and three emissions. Scope one is almost negligible in many cases. Scope two is more straightforward – you can calculate the energy consumed. But scope three is immense; it encompasses almost everything, and it dwarfs the other scopes. The problem is that you don't directly influence scope-three emissions. [...] By far the most important and difficult question in this area is the data quality. (G)

> Greenwashing is likely a very big problem. [...] For example, in Japan, they have Japanese government bonds and these new green bonds which are supposed to be used for energy transition, for example. But we have no way of reconciling that. And I guess, you know, at a corporate level, that sort of problem becomes even more pronounced. How do you monitor? [...] You know, it's the broad industry problem: lack of transparency. (F)

> There is still, I think, a quality issue. [...] This is because ESG data is not reported in the same way as financial information. So, while we do have some reported information, a lot of the information is actually made up of the estimates. So, it's third-party estimates, it's, you know, models based on peer performance, etc. So, I think that is one challenge that we tend to use modelling and estimates to quite a large extent already. (A)

> Timeliness is always an issue as well. That will be rectified with new reporting standards. But right now, we might have carbon emissions numbers that are one and a half years outdated. So that's a problem. (B)

Beyond data validity, our interviews revealed two additional challenges related to data quality: multidimensionality and a lack of standardisation (i.e., the absence of comparable key performance indicators). In contrast to financial performance, which relies on a limited set of well-established metrics based on accounting and non-GAAP measures of profit and cash flow, ESG metrics are inherently multidimensional and remain non-standardised, as our interviewees explained:

> So, we cannot keep on expanding the areas we look at in a completely uncontrolled way and are trying to make this process much more controllable, consistent, and comparable across firms. [...] I recently received a questionnaire from an institutional investor in which there were 1,570 questions. I mean, it is completely unreasonable to think that we will send many people for many days or weeks to try to answer 1,570 questions. [...] Nobody ever asks us 1,500 questions on financials. It does not happen. When I say cash flow or EBITDA everybody more or less knows what I mean. (C)

> You can't compare between companies, can't compare the two years. You can't compare at all. When I say can't, you can, but it's difficult. (G)

Not all interviewees appeared to use advanced proprietary scoring systems, contrasting with claims in the literature that ESG is now widely integrated in fund management beyond sustainable funds (Edmans and Kacperczyk 2022). Those who integrated ESG information more extensively justified their approach by emphasising the potential for higher financial returns (Cremers et al. 2023). This aligns with the financial value paradigm in sustainable investing.

There is no conflict between returns and sustainability. I mean, in the long run, in order to persist as a company and continue to generate returns, of course, you have to adapt in terms of sustainability. […] COVID and high interest rates have punished many of the sectors that are connected to ESG investments like renewable energy, which are quite capital intensive. So, performance has not been good during, specifically, 2022 and 2023. It's been a bit better this year and so far. […] Of course, you can always find periods of time where ESG has underperformed mainstream strategies. But we still see when we look at long time series that sustainability has been a good investment theme. (A)

In sum, it seems like the interviewees consider issues related to data quality as the main driving force behind the development of proprietary scoring systems. Validity and multidimensionality, emphasised as major challenges, require experts to discern the financial materiality of ESG information, a skill we further elaborate on in the following section.

3.2 How Intuitive Expertise Is Used in ESG Investing

In this section, we present insights from our interviews on the intuitive expertise fund managers use to integrate ESG information into the investment process. Overall, the interviewees reported no fundamental change in the role of the fund manager, which underscores experiential learning of fund managers (Mu and Jiang 2024). Hence, they seem to view ESG only as an additional factor that may influence the risk–return trade-off. As is evident in the quotes below, ESG risks appear to be an issue.

I think it's business as usual – there are always new factors to consider when analysing corporations, financial securities, or other investments. […] Over the last 12 to 20 years, however, it's become just part of the game. There are two main types of risks to consider: physical risks, which have always been there (e.g., earthquake risks for real estate in Tokyo or California), and the newer transition risks, which are man-made and tied to climate change. These add new dimensions to risk assessment, alongside opportunities. (G)

A portfolio manager needs to understand sustainability risks and sustainability opportunities, just as any other type of risk, the opportunity that the company faces. (A)

The quotes above align with the financial value paradigm in fund management (Starks 2023) and are consistent with Tuckett and Taffler's (2012) depiction of fund managers' work environment, characterised by high-performance expectations. Fund managers employ experiential learning (Mu and Jiang 2024) to navigate emerging risks (including transition risks) and opportunities associated with ESG. However, distinct nuances in how expertise is applied when analysing ESG information have emerged, which we describe below.

3.2.1 Selecting Financially Material ESG Information

As previously mentioned, a major obstacle to deeper integration of ESG information into investment decisions appears to be its multidimensional nature and the lack of standardisation. According to our findings, fund managers use ESG ratings primarily for negative screening and exclusions to mitigate risks in their stock-picking strategies. However, when selecting stocks for inclusion, they rely on their expertise to reduce ESG information into a financially material score through proprietary scoring systems. Several interviewees emphasised the importance of skills that enable experienced fund managers to filter out financially material information, thereby reducing multidimensionality and improving decision-making.

> Also on the materiality side, on the integration side, we always have to make an assessment of whether any kind of data point is financially material for the company and material for the company's performance. So that's a challenge we are facing. (B)

> I think that with the new sustainability reporting standards, the companies are required to make a materiality analysis. And I mean, of course, many companies have done this previously as well, but I think it's clearer now that you actually report only on those issues that are material. And that means, of course, financially material. (A)

> For the last couple of years already, we have been trying to organise this process in such a way that we can do it in a similar fashion as we do financial reporting, that we talk the same language and we have a certain set of data that we consider complete but also sufficient. (C)

> If there is a transition risk, hopefully, we would find through our secondary research the financial risk exposure due to physical risk or anything like that. In general, through analysts that cover it, which is outsourced by us as we use research houses to cover the stocks for us, we should find it there. (G)

Our interviewees emphasised that it is important to judge whether certain ESG information is material or not. Challenges regarding subjectivity in interpreting disclosed ESG information driving differing judgments have been echoed in the literature (Christensen et al. 2022; Du Rietz, 2014; Raghunandan and Rajgopal 2022). Also, as Dechow (2023) notes, the materiality of ESG information is dynamic, an issue that appears immaterial today may become critical in the future, making materiality assessments particularly challenging. During the interviews, fund managers explained their attempts to understand the financial materiality of ESG information by both choosing certain dimensions relevant for a firm's profitability (to be included in the scoring systems) and omitting others, as well as reducing the number of performance indicators. This resembles using experiential learning to apply financial materiality criteria to ESG information.

In sum, fund managers rely on expertise to reduce the multidimensionality of ESG information, using the resulting insights to both exclude stocks through negative screening and guide inclusion through proprietary scoring systems.

3.2.2 Validating ESG Information

Our interviews reveal a strong dependence on intuitive expertise when making stock-picking decisions. Intuition appears particularly crucial for validating ESG information, as its low quality represents a major limitation. A key skill of fund managers, therefore, lies in complementing analytical reasoning with intuitive judgment, often exercised through direct engagement with the management of portfolio companies.

The significance of corporate management as a critical source of ESG information is also well documented in the literature (Block et al. 2021; Gillan et al. 2021; Welch and Yoon 2023). Given the ongoing challenges with ESG data quality, as previously discussed, these interactions are particularly important. The following quotes illustrate the significance of engaging with company managers:

> It's very much a people's business. We talk to the entrepreneurs. So, it's very much a people's business based on the person-to-person interface. We get quite a lot of information by simply interacting with our entrepreneurs. What kind of people are they? How do they deal with their employees? I mean, there are so many soft aspects that are very difficult to capture otherwise. (C)

> We listen to management and their stories about the company: 'What was the story the management had? And then we should ask ourselves: Is it a good story? Yes, it sounds good. Does he/she believe in himself/herself? Yes, he/she does. Does he talk rubbish? No, he doesn't.' And then we meet in the next quarterly meeting after half a year. And if he changes the story and talks about something else you should be very, very suspicious. (E)

> So of course, if you are a quant portfolio manager, this (eds. proprietary) scoring model will be one of the models that are used in order to actually make investment decisions. So, the score that this company gets will play a part in portfolio construction. If you are a fundamental portfolio manager, you will use this information more as the source of knowledge of the company, as the source of finding out which questions to ask the companies and which areas to explore when it comes to strategy and transition that these companies are facing. (A)

The importance of understanding and evaluating management when making investments has been discussed in the literature (e.g., Grant and Nilsson 2023; Gompers et al. 2020). It is one of those areas where the use of intuitive expertise is more visible. It is therefore not that surprising that fund managers also place a lot of emphasis on firm management in their efforts to understand ESG information.

3.2.3 Balancing Over- and Underreaction in an Agile ESG Investment Approach

When discussing their investment process, our interviewees frequently referred to intuitive expertise in market timing and stock picking, often described as professional judgment. According to our interviewees, a key skill for fund managers is maintaining an agile approach, i.e., resisting overreaction while also avoiding underreaction, with the following quotes explaining the skill in general market timing and stock picking:

> I think what you want to overcome is emotional bias, as you need to be sort of flexible around views [...] making sure you are thinking clearly [...] to realise when I'm in a position mentally where I am making good decisions as opposed to when I am in a mental state where I am making suboptimal decisions. [...] For example, 2016, you get these Trump tweets that come out. [...] And, you know, often the algos would read these tweets and get chopped up. [...] Whereas the discretionary macro portfolio manager might be sitting there saying, 'Well, you know, it's kind of expected, or I'm not reading too much into this, or let's see what the official response comes out.' So, I'll use my discretion to not necessarily get triggered on every single price action. (F)

If the market is very optimistic, then you should have a little distance from it. If the market is very pessimistic, you should have a distance from it. You should try to work almost the same. And that is very, very hard. So, if you manage these basic problems then you are from day one an above-average manager. (E)

You should invest in companies you have faith in, where you believe the management is a good management. And you should invest in a company that can show a rather good history when it comes to profitability and the variation in profits, and then all the basic ones. And if you are wrong, you should also have the ability to sell the stock. It is very hard sometimes for people when they have invested to sell a bad stock. [...] If a good report comes out and the stock goes up, you shouldn't say 'Oh, now it's too expensive to buy.' You should perhaps say 'Fantastic, now it is this good company that we really believed it was.' (E)

Striking a balance between overreaction and underreaction in an agile investment approach appears to be particularly crucial when integrating ESG information into the investment process. The interviewees highlighted market inefficiencies, including market bubbles, linked to ESG information characteristics discussed in previous section, most notably multidimensionality and validity, which hinder understanding of its financial materiality. As a result, a key skill for fund managers is leveraging their intuitive expertise to navigate these uncertainties. In other words, to avoid impulsive reactions to market bubbles while ensuring they do not overlook relevant information. The following quotes illustrate this approach:

When too many people talk about ESG and what's in it for the future, there is a tendency that companies say 'we are a sustainable company.' The company can produce some cells or solar panels, or you can just mount solar panels on the roof. That is not so interesting. But perhaps the investors would be very interested in that company because everyone says: 'Oh, this will grow by 100% a year for ten years,' and not everyone, but too many, are rushing to those companies. And you know, that is perhaps not a bubble, but it creates strange valuations. So, we always stay away from those trends. (E)

So, everyone talks about the 'greenium.' The issue is like, why would an issuer want to issue a green bond? Okay, partly, you hope that their intentions are good. And they are using these bonds for, you know, climate change or energy transition, etc. But they are also probably leaning on the fact that there are certain investors who have non-economic drivers of their investment decision and are willing to pay a premium for that. So, you know, there's some opportunistic pricing going on. Like people are incentivised, if they can label something green and sell it at a higher price, then that's what happens. [...] You know, the green label product, I think it's a much trickier thing to model, what the fair price should be. If you're continually paying a premium without sort of really being able to verify credentials or compliance etc., it's a pretty slippery slope. (F)

If we identify major issues and know we can fix them, that's actually great, because we are buying something that is called black and we'll make it green. (C)

The interview evidence aligns with previous literature that highlights the challenges in interpreting materiality of multidimensional ESG information (Christensen et al. 2022; Raghunandan and Rajgopal 2022), as well as a tendency to overemphasise ESG factors (Cao et al. 2023), both of which can contribute to distorted or skewed asset valuations. The interviews show how difficult it can be to achieve an agile investment approach. When the level of uncertainty is high, purely analytical models are seldom sufficient. In such types of circumstances, long experience of the fund manager, in the form of intuitive expertise, is important, while it seems that the expertise required is of a more general nature rather than specific ESG expertise. This finding also highlighted the points made in chapter 'Individual Foresight and Fund Management Expertise' in this volume about the role of individual foresight in the decision-making process. An agile investment approach that avoids ESG-linked market valuation bubbles shows the importance of market timing and stock-picking skills applied in the ESG investing context.

4 Conclusions

This study is based on six exploratory interviews with eight experts in fund industry, examining how they integrate ESG information and use intuitive expertise. Below, we present four key conclusions.

First, our study contributes to the literature by offering insights to the ongoing debate on the relationship between 'value' and 'values' in fund management (see Starks 2023). Despite discussions about the rise of values-oriented investments (Barber et al. 2021; Heeb et al. 2023), the interviews revealed that financial value remains the dominant motive among fund managers. We found no evidence that intrinsic values influence decision-making in ESG investing, which aligns with Fama's (2021) view that firms should prioritise ESG only if societal demands translate into significant economic incentives. Despite widespread rhetoric about 'mainstreaming' ESG investing (Edmans and Kacperczyk 2022), ESG integration appears to be a careful and strategic adaptation to external expectations, rather than a shift from return maximisation in fund management. The traditional financial paradigm likely explains the limited ESG information integration, and the use of exclusionary negative screening (Bolton and Kacperczyk 2021; Hong and Kacperczyk 2009; Krueger et al. 2020), mainly to reduce investment risk under uncertainty.

Second, the interviewees emphasised that the key competency for fund managers is assessing the financial materiality of ESG information (i.e., aspects most relevant to firms' financial performance). This is challenging due to the dynamic nature of materiality (Dechow 2023) and the generally low quality of ESG information. Interviews revealed that ESG information quality suffers from a range of issues: low validity due to greenwashing (e.g., Flugum and Souther 2025; Yang 2022), data scarcity, and usage of estimates; as well as lack of standardisation (e.g., Berg et al. 2022) and high multidimensionality. The interviewees consistently identified poor data quality as a major obstacle to effective valuation and ESG investing (echoing concerns raised by Christensen et al. 2022). These findings align with research highlighting widespread dissatisfaction with ESG ratings (e.g., Raghunandan and Rajgopal 2022). Available ratings are viewed as a starting point only, as they fail to reflect accurately firms' ESG commitment. Fund managers draw on analytical expertise to distil complex, multidimensional ESG information, starting with basic metrics for negative screening and then applying more advanced proprietary scoring systems to guide inclusion decisions.

Information overload mentioned by the interviewees, characterised by hundreds of performance indicators and complex materiality judgments, may be especially pronounced under the EU's ESRS impact materiality framework. This framework requires reporting both financially material and other environmental and social impacts, unlike the ISSB framework, which focuses solely on financial materiality. However, given the dynamic nature of ESG materiality, shaped by evolving regulatory and societal expectations (Dechow 2023), the EU's broader approach may prove more effective over time. It provides fund managers with a more comprehensive information base, recognising that impact issues may become financially material in the future. This wider scope may foster exploration of strategic opportunities and thus help fund managers avoid a potential competency trap (Mu and Jiang 2024), arising from a narrow focus on financial risk only.

Third, the interviews show that while analytical expertise is central in ESG investing, both in excluding and including stocks (i.e., stock picking), intuitive judgments are considered equally important. As noted earlier, according to the interviews, ESG ratings often lack full decision relevance, failing to reflect company-specific characteristics or genuine ESG commitment. As highlighted in the literature review, important ESG information, such as leadership commitment to ESG (Block et al. 2021), or the extent to which ESG is embedded in operations, are difficult to assess without direct interaction with firm management. The interviewees viewed such interaction as essential for validating their interpretations of ESG information. Although different types of ESG information, for example, used in proprietary scoring models, are highly important, they cannot solely replace intuition. These insights align with findings from other contexts (Gompers et al. 2020; Grant and Nilsson 2023).

Fourth, the interviewees emphasised the critical importance of an agile investment approach grounded in intuitive expertise, one that balances overreaction and underreaction to information. While this balancing is important for stock picking, especially when assessing 'green' or 'brown' labels, it is also crucial for market timing in ESG investing, helping to avoid potential market bubbles that may arise when investors rush toward 'green' assets. When uncertainty increases, both overreaction and inaction can lead to value destruction. Our interviewees noted that pricing inefficiencies are more likely when valuations rely on ESG information, given its inherent uncertainty and often low quality (as discussed earlier). Such mis-valuations can become 'a slippery slope' for investors, as described by one interviewee. This concern is echoed in the literature (e.g., Christensen et al. 2022 highlight pricing inefficiencies arising from difficulties in interpreting ESG performance). These challenges underscore the importance of direct engagement with companies and their managers. It is thus apparent that fund management is not only an analytical but also a communicative process, where soft skills including building trustful relationships and conducting open dialogues with company management are essential (Gompers et al. 2020; Grant and Nilsson 2023; Tuckett and Taffler 2012).

In sum, this study contributes to the limited existing literature by shedding light on how fund managers integrate ESG information through three key components: investment motives, the nature of ESG information, and the type of expertise applied. Particular emphasis is placed on the intuitive skills of active fund managers, which prove essential in navigating the persistent quality challenges associated with ESG information. Finally, we note that the research presented in this chapter is exploratory, based on interviews with eight fund management experts. As such, the conclusions are preliminary and intended to suggest potential directions for future research.

References

Anderson A, Robinson DT (2022) Financial literacy in the age of green investment. Rev Finance 26:1551–1584

Avramov D, Cheng S, Lioui A, Tarelli A (2022) Sustainable investing with ESG rating uncertainty. J Financ Econ 145:642–664

Barber BM, Morse A, Yasuda A (2021) Impact investing. J Financ Econ 139:162–185

Bauer R, Ruof T, Smeets P (2021) Get real! Individuals prefer more sustainable investments. Rev Financ Stud 34:3976–4043

Berg F, Kölbel JF, Rigobon R (2022) Aggregate confusion: the divergence of ESG ratings. Rev Finance 26:1315–1344

Berk JB, Van Binsbergen JH (2015) Measuring skill in the mutual fund industry. J Financ Econ 118:1–20

Block JH, Hirschmann M, Fisch C (2021) Which criteria matter when impact investors screen social enterprises? J Corp Finance 66:101813

Bollen NPB, Busse JA (2001) On the timing ability of mutual fund managers. J Finance 56:1075–1094

Bolton P, Kacperczyk M (2021) Do investors care about carbon risk? J Financ Econ 142:517–549

Cao J, Titman S, Zhan X, Zhang W (2023) ESG preference, institutional trading, and stock return patterns. J Financ Quant Anal 58:1843–1877

Chen L, Chen Y, Kumar A, Leung WS (2024) Firm-level ESG information and active fund management. J Financ Intermed 60:101122

Christensen DM, Serafeim G, Sikochi A (2022) Why is corporate virtue in the eye of the beholder? The case of ESG ratings. Account Rev 97:147–175

Cohen S, Kadach I, Ormazabal G (2023) Institutional investors, climate disclosure, and carbon emissions. J Account Econ 76:101640

Cremers M, Riley TB, Zambrana R (2023) The complex materiality of ESG ratings: evidence from actively managed ESG funds. Harvard Law School Forum on Corporate Governance. https://corpgov.law.harvard.edu/2023/02/14/the-complex-materiality-of-esg-ratings-evidence-from-actively-managed-esg-funds/. Accessed 7 Jan 2025

Dechow PM (2023) Understanding the sustainability reporting landscape and research opportunities in accounting. Account Rev 98:481–493

Dikolli SS, Frank MM, Guo ZM, Lynch LJ (2022) Walk the talk: ESG mutual fund voting on shareholder proposals. Rev Account Stud 27:864–896

Döttling R, Kim S (2024) Sustainability preferences under stress: evidence from COVID-19. J Financ Quant Anal 59:435–473

Du Rietz S (2014) When accounts become information: a study of investors' ESG analysis practice. Scand J Manag 30:395–408

Edmans A, Kacperczyk M (2022) Sustainable finance. Rev Finance 26:1309–1313

Fama EF (2021) Contract costs, stakeholder capitalism, and ESG. Eur Financ Manag 27:189–195

Flugum R, Souther ME (2025) Stakeholder value: a convenient excuse for underperforming managers? J Financ Quant Anal 60:135–168

Gantchev N, Giannetti M, Li R (2024) Sustainability or performance? Ratings and fund managers' incentives. J Financ Econ 155:103831

Garavaglia S, Van Landuyt BW, White BJ, Irwin J (2024) The ESG stopping effect: do investor reactions differ across the lifespan of ESG initiatives? Account Organ Soc 113:101441

Gillan SL, Koch A, Starks LT (2021) Firms and social responsibility: a review of ESG and CSR research in corporate finance. J Corp Finance 66:101889

Gompers PA, Gornall W, Kaplan SN, Strebulaev IA (2020) How do venture capitalists make decisions? J Financ Econ 135:169–190

Grant M, Nilsson F (2023) Intuitive expertise and financial decision-making. Routledge, New York

Heeb F, Kölbel JF, Paetzold F, Zeisberger S (2023) Do investors care about impact? Rev Financ Stud 36:1737–1787

Hong H, Kacperczyk M (2009) The price of sin: the effects of social norms on markets. J Financ Econ 93:15–36

Iliev P, Roth L (2023) Director expertise and corporate sustainability. Rev Finance 27:2085–2123

Kosowski R, Timmermann A, Wermers R, White H (2006) Can mutual fund 'stars' really pick stocks? New evidence from a bootstrap analysis. J Finance 61:2551–2595

Krueger P, Sautner Z, Starks LT (2020) The importance of climate risks for institutional investors. Rev Financ Stud 33:1067–1111

March JG (1991) Exploration and exploitation in organizational learning. Organ Sci 2:71–87

Michaely R, Ordonez-Calafi G, Rubio S (2024) Mutual funds' strategic voting on environmental and social issues. Rev Finance 28:1575–1610

Morgan Stanley Institute for Sustainable Investing (2024) Sustainable reality: modest outperformance, but flows only slightly positive. RO3865603-Sustainable_Reality_1H_2024_Report-FINAL.pdf. Accessed 13 Aug 2025

Mu W, Jiang X (2024) Absorptive capacity versus competency trap: experiential knowledge and investment in emerging technologies. Technovation 131:102973

Pástor Ľ, Stambaugh RF, Taylor LA (2022) Dissecting green returns. J Financ Econ 146:403–424

Raghunandan A, Rajgopal S (2022) Do ESG funds make stakeholder-friendly investments? Rev Account Stud 27:822–863

Sarafeim G, Yoon A (2023) Stock price reactions to ESG news: the role of ESG ratings and disagreement. Rev Account Stud 28:1500–1530

Sinclair M (2010) Misconceptions about intuition. Psychol Inq 21:378–386

Starks LT (2023) Presidential address: sustainable finance and ESG issues—value versus values. J Finance 78:1837–1872

Tao C, Hui D, Chen L (2020) Institutional shareholders and corporate social responsibility. J Financ Econ 135:483–504

Tuckett D, Taffler RJ (2012) Fund management: an emotional finance perspective. https://rpc.cfainstitute.org/sites/default/files/-/media/documents/book/rf-publication/2012/rf-v2012-n2-1.pdf. Accessed 13 Aug 2025

Verma S, Rao P, Kumar S (2024) Is investing inherently emotionally arousing process? Fund manager perspective. Qual Res Financ Mark 16:380–400

Welch K, Yoon A (2023) Do high-ability managers choose ESG projects that create shareholder value? Evidence from employee opinions. Rev Account Stud 28:2448–2475

Yang R (2022) What do we learn from ratings about corporate social responsibility? New evidence of uninformative ratings. J Financ Intermed 52:100994

Analysing Fund Managers' Accountability

Frank Hartmann⬤, Janina Hornbach⬤, and Anna-Carin Nordvall⬤

Abstract This chapter examines fund managers' accountability as an intermediate organisational and psychological mechanism between formal performance management systems and decision-making behaviour. We challenge the simplistic 'what you measure is what you get' assumption underlying many applications of accountability, arguing that accountability is not merely a contractual or metric-based mechanism but involves a complex social and psychological process. Drawing on ideas from agency, stakeholder, and legitimacy theory, we analyse how formal controls, informal norms, and self-imposed standards interact in the volatile environment that makes up fund management. We explore the tensions between short-term financial targets and long-term sustainability goals, particularly under growing Environment, Social and Governance (ESG) and Sustainable Development Goals (SDG) pressures. We argue that accountability can enhance deliberation and transparency, while excessive process imposition may crowd out intuitive expertise, foster short-termism, and induce gaming behaviour. We conclude that effective accountability systems must integrate quantitative performance measures with qualitative, culturally embedded practices that support ethical reflection and balanced trade-offs between investor returns and societal value.

Keywords Accountability · Performance · Sustainability · Value Creation · Intuitive Decision Making

F. Hartmann (✉)
Northeastern University, Boston, MA, USA
e-mail: f.hartmann@northeastern.edu

J. Hornbach
Mälardalen University, Västerås, Sweden

A.-C. Nordvall
Department of Business Studies, Uppsala University, Uppsala, Sweden

125
F. Nilsson (ed.), *Exploring Fund Management Expertise*, Contributions to Finance and Accounting, https://doi.org/10.1007/978-3-032-08545-0_8

1 Introduction

In this chapter, we explore essential aspects of the behaviour of fund managers through the lens of fund managers' accountability. We start from the relatively trivial observation that fund managers face a complex and dynamic performance management context, in which several incentive and organisational control systems aim to determine their decision-making behaviours. We argue that while one crucial objective of such incentive and control systems is to enhance the performance of fund managers, the intermediating effects of the imposition of accountability through the use of such systems are fundamental. This imposition of accountability through performance management, in turn, affects fund managers' decision-making behaviours, but the relationships are non-trivial. Too often, it is believed that 'just' defining performance measures, coupled with rewards, will provide managers with the right motivation and direction. This principle of 'what you measure is what you get' (WYMIWYG) is, we believe, an overly simplified adage covering a complex reality. This may be a reason why it is indeed hard to steer fund managers into persistently higher performance, as observed at the start of this book (see chapter 'Performance and Fund Managers' Expertise,' in this volume). For one thing, the interest explicated in the cognitive makeup and expertise of fund managers also requires a better understanding of how fund managers react to imposed accountability in terms of how behavioural biases, emotional factors and organisational pressures affect the expertise practice of the fund manager leading to distorted accountability. There is a need to understand the reaction of fund managers to imposed accountability, which demands a nuanced analysis, considering psychological, organisational and contextual factors, instead of assuming solely expertise actions (Lerner and Tetlock 1999). Our essay highlights that accountability is a crucial analytical step in understanding fund managers' decision-making behaviours, and, as it were, forms the 'missing link' between incentive and control systems and those behaviours. We graphically illustrate this link in Fig. 1 below as well as the overall structure of this chapter. We look at how the management control system affects decision making by fund managers. We consider the management control context in terms of shareholders and stakeholders as well as uncertainty, which is captured by the acronyms VUCA and BANI which we will explain later. We analyse accountability, denouncing the traditional view of WYMIWYG and replace that with more accurate effects of accountability imposition. Our methodology is one of reviewing the relevant literature and theoretically building on it (see Appendix for more details).

Throughout this chapter, we define accountability rather classically as the perceived obligation of a decision maker to justify his or her decisions to others (Lerner and Tetlock 1999). This perception of some future obligation lies, we believe, at the core of organisational incentive and control systems, since they crucially aim to incentivise people to make the right decisions. Asking people to explain what they did and what not is expected to be crucial in helping people make the 'right' decisions. Being pressed to justify, and perhaps even defend decisions, forms a crucial step, but a far from an easy one, in making such systems have any behavioural effect.

Legend:

VUCA (Volatility, Uncertainty, Complexity and Ambiguity)

BANI (Brittle, Anxious, Non-Linear and Incomprehensible)

WYMIWYG: 'What You Measure Is What You Get'

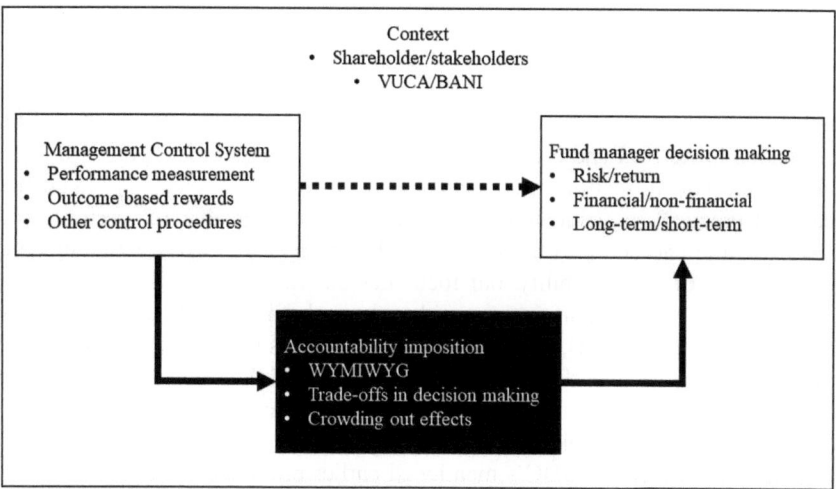

Fig. 1 Structure of the chapter. *VUCA* volatility, uncertainty, complexity and ambiguity, *BANI* brittle, anxious, non-linear and incomprehensible, *WYMIWYG* 'what you measure is what you get'

Moreover, the often-heard complaint that incentives invoke the 'wrong' decisions necessitates an interest in the workings of such accountability systems. Later in this chapter, we will specifically refer to process accountability if the imposition of accountability forces decision makers to deliberate about the steps and the process followed in their decision making. This form of accountability is often contrasted with outcome accountability, which relates to a decision maker somehow bearing the consequences of decision outcomes (Dalla Via et al. 2019; Lerner and Tetlock 1999).

Our analysis in this chapter particularly aims to articulate how accountability imposition acts as an intermediary between the managerial context, performance management, and managerial decision-making behaviour (see Fig. 1). This is especially suitable since fund management and fund managers differ significantly in their tasks and objectives, the types of funds in which they are employed, and the contexts in which they operate. Amidst such diversity, fundamental principles easily get lost. In our analysis, we also pay attention to relatively new trade-offs in fund management policies due to increasing societal apprehensions of investment funds, like an increased demand for sustainability and disclosures, asking for attention to non-financial 'performance' as discussed in chapter 'Integrating ESG Information in

Active Fund Management,' in this volume. The effects of societal pressures, which are formally manifested as UN Sustainable Development Goals (SDGs), can place substantial pressure on organisations and their management to provide transparency in their environmental and social sustainability reporting. At the same time, it is currently notable that public opinions on potential trade-offs, such as profitability vs. Environmental, Social and Governance (ESG) goals, short term vs. long term values, stakeholder expectation or reputational risks between financial and nonfinancial performance are also rising. These latter opinions underline the generic principle that investment funds must satisfy their stakeholders, whose financial-economic prosperity provides a fundamental *raison d'être*, and whose future simply depends on the financial returns that investment funds make (see also chapter 'Integrating ESG Information in Active Fund Management,' in this volume).

In the subsequent sections in this chapter, we will analyse selected fundamental ideas and practical implementations of being held accountable for performance, in the dynamic and complex context of fund management. Given the complexity of the concept of accountability, our focus lies on what is common and principal in performance management settings, rather than what is variable across contexts. In the following paragraphs, we will particularly discuss the evolving concepts and practical applications of performance related to accountability. We start with familiar financial performance indicators, in which some intricacies of accountability become visible. We also take a look at how ESG performance factors further complicate the picture, for which the SDG's mentioned earlier provide a societal thrust (also discussed in chapter 'Integrating ESG Information in Active Fund Management,' in this volume). Finally, we will highlight some pitfalls of not understanding the full effects that accountability impositions have on managerial behaviours. We will, for example, review the crowding-out effect that simplistic performance measurement may have on fund managers' intuitive expertise, which may be a dysfunctional effect of imposing accountability.

Overall, the sections explore how accountability supports and underlies fund management performance incentivisation, resulting in challenges to the congruence of the behaviour of fund managers as individuals, the organisational structures they work in, and the stakeholders they are ultimately accountable to. By exploring these dimensions, we seek to deepen insight into the expertise of fund managers and the challenges they face in navigating the current highly intricate and volatile environment of the financial industry.

2   Accountability and Performance Measurement

2.1   The Traditional View

We will call the traditional view of accountability the one in which fund managers' behaviour is primarily steered by implementing some form of performance measurement. The term performance management then refers to the process of choosing performance measures, administering their implementation, and providing a continuous cycle of monitoring actual performance against such measures. This way of imposing accountability could be labelled outcome accountability, and we will sketch some misunderstandings about it later. In this section and the next, we will highlight some ingredients of what such typical performance measurement and management entails in settings in which multiple definitions of what constitutes 'good performance' are available. None of this do we regard as controversial or typically innovative. Rather, our goal is to provide important nuances to any idea that the conceptual and operational definitions of what good fund performance is, are themselves trivial. Even the simplest and schematic representation of what constitutes good performance in actual settings invites a deeper analysis of how such good performance becomes something that can be measured and managed.

One dimension concerns the type of metrics entering performance management, in which we typically distinguish between *financial* and *non-financial* indicators (metrics). Obviously, achieving satisfactory financial performance is the first and foremost challenge fund managers have to face. However, when it comes to incentives and controls, it must be acknowledged that financial performance can be measured in many ways and that the financial nature of the metric should not be confused with the underlying performance dimension. Typical financial indicators such as return on investment (ROI), Alpha ratio (performance compared to the market), and Sharpe ratio (performance adjusted for risk) may be used. Such measures may be applied in the form of *absolute targets* or as *benchmarked targets*. In the former case, fund managers are held accountable for a fixed number. In the latter case, we speak of relative performance evaluation, since the ultimate performance judgment also depends on the performance of other funds or fund managers. The use of absolute or relative performance targets may seem just a nuance, but it covers an intricate set of technical and motivational mechanisms. For example, a benchmark-driven paradigm may not adequately capture the richness of fund performance because of the distinct risk-return characteristics of the asset classes and investment strategies (Jensen 1968). For instance, when a fund's performance invested in high-growth technology stocks is compared to indices encompassing a wide variety of industries, distinct patterns of volatility and return and dysfunctional motivational signals are given. Relative performance indicators may also enhance managerial game-playing, since one's performance levels may be enhanced by manipulating the benchmark, rather than increasing one's effort (Hartmann and Schreck 2022).

A third dimension, concerns whether performance indicators cover *short-term* or *long-term* consequences of managerial decision making. Short-term performance indicators are conceptually those that provide insights into short-term decision outcomes. Over the last decades, the label 'short-term' has received a somewhat pejorative connotation (e.g., Hartmann et al. 2020; Holland 2011; Zhu et al. 2025). This is because organisational performance is considered a long-term objective and taking short-term performance indicators as the primary target might come at longer-term costs. For example, when judging decisions using spot market terms and immediate investment returns, short-term signals may produce misleading conclusions about how effective a manager is in the long run (Hartmann and Schreck 2022). For example, a manager might achieve significant gains over a short period, but such performance may not be sustainable or a true reflection of a sound investment strategy (Berk and van Binsbergen 2015). On the other hand, long-term performance assessment conceptually aims at identifying more profound and more fundamental value drivers. Such indicators, notably hard to find, give a comprehensive look at how well a manager has applied, over time, a successful investment approach in place of various cycles of markets (e.g., Zhu et al. 2025). Yet, deciding the appropriate time scales for these assessments can be difficult. If the importance of short-term performance is emphasised, it can lead to less effective decision-making, i.e., adopting riskier decisions that can lead to loss of long-term value (Harris 2014). Focusing on short-term and long-term performance is essential for making informed and responsible investment choices. In addition, performance evaluation is not just about the right metrics regarding their informativeness, but also about their timeliness. The quest for good accountability is, in that sense, often a matter of trade-off. What is easy to describe as good performance *ex post*, is often distinctly different from what at any moment of performance evaluation or decision making is available (Lerner and Tetlock 1999).

Each performance measurement involves making implicit or explicit choices on these dimensions. Conceptually, they provide a different view of performance and, managerially, they will steer behaviour differently. Perhaps, as a result of this conceptual diversity, many approaches in this matter are quite scattered (Cohen et al. 2013; Hartmann et al. 2020). Arguably, this is the cause of continued discussion about optimal performance measurement, lack of generic satisfaction with performance measurement practices, and a practice that applies certain standard performance contracts despite such dissatisfaction (Dyckhoff and Souren 2020).

2.2 The Impact of ESG on Performance Measurement

In recent years, the SDGs have put pressure on organisations, where ESG factors have become substantial to organisations to act as performance assessment standards to reduce their negative impact on society (earlier discussed in chapter 'Integrating ESG Information in Active Fund Management' in this volume). From the conditions discussed above, with intricate performance management systems, diverse stakeholder demands, and an evolving global economic landscape that requires responsiveness and adaptability from fund managers, now also including ESG factors in this equation, exacerbates the multiple dimension issue of accountability even further. In organisations, ESG factors have become common practice in meeting external demands, with all bodies within the organisation being permeated by this, including fund managers. In the fund managers' context, this means that investments should focus both on improving financial performance and, at the same time, promoting sustainable practice, where impact investing goes beyond financial returns. For fund managers' accountability, it would involve further trade-offs between two seemingly dichotomous decisions—maximising financial profit or investing in social sustainability—where the trade-off considerations include the fund manager's risk judgment of becoming responsible for the choices he makes and the consequences of the decision he makes. For example, trade-off situations could occur where social sustainability investment align or conflict with financial objectives such as economic downturn, stable period situations, crisis or high market volatility. It could also include cognitive biases in terms of risk perception or time horizon. As demand builds within the broader ethos of what is expected of modern investors, the increasingly integrated nature of what fund managers do and how they operate brings further complexity to the mix of investment strategies, stakeholder expectations, regulatory requirements and ethical considerations. This creates a new complexity, with growing societal pressure on fund managers to have their strategies reflect the broader expectations of increasingly elevated information, values, and ethics from today's investing population, but also creates even greater tension between the different expectations, in terms of short-term and long-term performance. In this situation, accountability extends beyond merely justifying choices, where fund managers may be forced to take responsibility for the outcomes of their investment actions, whether positive or negative. Holland (2011) presents an optimistic viewpoint, highlighting the increasing influence of SDGs and the rising significance of ESG factors as a hallmark of organisational investment practices. However, Holland (2011) was perhaps too optimistic, and especially over de last decade, counterforces in society are clearly visible, as fund managers must contend with numerous factors beyond just ESG criteria as they strive to meet increasing expectations. This scrutiny extends to their performance metrics, requiring new methods for analysing and modelling sustainability indicators.

As fund managers endeavour to promote sustainable investment practices while acting as stewards of investor capital, they face intensified pressure to integrate financial and non-financial performance indicators within a cohesive assessment framework (Chen et al. 2024). This integration of sustainable investment practices while reinforcing their role as stewards of investor capital not only complicates their operational landscape but also amplifies the expectations placed upon them regarding the accountability for their investment decisions.

2.3   Economic Context and Performance Measurement

The economic dynamics refer to how economic variables change over time and how these changes impact economies. The current global economic dynamic is identified by the uncertain environment in which funds, not unlike most large financial performance-driven organisations, operate. Such an environment is described as high in VUCA (Volatility, Uncertainty, Complexity and Ambiguity) or BANI (Brittle, Anxious, Non-Linear and Incomprehensible; Seeber-Quayle 2024). These factors have a dramatic and tangible impact on fund managers who simply have to move beyond short-term financial indicators, at least in their contemplations and narratives. This also implies that the accountability of fund managers includes an ever-broader scale of tasks and environmental challenges that they must deal with, emphasising they are required to look beyond short-term financial metrics, considering a broader array of responsibilities shaped by societal expectations and non-financial factors, discussed in the above paragraph. Here, we describe a trend towards a more complicated set of accountabilities, driven by society's non-financial desires, that runs through the entire investment industry, and which no fund manager can escape.

The landscape within the dynamic and uncertain environment (VUCA and BANI) in which fund managers operate with an increased societal pressure is subject to change towards a dualistic focus; fund managers need to cope. To encompass a less dualistic approach for fund managers where they can operate more freely without multiple, sometimes conflicting, requirements is needed. Through this lens, both managers and stakeholders are called to cultivate a more balanced approach that supports long-term sustainability alongside immediate financial aspirations. Here, there exist different views on how fund managers can accommodate this. For example, agency theory (Eisenhardt 1989) highlights the critical relationship between fund managers (agents) and investors (principals), as the manager must anchor their decisions on performance to yield high returns and build investor trust. Thus, the fund manager's responsibility is dualistic, where the investor's interest is weighed against societal benefits. If these do not align, the fund manager must prioritise the investor's interest over societal benefit. This, of course is industry-dependent—from the industry's impact, regulatory context or technological evolutions, such as oil or gas that could create more pronounced trade-offs, to more social impact industries such as renewable energy where the trade-offs could be perceived as more seamless, reducing the conflict. In such cases, sustainability is often secondary, and the question remains whether the industry can evolve to become entirely sustainable and how far the fund manager's responsibility extends. Also, the risk is argued to be shared between principals and agents, which could imply a lower pressure and need for accountability for the fund manager, but it seems not to be the case.

Another view is presented in stakeholder theory (Parmar et al. 2010). It is argued that successful fund managers create value for all organisational stakeholders, not just shareholders. Organisations can build long-term relationships and achieve sustainable success by satisfying the needs and expectations of a broader set of stakeholders. The question is whether fund managers genuinely feel they have the flexibility to do so, as much focus is placed on pleasing investors' demands, which is also a prevailing expectation within the organisational culture. This could lead to a case where fund managers are constrained in their ability to innovate or adopt sustainable practices and are urged to do so. However, even if a fund manager considers the dynamic and uncertainty of VUCA and BANI and integrates ESG factors into their strategies to justify their choices regarding societal benefit and satisfying both the organisation and the investors, the question of long-term and short-term results still resurfaces. By prioritising short-term gains, the fund manager may fulfil the investor's interests but risks jeopardising long-term sustainable business practices. Further, legitimacy theory (Gulluscio 2023) argues that legitimacy is granted by various stakeholders, including customers, employees, investors, regulators, and the public, who have different criteria for legitimacy, shaping siloed demands on how the criteria should be fulfilled, and operate as implicit social contracts within the organisation. This precarious situation where demands come from several different directions and include various dimensions of expectations makes it impossible for the fund manager to achieve satisfactory results, where their decisions and actions must withstand scrutiny across moral, pragmatic, and cultural dimensions, reinforcing the obligation to uphold ethical standards and demonstrate accountability for the long-term consequences of their investment choices. Surely, the requirement to explain one's decisions is severely hampered.

The different views of organisational theories show that the evolving landscape already affects or will ultimately affect the fund managers soon. It necessitates a paradigm shift in understanding how they will cope and prioritise between the different demands. Also, this makes our understanding of the accountability mechanisms even more critical. Here, the accountability trends lean towards broader responsibilities where fund managers must navigate a complex set of accountabilities, which signifies that fund managers cannot solely focus on maximising returns—they also need to account for the implications of their decisions on various stakeholders and society at large. Further, the impact of dual accountability is of utmost importance, where the fund manager must balance the interests of investors with societal benefits. This conflict may lead to dilemmas where fund managers prioritise short-term financial gains over long-term sustainability, emphasising the tension between meeting immediate investor demands and adhering to ethical and socially responsible investing practices. As accountability mechanisms evolve, fund managers must incorporate a multidimensional perspective that recognises the importance of legitimacy and stakeholder relationships. This emphasis on broader criteria for success will likely influence decision-making processes to re-evaluate fund managers' accountability strategies and operational practices. These views provide partially overlapping and partially competitive opinions on the performance measurement landscape. What they have in common, however, is that they each point to complications in how fund managers can be held accountable by senior fund management, using appropriate management control system elements. In other words, the challenge is to ascertain that these managers will be able to satisfy their stakeholders by demanding accounts of their behaviours as one of those elements. In addition, they also make collectively clear the challenges of the imposition of accountability that is meant to make fund managers become, somehow, more rational or thoughtful.

3 Dimensions of Accountability

In the previous section, we outlined the complex expectations and demands that fund managers face, and need to deal with, in their daily decision-making. To illustrate the different tensions of accountability that fund managers encounter, we need to dig deeper into the fundamental connotations of the accountability concept itself.

Accountability, though a seemingly clean and straightforward concept, is, in reality, a rich and intricate web of expectations, demands and rules that guide and inform the behaviour of individuals (Frink and Klimoski 2004). As we will outline in this chapter, these demands and expectation work through different mechanisms, ranging from a need to justify performance and decisions to others (Lerner and Tetlock 1999), to abiding by collective norms (Frink and Klimoski 2004), and internal convictions and values (Schlenker 1997). These mechanisms are not easily delineated, though, contributing to a plethora of different accountability mechanisms that not seldom conflict with each other and cause dilemmas and trade-offs.

In traditional accounting research, accountability is typically characterised as a top-down control mechanism that steers behaviour through rigorous performance and control systems, variance analyses, and compensation schemes (Merchant and Otley 2006). These systems usually seek to reduce opportunistic behaviour, align behaviour with organisational goals, and improve overall performance. The mechanism of accountability through which these systems operate lies in the perceived expectation of individuals of having to justify outcomes and decision-making strategies, be accountable for their behaviour in terms of assuming consequences of their performance, and, in a transparent manner, report performance outcomes (Lerner and Tetlock 1999).

However, these systems also introduce the need for various trade-offs. First, while fund managers shape their investment approach according to their perceptions of the market and economic signals in particular, their approach also needs to be consistent with the fund's specific goals, as specified by the formal systems that these managers operate under (Hartmann et al. 2020). Fund managers are seen as guardians of investors' capital and are expected to make well-informed decisions, but it is ultimately the performance management and control systems that influence their behaviour and decisions. Therefore, it must be noted that the definition of an 'informed decision' is not as straightforward as it seems and is potentially influenced by the specific control and reward system in place. Linking back to a previous example in this chapter, if a control system rewards short-term returns on investment, fund managers are less inclined to make investment decisions that are sustainable and profitable in the long run but provide only limited returns in the short run. As a result, informed decision-making is mitigated by what is immediately justifiable and rewarded.

Second, there are limits to what individuals can grasp, measure, and weigh when considering future actions (Butler 2001). Although standard economic theory would have us assume decisions to be informed solely by the information gathered, we contend that experience, expertise, intuition, and even the sense of 'knowing' also contribute to shaping decision results (Frink et al. 2008; Kahneman and Tversky 2013). This, in terms of encountering market conditions in the past and the future, interpreting market information, or recognising patterns to identify risks. Also, fund managers intuitively or instinctively feel the market movements or trends with an intuitive conviction that the decision is correct. These considerations are a result of tacit knowledge. We propose that this results in a distinction between decision-making based on the information as perceived and the best possible decision-making given all relevant information available. In this distinction, arguably between optimal and actual decision-making behaviour, formal accountability plays an important, but often not well-understood, role. If fund managers are held strictly accountable for 'informed decisions', they may be constrained to those options that can be fully justified, or they may resort to evasion tactics and gaming behaviour to circumvent formal accountability demands (Messner 2009). This represents a deep problem in designing performance management systems, which is not typically articulated.

What is often forgotten when we talk about accountability is that accountability is much more than a formal structure of compliance and control; accountability is what makes up social systems and relations (Frink and Klimoski 2004; Lerner and Tetlock 1999). This implies that accountability structures can operate implicitly through, for instance, unwritten professional codes of conduct, mutual expectations and norms, all of which affect what is considered to be a '(un)desirable' investment strategy or a 'good' or 'bad' fund performance. These mechanisms work because individuals want to feel approved by others (Baumeister and Leary 1995). Given the complex environment that fund managers operate in, this implies that fund managers frequently find themselves in situations where they need to weigh the demands from many different stakeholders, including investors, managers, senior executives, peers, and society at large, all of which have different definitions of 'right' and 'wrong', 'acceptable' and 'unacceptable', and 'good' or 'bad'. This complexity can generate intractable ambiguities, which paradoxically worsen the problems that accountability is designed for in the first place (Merchant and Otley 2006). A fund manager may encounter expectations from investors to maximise financial returns on their investments, which may motivate the fund manager to choose a high-risk investment profile. However, the fund manager may also get signals from management to seek a balanced risk profile to secure stable returns on investment over time. Yet another demand may involve societal and regulatory expectations of fund managers to apply sustainable investment strategies that may exclude certain funds but include other, less profitable ones. This may conflict with investors' demands for high-risk, high-profitability funds. The implicit need to adhere to varying standards and expectations can result in goal ambiguity, confusion, and anxiety (Messner 2009), all of which may lead to impaired decision-making and performance.

In most investment firms, employees co-create a common understanding of what is 'normatively right', which is based on hidden codes of conduct and the nature of the organisational climate in place (Frink and Klimoski 2004). It is widely understood that in a company culture, risk-taking or compliance with regulatory standards becomes a normative guideline at the individual decision-making level (Lerner and Tetlock 1999; Messner 2009). This view emphasises the need for an enabling organisational culture in which actions are directed toward organisational objectives.

The complexity of accountability is further augmented when individuals have to weigh in their own, self-imposed sense of accountability (Schlenker 1997). Individuals are drawn to maintaining a positive image of themselves (Baumeister et al. 2001), which implies that they generally strive to behave in ways that confirm that positive image (Bandura 1999). However, given the complexity of accountability relationships that fund managers encounter in organisations and beyond, this goal is easily threatened when demands become incompatible. Discrepancies often lead to heightened cognitive load in an attempt to reduce this discrepancy, which can increase anxiety and impaired decision-making (Bandura 1999). For example, a fund manager at an investment firm who discovers financial inconsistencies in a project but fears the economic and reputational repercussions of reporting them, may face this kind of dilemma. The fund manager is subject to the external pressure of colleagues to remain silent, as well as their own professional duty and self-imposed standards of what is the 'morally right thing to do'. This tension may force the fund manager into rationalisation processes—a coping mechanism that allows the fund manager to justify a choice to remain silent while evading any damaging consequences of this inaction to the self (Bandura 1999). Even though organisations aim to develop well-functioning accountability systems that facilitate ethical and professional conduct, the dynamics of self-evaluation, peer impression, and rationalisation can result in unintended actions that deviate from the organisation's values, intentions and purposes.[1] This again emphasises the importance of an organisational culture that protects fund managers from repercussions when they appropriately challenge behaviour to benefit the organisation, thereby avoiding negative consequences through social disciplinary effects, such as reputational loss, social isolation, and status threats (Lerner and Tetlock 1999; Schlenker 1997).

In sum, a comprehensive understanding of the different facets of accountability is necessary if meaningful accountability structures are to be achieved. Accountability is often associated with formal rules and structures, but, as we have illustrated, goes way beyond that. Moreover, accountability is not a clean and unified concept, but instead spans a whole range of individual, social, organisational and even societal expectations that managers may be required to respond to. This makes the design of organisational incentive and control systems anything but a straightforward implementation of a WYMIWYG principle.

---

[1] The dissertation by Hornbach (2023) explores the 'human' facet of accountability, showing how internal, self-regulatory mechanisms facilitate potentially unintended organisational outcomes.

4   Unintended Consequences of Simplistic Accountability Imposition

4.1   The Received View on Accountability Mechanisms

It is now time to tie together the various ingredients our exposé on accountability has invited. We will do so by rehearsing the standard view on accountability. We labelled this view as outcome accountability, as it involves the idea that decision-makers are somehow accountable for scoring well on chosen performance measures, which typically define the desired outcomes a fund manager has to achieve.

Outcome accountability logic operates on the principle that individuals will align their behaviour with the specific performance outcomes for which they are held accountable—a mechanism we summarised as "WYMIWYG." This principle is consonant with agency theory, which models the relationship between a principal (e.g., an investor or firm) and an agent (e.g., a fund manager) as a performance contract. This theory assumes agents are self-interested and effort-averse, while principals seek to align agent behaviour with organisational goals through performance-based incentives (Eisenhardt 1989). According to agency theory, organisations steer the behaviours of their managers via performance contracts that lay down value-creating performance measures and appropriate financial incentives. Although agency theory is largely seen as too simplistic to provide solid practical advice, the other views we presented above still adopt the core assumption of agency theory, which is that people are incentive-driven. Agency theory defines the owners of the firm as the most critical stakeholders. The other approaches extend the range of stakeholders beyond shareholders, but still principally rely on performance measures and incentives to please these stakeholders. By tying rewards to observable outcomes, outcome accountability mitigates agency problems such as moral hazard or shirking. When performance is measured clearly and unambiguously, agents are expected to act to maximise the desired metric, thereby fulfilling the principal's objectives.

However, this mechanism becomes significantly more complex when multiple, potentially conflicting, performance measures are introduced. In practice, fund managers are evaluated on short-term financial metrics (e.g., quarterly returns) and long-term value creation, risk management, ESG compliance, or client satisfaction. From an agency theoretical perspective, this creates a multi-tasking problem. When multiple objectives are not equally measurable or incentivised, agents are likely to focus on those that are more easily quantified and rewarded. Consequently, this may lead to short-termism, underinvestment in intangibles, or manipulation of performance indicators, distorting the intended alignment between agent and principal.

This complexity undermines the ability to design a foolproof incentive system for fund managers. While outcome accountability can drive performance improvements in well-specified contexts, it struggles to function optimally when goals are plural, intertemporal, or subjectively evaluated, also discussed in chapter 'Performance and Fund Managers' Expertise' in this volume. Balancing short- and long-term goals or financial and non-financial metrics requires sophisticated contract designs that are often difficult to implement or enforce. Moreover, ambiguity in evaluation criteria can create strategic behaviour or gaming, further weakening the accountability mechanism. Thus, the theoretical elegance of outcome-based contracts is challenged by the messy realities of multi-dimensional performance environments.

In sum, this complicates the design and implementation of an effective accountability system for the fund's upper management. It becomes difficult to specify contractually how performance should be assessed (see also chapter 'Performance and Fund Managers' Expertise,' in this volume), how trade-offs among objectives should be weighed, and how to prevent gaming or misreporting. Ambiguous or overly complex metrics also increase the administrative burden of monitoring and evaluation.

For individual fund managers, the presence of competing and potentially ambiguous performance criteria complicates decision making. Fund managers may face uncertainty about which behaviours are rewarded, leading to inconsistent or overly conservative choices. They may also engage in impression management or strategic behaviour to meet the most salient metrics, even when such actions are misaligned with broader organisational goals (and the goals by the fund investors). Thus, while theoretically efficient, outcome accountability becomes practically fraught in multidimensional and dynamic performance environments.

4.2   Accountability and Expertise Decision Making

An alternative view, which is gaining dominance, challenges the received doctrine underlying much accountability thinking. Both theoretical and empirical literature in judgment and decision-making suggest that accountability, explicitly now defined as the expectation to justify one's reasoning stepwise, triggers a cognitive shift toward analytic and explicit thought (Lerner and Tetlock 1999). As the received doctrine states, individuals under such accountability exhibit heightened attentional focus and engage more systematically with information (Dalla Via et al. 2019). Yet, while such strategies may promote rational and deliberate analyses (Lerner and Tetlock 1999), they may inhibit performance on tasks requiring intuition, expertise, or sudden insight. This is especially relevant for problem types where non-analytic processes, such as restructuring and spontaneous realisation, are crucial for success, as is central to decisions that require the decision maker's intuitive expertise (Grant and Nilsson 2020).

Insight problem solving is marked by a sudden, often inexplicable emergence of a solution, commonly referred to as the 'Aha!' experience (Bowden et al. 2005). Unlike analytic problem solving, which proceeds through conscious, stepwise logic, insight involves reaching a solution after an impasse through an unconscious restructuring of the problem (Knoblich et al. 1999). Because insight-based solutions are opaque and difficult to verbalise, they clash with the demands of accountability, as the demand to explain one's reasoning. Such accountability favours transparent, justifiable processes leading to decisions. As a result, individuals subject to account-ability may gravitate toward analytic strategies even in tasks where intuitive expertise would be more effective. One could say that accountability crowds out insight.

In experimental studies, which are rarely about financial decisions such as those taken by fund managers, one task has become exemplary. The so-called Remote Associates Test (RAT; Mednick 1962) asks decision makers to 'come up' with a solution to a word riddle. For example, to the cues of 'cheese', 'trap' and 'tail', the solution sought is 'mouse'. Although solvable through analytic means, RAT problems are often resolved via insight, with solvers suddenly perceiving connections among distantly related words. Apparently, this task seems distant from those solved by fund managers, but as is often the case in psychology, its simplicity covers a fundamental cognitive process. Performance on the RAT correlates with creative abilities and is enhanced by broad, diffuse attention to many potentially important, yet vague, contextual information cues. Analytic approaches, by contrast, involve narrowing focus and sequentially testing associations. This method is more compatible with accountability but less conducive to insight (Eskenazi 2015).

Interestingly, recently, neuroscientific research has found that this distinction seems to operate at the level of the brain. Insight, as the outcome of intuitive expertise, appears linked to increased right hemisphere activity, which is involved in integrating different concepts and meanings (Mednick 1962). The mechanism has been studied widely, including by studies focusing on brain activity. EEG studies in particular, which observe brain activity through changes in brain wave frequency, show greater right frontal-temporal activity during insight problem solving, suggesting a neural basis for the attentional and cognitive states supporting insight (Sandkühler and Bhattacharya 2008).

In sum, the theoretical and empirical literature suggests that the traditional frame-work, in which accountability is associated with increased attention, concentration, and rationality, needs an important nuance. Accountability, which demands the expli-cation of one's thought process steps, holds a danger of leading to fewer insight-based solutions by discouraging opaque cognitive processes. Instead, it fosters a prefer-ence for analytic strategies that are easier to justify, potentially suppressing intuitive and expert-level insights, especially on tasks like the RAT that reward spontaneous connections. For the role of fund managers as holding increasing levels of expertise, this is an essential caveat in the design of performance measurement and control systems. Although insights do not equate foresight, they may share a common ground in a hard-to-explicate cognitive ability, which process accountability fundamentally touches. In that sense, the relationship between insights and foresights remains an intriguing line of thought.

4.3 Other Behavioural Effects of Accountability Imposition

Temporal discounting concepts (see for a recent discussion: Loewenstein and Carbone 2024) in behavioural economics and finance describe this challenge, revealing that investors value future rewards (or costs) lower than the corresponding rewards (or costs) received now, i.e., short-term goals, and the further in time a reward is, the more its value is discounted. Since investors are cognitively biased towards short-term returns, this limits the fund manager's scope for pursuing long-term goals and sustainability. One could argue that fund managers should strive to create added value beyond immediate returns. However, this requires an awareness of how short-term decisions can influence their long-term outcomes and the ability to communicate these trade-offs to investors. Thus, once again, accountability falls back on the fund manager, further increasing the pressure on them.

Another cognitive process that accountability is likely to affect is information retrieval. Accountability affects how much cognitive effort individuals exert when processing information. Previous research has found that individuals who are accountable tend to be more self-critical in justifying decisions and more thorough in screening available information before making a decision (Lerner and Tetlock 1999). However, suppose fund managers need to tackle various, often conflicting, demands from different stakeholders. In that case, cognitive effort is likely to turn into cognitive overload, causing negative affect (Bagley 2010) and judgment biases (Lerner and Tetlock 1999). The need to integrate different demands from different stakeholders can make it more cognitively demanding to filter and distinguish relevant from irrelevant information, resulting in impaired judgment and decision-making (Tetlock and Boettger 1989). This may cause fund managers to focus on some information, but ignore others, leading to investment strategies that may overly emphasise short-term financial returns to the disadvantage of long-term sustainability. This, again, illustrates the fine line between accountability being a driver and an impediment to 'good' decision-making.

5   Conclusions

In this chapter, we devoted attention to the way in which organisational incentive and control systems affect fund managers' decision-making behaviours. We aimed to highlight accountability as a crucial intermediate process comprising a large set of informational, societal, and cognitive factors. Its vital importance resides on the one hand in providing a better explanation of managers' responses to organisational incentive and control systems. Without attention to the psychological mechanisms through which organisational incentive and control systems affect behaviour, we may simply hang on to simplistic truths about our ability to steer managerial behaviour. The adage WYMIWYG is still too often heard but should be discarded. On the other hand, we believe that understanding the mechanism of accountability in particular provides new views on how managerial behaviour occurs. Accountability does not just mean responsibility for certain performance outcomes but involves a highly complex process of cognitive and social factors that make up the decision-making context. Fund managers are not simply achieving goals, but are making trade-offs, weighing considerations, and preparing for explanations. We have illustrated several factors that make this process complex. In particular, we highlighted that the performance context complicates decision making through its effect on the linearity between performance measures and behaviours that classic agency theory assumes.

For our interest in accountability as such, the exposition of fund managers' roles and tasks becomes one of a professional domain steeped in complexity, contradiction, and mounting performance pressures. Given this book's larger interest in explaining fund (managers') performance at the macro level through a micro interest in issues such as expertise and intuition, this chapter provided a multifaceted nature of accountability. In fund management, both the classical paradigm of performance-based evaluation prevails, as well as a contemporary influx of nonfinancial imperatives such as sustainability and ethical investment mandates.

Our starting point was relatively easy to find and was not specific to the industry. Performance management systems are and should be seen as levers to motivate desirable decision-making behaviours in fund managers. Yet this mechanical view, known under the adage WYMIWYG, should give way to a more cautionary tale. Accountability, we argued, is not merely a contractual requirement enforced through metrics and incentives, such that the dominant agency paradigm would have it. Instead, it is a psychological and social phenomenon, rooted in expectations, shaped by organisational cultures, and governed as much by norms and peer interactions as formal reporting structures.

Three core conclusions emerge from this discussion.

First, accountability should be regarded as something that is a mix of socially constructed and objective elements, rather than just a mechanically implemented tool based on WYMIWYG logic (e.g., Frink and Klimoski 2004; Messner 2009; Schlenker 1997). Despite being widely understood through the lens of incentives and controls, accountability is deeply embedded in the social fabric of organisational life (Lerner and Tetlock 1999). Fund managers are not only answerable to formal systems but also to the unspoken codes and norms of their professional community. They must navigate conflicting performance demands, even those that remain implicit, from peers, executives, regulators, and their own ethical standards. They operate in ambiguous, changing and uncertain environments, where any simple performance contract rapidly becomes stale. This layered complexity suggests that any accountability system must go beyond checklists and compliance metrics; it must attend to the relational and cultural dynamics of the decision-making environment. Practically, this means that investment funds should invest in fostering enabling cultures that support ethical reflection, protect principled dissent, and reinforce peer-based learning. This requires less emphasis on rigid outcomes and more attention to how decisions are made and justified within social and professional networks.

Second, oversimplified performance metrics and process accountability can undermine expertise. Traditional accountability mechanisms, particularly those grounded in performance metrics or process accountability, often overlook the nuanced cognitive processes involved in expert-level decision-making. Academic studies provide strong evidence that such systems might discourage intuitive, creative, or insight-driven problem solving. Fund managers operating under tight performance scrutiny may abandon complex, long-term strategies in favour of analytically defensible but strategically suboptimal ones. Fund organisations should acknowledge and make room for intuition and expertise by avoiding overemphasising strictly quantifiable outcomes (in line with conclusions in other chapters). They should tone down accountability procedures that demand the retrieval of all decision-making steps, especially in complex environments requiring judgment beyond formulaic logic.

Third, ESG and SDG imperatives complicate accountability frameworks. Despite a range of optimistic announcements (Eccles et al. 2014; Holland 2011), the actual influence of environmental, social, and governance (ESG) criteria, along with pressure from the UN Sustainable Development Goals (SDGs) is still under development. However, the thought of performance as an expanding concept is seriously established. Fund managers are now expected to optimise not only financial returns but also social outcomes, even if the former is more explicit and dominates the latter. Principally, dual obligations such as these introduce internal cognitive conflict. This dual accountability requires a careful balancing act that current systems are ill-prepared to support. Thus, a need is rising for more integrated performance frameworks that allow fund managers to evaluate trade-offs transparently and systematically. Such frameworks must also empower fund managers to communicate their rationale to stakeholders with divergent expectations.

The future of fund management depends not just on optimising returns but on legitimising the decision-making process—balancing quantitative discipline with qualitative integrity and short-term efficacy with long-term societal value.

References

Bagley PL (2010) Negative affect: a consequence of multiple accountabilities in auditing. Audit J Pract Theory 29:41–157

Bandura A (1999) Moral disengagement in the perpetration of inhumanities. Pers Soc Psychol Rev 3:193–209

Baumeister RF, Leary MR (1995) The need to belong: desire for interpersonal attachments as a fundamental human motivation. Psychol Bull 117:497–529

Baumeister RF, Bratslavsky E, Finkenauer C, Vohs KD (2001) Bad is stronger than good. Rev Gen Psychol 5:323–370

Berk J, van Binsbergen JH (2015) Measuring managerial skill in the mutual fund industry. J Financ Econ 118:1–20

Bowden EM, Jung-Beeman M, Fleck J, Kounios J (2005) New approaches to demystifying insight. Trends Cogn Sci 9:322–328

Butler J (2001) Giving an account of oneself. Diacritics 31:22–40

Chen L, Wang Y, Peng J, Xiao Q (2024) Supply chain management based on uncertainty theory: a bibliometric analysis and future prospects. Fuzzy Optim Decis Making 23:1–38

Cohen A, Hall M, Waisman A (2013) Performance evaluation in the investment management industry. J Portfolio Manag 39:25–41

Dalla Via N, Perego P, Van Rinsum M (2019) How accountability type influences information search processes and decision quality. Account Organ Soc 75:79–91

Dyckhoff H, Souren R (2020) Performance evaluation: foundations and challenges. Springer International Publishing, Cham

Eccles RG, Ioannou I, Serafeim G (2014) The impact of corporate sustainability on organizational processes and performance. Manag Sci 60:2835–2857

Eisenhardt KM (1989) Agency theory: an assessment and review. Acad Manag Rev 14:57–74

Eskenazi P (2015) The accountable animal. Unpublished PhD dissertation, no. EPS-2015-355-F&A, Erasmus University Rotterdam

Frink DD, Klimoski RJ (2004) Advancing accountability theory and practice: introduction to the human resource management review special edition. Hum Resour Manag Rev 14:1–17

Frink DD, Hall AT, Perryman AA, Ranft AL, Hochwarter WA, Ferris GR, Todd Royle M (2008) Meso-level theory of accountability in organizations. In: Martocchio JJ (ed) Research in personnel and human resources management. Emerald Group Publishing Limited, Leeds, pp 177–245

Grant M, Nilsson F (2020) The production of strategic and financial rationales in capital investments: judgments based on intuitive expertise. Br Account Rev 52:100861

Gulluscio C (2023) Legitimacy theory. In: Idowu S et al (eds) Encyclopedia of sustainable management. Springer International Publishing, Cham, pp 2209–2215

Harris E (2014) Feel the risk: strategic investment decisions in an uncertain world. In: Otley D, Soin K (eds) Management control and uncertainty. Palgrave Macmillan, London, pp 162–177

Hartmann F, Schreck P (2022) The undesired effects of performance rankings. Control Manag Rev 66(6):44–47

Hartmann F, Kraus K, Nilsson G, Anthony R, Govindarajan V (2020) Management control systems, 2nd edn. McGraw Hill, London

Holland J (2011) A conceptual framework for changes in fund management and accountability relative to ESG issues. J Sustain Financ Invest 1:159–177

Hornbach JJ (2023) Accounting for accountability: theoretical and empirical explorations of a multifaceted concept. Doctoral thesis no. 219, Department of Business Studies, Uppsala University

Jensen MC (1968) The performance of mutual funds in the period 1945-1964. J Financ 23:389–416

Kahneman D, Tversky A (2013) Prospect theory: an analysis of decision under risk. In: MacLean LC, Ziemba WT (eds) Handbook of the fundamentals of financial decision making: part I. World Scientific Publishing, Hackensack, pp 99–127

Knoblich G, Ohlsson S, Haider H, Rhenius D (1999) Constraint relaxation and chunk decomposition in insight problem solving. J Exp Psychol Learn Mem Cogn 25:1534–1555

Lerner JS, Tetlock PE (1999) Accounting for the effects of accountability. Psychol Bull 125:255–275

Loewenstein G, Carbone E (2024) Self-control ≠ temporal discounting. Curr Opin Psychol 60:101924

Mednick S (1962) The associative basis of the creative process. Psychol Rev 69:220–232

Merchant KA, Otley DT (2006) A review of the literature on control and accountability. In: Chapman CS, Hopwood AG, Shields MD (eds) Handbooks of management accounting research, vol 2. Elsevier, Amsterdam, pp 785–802

Messner R (2009) The limits of accountability. Account Organ Soc 34:918–938

Parmar BL, Freeman RE, Harrison JS, Wicks AC, Purnell L, De Colle S (2010) Stakeholder theory: the state of the art. Acad Manag Ann 4:403–445

Sandkühler S, Bhattacharya J (2008) Deconstructing insight: EEG correlates of insightful problem solving. PLoS One 3:e1459

Schlenker B (1997) Personal responsibility: applications of the triangle model. In: Cummings LL, Staw BM (eds) Research in organizational behavior, vol 19. JAI Press, Greenwicht, pp 241–301

Seeber-Quayle S (2024) How effective thinking habits help leaders to be more effective. Lead Lead 113:58–63

Tetlock PE, Boettger R (1989) Accountability: a social magnifier of the dilution effect. J Pers Soc Psychol 57:388–398

Zhu R, Zhang Y, Zeng H, Guo L (2025) Solve the cause, not the symptom: managerial myopia and environmental investment preferences. J Environ Manag 373:123873

Does Expertise Matter? Concluding Reflections

Fredrik Nilsson⒤, Martin Abrahamson⒤, Katarzyna Cieslak⒤,
Michael Grant⒤, Haojun Hu, Melissa Innes⒤, Inna Neskorodieva⒤,
and Anna-Carin Nordvall⒤

Abstract The final chapter of the book provides the reader with a concise summary and integrated analysis of chapters 'Performance and Fund Managers' Expertise,' 'Searching for Expert Fund Managers,' 'Judgments and Decisions by Expert Fund Managers,' 'Individual Foresight and Fund Management Expertise,' 'Artificial Intelligence in Discretionary Fund Management,' 'Integrating ESG Information in Active Fund Management,' and 'Analysing Fund Managers' Accountability.' The focus lies on the insights gained from the individual chapters, as well as what can be learnt in general, contributing to a deeper and more comprehensive understanding of fund management expertise. The chapter illustrates what fund management expertise is, how it is used and why it matters. It concludes by offering suggestions for future research as well as some practical implications.

Keywords Expertise · Financial decision-making · Fund management · Judgment · Performance

F. Nilsson (✉) · M. Abrahamson · K. Cieslak · M. Grant · H. Hu · I. Neskorodieva ·
A.-C. Nordvall
Department of Business Studies, Uppsala University, Uppsala, Sweden
e-mail: fredrik.nilsson@fek.uu.se

M. Abrahamson
e-mail: martin.abrahamson@fek.uu.se

K. Cieslak
e-mail: katarzyna.cieslak@fek.uu.se

M. Grant
e-mail: michael.grant@fek.uu.se

H. Hu
e-mail: haojun.hu@fek.uu.se

M. Innes
School of Business and Creative Industries, University of the Sunshine Coast, Sippy Downs,
QLD, Australia
e-mail: minnes1@usc.edu.au

I. Neskorodieva
Karazin Business School, V.N. Karazin Kharkiv National University, Kharkiv, Ukraine

F. Nilsson (ed.), *Exploring Fund Management Expertise*, Contributions to Finance and
Accounting, https://doi.org/10.1007/978-3-032-08545-0_9

1 Overall Analysis and Conclusions

This book explores what fund management expertise is and how it is used. The book offers insights into various facets of decision-making among fund managers, for example, the fundamental question of how they respond to new information shaping their investment decisions. Even though the capital market in general, and the fund industry in particular, have always been characterised as dynamic and uncertain, they have recently begun to be affected by new societal developments—such as demands for sustainability, the rise of artificial intelligence, and, as a result, a call for multiple accountabilities. These significant developments affect how fund managers use their expertise, as well as what constitutes their expertise and how it is developed.

One well-established concept that is used to capture the level of expertise is performance, more specifically, that an expert should show 'highly superior performance, consistently over a long period of time, within a specific domain and its related tasks.' (Grant and Nilsson 2023, p. 9). In line with this theoretical starting point, the literature review in chapter 'Performance and Fund Managers' Expertise' shows that the vast majority of research in finance has centred on whether actively managed funds can persistently show financial outperformance. The explorative studies presented in this book move that discussion from the aggregated level of a specific fund to the level of the individual fund manager. The assumption being that the core activity of any fund manager is to achieve financial returns to investors, measured as outperformance in comparison to a relevant benchmark.

However, as shown in chapter 'Performance and Fund Managers' Expertise,' measuring outperformance—both at the fund level and at the level of individual fund managers—is difficult. First, measuring fund level performance poses several methodological challenges, such as determining an appropriate benchmark, deciding whether outperformance should be measured in percentage terms (alpha) or in absolute values (added value), and accounting for Type I and Type II errors (i.e., falsely claiming outperformance or failing to detect genuine outperformance). Additionally, there is the question of how to account for market dynamics and changes over time. Second, measuring performance at the individual fund manager level introduces further complexities. These include high turnover among fund managers, many of whom leave the profession entirely, and the significant stochastic component of the stock market, which makes it almost impossible to outperform consistently year after year. To conclude, measuring outperformance over an extended period of time, at both the fund and individual fund manager levels, is complex and ambiguous, as shown in chapters 'Expertise in Fund Management' and 'Performance and Fund Managers' Expertise.' Still, few practitioners and scholars would argue that expertise in fund management does not exist (e.g., Barras et al. 2022; Berk 2005).

Thus, one important conclusion drawn in the book is that financial outperformance, compared to a benchmark, is not sufficient to evaluate whether a fund manager possesses expertise or to what extent. Contributing to these measurement difficulties is the question of how other members of the organisation, as well as the fund's owners, are involved. At the same time, these actors can be seen as distinct stakeholders affecting fund performance, potentially giving rise to agency issues. For example, a common objective for the fund company is to increase the inflow of capital into its funds. This objective may affect the ability to generate outperformance for the fund's investors.

Because of the obvious challenges in using financial outperformance as the sole indicator of fund manager expertise, there is a need to consider alternative ways of capturing it. Naturally, a fund manager's track record in generating financial outperformance—approximated, for example by a 'good enough' rating from a rating agency—remains important and is something that recruiters in the fund management industry take into account. At the same time, as shown in chapter 'Searching for Expert Fund Managers,' recruiters also appear to look for characteristics that can be assumed to foster and facilitate the development of expertise. The idea seems to be that searching for these characteristics will help recruiters identify experts who have the ability to deliver outperformance. Some of the traits that are used to identify an expert fund manager include; staying in the game over time, having experience of both bull and bear markets, showing a 'nerdy' interest in the assets under management, being a good listener and observer, having an interest in society and its challenges, being intrinsically motivated to make money and grow the fund, and showing commitment to deliberate learning throughout one's career. In addition, an expert fund manager can be expected to demonstrate notable working capacity, intelligence, grit and internal motivation. Moreover, since fund management has developed into being more of a team-based activity than in the past, 'soft skills'—such as emotional intelligence and the ability to contribute to collaborative learning—have become increasingly important. Previously, it might have been enough to show high returns of the managed fund to be considered an expert fund manager. That no longer seems to be the case.

Furthermore, the explorative studies highlight the importance of the fund managers' investment strategies and how these affect judgments and decisions. In this respect, as outlined in chapter 'Judgments and Decisions by Expert Fund Managers,' intuition and heuristics appear to play a vital role in expert fund managers' judgments and decisions. They have developed this particular kind of expertise through long-term experience, analytical and social skills, as well as an ability to leverage insights that extend beyond quantitative analyses. Thus, in line with earlier research (e.g., Backman et al. 2024; Grant and Nilsson 2020), the chapter shows that fund managers' decision-making consists of both qualitative and quantitative assessments, combining intuition and analysis—what Grant and Nilsson (2023) refer to as intuitive expertise. This important finding once again demonstrates that experts in the broader field of accounting and finance, do not rely solely on formal models and quantitative analysis, as is often claimed in the literature (Ibid.). Instead, there is an interplay between analysis and intuition in the process of making judgments and decisions.

An example of this interplay is the ability to monitor changes in external business environments and know when to pivot an investment strategy. This 'knowing' aptitude should not be underestimated in terms of recognising expertise in the realm of fund management. As discussed in chapter 'Individual Foresight and Fund Management Expertise,' individual knowledge and experience, along with emotional intelligence and future thinking skills, are central to foresight ability at work. Given the tacit nature of fund manager work—for example, the way they build relationships with key stakeholders or utilise intuitive decision-making following company-fund manager meetings—establishing a greater understanding of a fund manager's past industry and firm-level experiences and commitment becomes crucial to understanding their future performance. Adding to the earlier discussion in this chapter, exploring alternative ways to measure performance, such as their reputation as a loyal and trustworthy colleague, could lead to foresightful capacity building through collaborative learning. Furthermore, given the turbulent environment in which fund managers operate and the potential for emotional triggers and responses to have detrimental effects on investment decisions, high emotional intelligence is arguably—as pointed out earlier—an essential skill for expert fund managers, considered vital to performance outcomes.

Regardless of the individual skills and abilities of fund managers and how these are measured, the way in which fund managers pursue their work is also of great interest. As previously surmised, utilising machines—such as AI—in the process of investment analysis seems appropriate. The overwhelming volume of data available to anyone seeking to make sense of broader environmental factors is unfathomable. Thus, given the advances in what machines can do today, fund managers would be remiss not to adopt these practices to evaluate data that can positively contribute to explain what has happened. However, fund managers' decision-making also involves interpreting why events occurred and predicting what is likely to happen next. As discussed in chapter 'Artificial Intelligence in Discretionary Fund Management,' tasks that rely heavily on analysis, such as processing digital public data and preparing data sets, can be assisted by machines. In contrast, tasks that depend on intuition, such as direct communication with invested firms or investors, are much harder for machines to perform. However, even in these areas, machines can support fund managers by handling preparatory and follow-up work that requires analytical capabilities. Despite the promising potential of these technologies to enhance human expertise, the interviewees remain hesitant about embracing them. Possible explanations for that surprising finding are that machines are not yet very good at capturing future uncertainties and understanding the intentions of managers in companies that provide investment opportunities. In that regard they lack human foresight.

One example of an area in which machines seem to struggle is the analysis of how Environmental, Social and Governance (ESG) factors can affect financial risks and returns, ultimately leading to possible outperformance. These factors, even though they are considered by many to be a global challenge, and thus important both for companies and society at large, appear to be difficult to analyse and quantify from a financial perspective. This may help explain the results reported in chapter 'Integrating ESG Information in Active Fund Management,' namely that fund managers largely continue to perceive their accountability as being limited to financial returns. Accordingly, the interviewees use ESG factors primarily for negative screening, and in line with that, consider financial outperformance to be the core task of fund managers. Consequently, superior returns appear to prevail over ESG when there is a conflict between the two. Nonetheless, the environmental and social work of companies, may, over the long term, translate into financial materiality. Such a shift could be driven by changes in top-down regulations or, perhaps more significantly, by bottom-up shifts in consumer preferences, as increased awareness influences purchasing decisions toward more sustainable products and services. The ability to navigate this dynamic materiality to discern risks and opportunities, and their financial implications, becomes a crucial aspect of fund managers' expertise. A growing emphasis on sustainable investment practices highlight new dimensions of expertise and accountability, challenging the performance practices of fund managers and their commitment to act for the collective good rather than for their own gain.

Applying a behavioural perspective, a relevant question to ask is whether fund managers can navigate a landscape where values and non-financial performance are becoming increasingly important, while also being expected to incorporate sustainability and sustainable practices. These developments are introducing new and multiple forms of accountability, as discussed in chapter 'Analysing Fund Managers' Accountability.' Even so, and as pointed out earlier, the focus on financial outperformance remains very strong. One possible explanation for this is that the performance measurement systems, designed to affect behaviour and to hold agents accountable, have not been updated to reflect the influx of new non-financial imperatives such as ESG. Another possible explanation is that accountabilities are not easy to change, as they are largely psychological and social phenomenon rooted in expectations from a wide range of stakeholders. Together, these two explanations make decision-making difficult for fund managers, since established—and to some degree obsolete—processes and methods do not provide guidance in this new context. As a result, fund managers can find themselves caught between their own objectives, and emotional responses towards other stakeholders, while their expertise is not fully in line with the most recent developments, such as AI and ESG.

After these reflections it is now time to give an answer to the question posted in the introduction to this chapter: Yes, expertise does indeed matter! The explorative studies reported in this volume provide the reader with insights into what expertise consists of and how expertise can translate into high and consistent performance. The complexities of the fund management process—especially how judgments and decisions are made—are also evident, as well as the difficulties in measuring how value is created and distributed among stakeholders. The book shows that there is an obvious need to problematise and reconsider the role, definition and evaluation of expertise in fund management. This need is even more urgent than before because of important developments mentioned earlier, affecting the fund management industry, such as sustainability, artificial intelligence and multiple accountabilities. The explorative findings of the studies presented in this volume also point to certain significant areas that are in need of more research. Below we identify some areas that we find especially important and thus worthy of more research resources allocated to them. These areas could be studied separately, or preferably, together in a research programme. Before presenting suggestions for future research some methodological reflections will be provided.

2 Implications for Scholars and Practitioners

Unsurprisingly, considering its roots in finance and economics, the dominant methodological paradigm in fund management research is quantitative, using large datasets from sources available to researchers and practitioners. The focus of these research endeavours is to a large extent directed towards studying outperformance of funds and to what extent that can be related to the expertise of fund managers (e.g., Clare et al. 2022; Cremers et al. 2019). As discussed in many of the chapters in this book, results from this stream of research, question whether fund management is commensurate with expertise. However, there are several methodological challenges associated with these types of studies. One of them is the significant stochastic element in fund management, which requires that quantitative studies use very large datasets and sophisticated methods in order to produce robust results. Another challenge relates to the level of analysis and the lack of data on individual fund managers—for example, due to high turnover among fund managers. There is also a need to better understand how investors identify and select expert fund managers to manage their investments. Consequently, if we want to deepen our understanding of fund performance and expertise in fund management, we arguably need to complement quantitative methodologies with qualitative ones. Hence, we suggest that qualitative methods could be used to a much greater extent, examining multiple levels of analysis—from the fund itself to the individuals working within it. Most of the suggestions for future research are written in that spirit even though both mixed methods and quantitative studies can be appropriate, depending on the specific research question to be answered.

Several of the book's chapters emphasise the need for longitudinal studies that track performance and fund managers' development over time, aiming to increase our understanding of the development of expertise and the factors influencing decision-making. One recurring theme in the book is value creation—or where expertise adds significant value in fund management—often referred to as outperformance. Here, we suggest comparative studies of active and passive management under varying market conditions to examine the effectiveness of different fund management strategies. This would contribute to our limited knowledge and understanding of the investment process. It would also add to previous research in the field, which has primarily used methods that suffer from post-hoc or hindsight biases (Ross 1989). For example, interview statements from participants about their own or others' expertise may have been influenced by the way they believe, or want to believe, their expertise appears, rather than how it actually manifests. Furthermore, with a focus on the cognitive processes related to intuitive expertise, there is a need to explore this in real-time settings to avoid such biases (Schwarz 2012). The argument for using methods that measure intuitive expertise in practice and in real-time is also relevant for understanding the effect of external factors on decision outcomes and managerial behaviour.

A related research endeavour takes its point of departure in how fund managers process information. Since this lies at the heart of their work, a key focus is on their agility in the face of changing conditions—particularly how they respond to new information that shapes their buy and sell decisions. As shown in the book, expert fund managers are distinguished by their ability to strike a balance between self-conviction and adaptability, risk tolerance and risk avoidance, and overreaction and underreaction. While expertise can be cultivated over years of practice and learning, certain innate personal traits may also facilitate its development. For example, the book shows that HR managers tend to favour candidates with a history of multiple prior employments—a preference that aligns with the search for the personality trait of openness (Goldberg 1990). This trait may be associated with the ability to overcome underreaction to new information, avoiding decision-paralysis because of fear of making a wrong decision, and being decisive in spite of high uncertainty. Conversely, the ability to avoid overreaction, which is equally important as outlined in the context of sustainable investing, may be linked to the trait of conscientiousness (Ibid.). Conscientiousness has previously been associated with overall career success (Alderotti et al. 2023). Thus, further investigation into the personality traits of successful fund managers is clearly warranted. Such research could also explore gender-related dimensions, given the well-documented gender differences in personality traits (Bunnett 2020).

As posited in the book, fund managers can develop foresight capacity—useful for pursuing intuitive expertise—through cultivating skills related to emotional intelligence, intuitive decision-making, and future-thinking. Future research could explore the value of individual foresight in relation to fund manager performance and other associated processes and outcomes, such as emotional intelligence, intuitive decision-making and social capital. This would help determine the relevance of these abilities to fund manager expertise. Moreover, to evaluate whether firms should recruit and develop fund managers who demonstrate skills associated with collaborative learning, relevant past industry or fund experience, and a commitment to ESG factors, future studies could seek to observe and measure the influence of these factors on fund manager performance. Ultimately, in the pursuit of fund manager expertise, fostering foresightful, inspired values in professionals who invest in companies that prioritise ESG objectives would go a long way to encouraging sustainably focused fund management in the future.

A shift in emphasis toward intuition and foresight also raises the question: How do fund managers themselves assess the level of their 'intuitive expertise'? It is possible that some believe they possess intuition, when in fact this may simply be a quick reaction based on insufficient experience. At the same time, more experienced professionals may doubt themselves because they have a deeper awareness of risks and complexities. This could be a manifestation of the so-called Dunning–Kruger effect (Kruger and Dunning 1999), where confidence is not aligned with actual abilities. Such a distortion in self-assessment is likely to be particularly relevant under conditions of uncertainty and unstable data, for example, as when working with ESG. Even experienced fund managers may show excessive caution, procrastination, or self-doubt, especially if they feel external pressure or high levels of accountability (Schwarz 2012; Taffler et al. 2017). Therefore, distorted perceptions of one's expertise, whether in the form of over- or underestimation, may affect investment decisions, especially in complex and rapidly changing environments. Addressing these questions may provide valuable insights for improving the professional development of fund managers and the quality of investment decision-making.

Equally important is developing a better understanding of how new information technology, particularly AI and BD, affects how fund managers make judgments and decisions. One such area highlighted in several chapters is the acquisition of information through direct interactions with managers of portfolio firms. These interactions have also been recognised as critical in previous research (e.g., Barker et al. 2012; Gompers et al. 2020; Tuckett and Taffler 2012). As AI tools continue to evolve, they are expected to offer alternative sources of decision-relevant information. These sources range from drone imagery of corporate facilities (Mukherjee et al. 2021) to the analysis of speech content from earnings calls (Flugum and Souther 2025). Given the ongoing advancement of AI, further research into human–machine interaction is warranted—particularly to explore the conditions under which AI-generated inputs may offer greater decision-making value than traditional interactions with portfolio firms, which often rely on trust and may serve as a source of privileged or insider-like information.

In this connection, it is vital to abandon the 'human versus machine' paradigm and instead adopt a more practical 'human + machine' perspective (Cao et al. 2024). While this approach is grounded in real-world fund management practices, it requires more empirical investigation. First, fund management is a process of value creation and co-creation. Yet, it remains unclear how machines influence this process, and how fund managers use their expertise in response. Do machines amplify market noise, obscure information, or hinder value creation and market price accuracy or do they instead enhance market efficiency? Additionally, how do fund managers apply their expertise to navigate these uncertainties, and how are outcomes shaped when considering fund investors? Second, since full automation is not yet feasible, machines currently act as specialised tools that support specific tasks. Their effectiveness, and fund managers' evolving expertise in these areas, are shaped by human intentions and attention allocation, which warrants further study. Third, fund managers' characteristics include experience and background (e.g., education, certificates and experiences), as well as personality traits and the ability to handle emotions. These factors shape how technology is used and how expertise develops. While this book demonstrates that individual characteristics influence investment decisions, what remains under-explored is how these interact with machines and ultimately shape investment behaviours and outcomes.

Finally, with these suggestions for future avenues of research as a back-drop, we would like to address some of the practical implications that can be drawn from the findings reported in this book.

First, there is a need to rethink and redesign the performance metrics currently in use. As discussed at length, outperformance is an important metric, but it remains too crude to capture the full value of the products and services provided by fund managers or to help investors assess the level of expertise provided. In addition, performance metrics appear to focus narrowly on objectives that are increasingly being challenged by non-financial concerns, such as sustainable business practices and ethical considerations.

Second, and closely related, are the multiple accountabilities that fund managers are exposed to, which create tensions and challenges when making judgments and decisions. As already pointed out, new performance metrics need to be designed and used to support fund managers in their everyday work. However, there is also a need to question whether the current paradigm in finance—focusing almost exclusively on financial outperformance—is really sustainable, even from a purely financial perspective.

Third, following this line of argumentation, the expertise of fund managers needs to be broadened beyond traditional financial modelling and analysis to accommodate significant societal changes, most prominently seen in the development of ESG and AI. Although some practitioners argue that new technologies cannot replace human expertise, there is a lack of solid argumentation as to why this should be the case. The same logic applies to sustainability concerns. Hence, in order to position oneself as an expert fund manager for the future, there are good reasons to embrace these changes and turn them into a competitive advantage.

Fourth, and related to the influential education industry of which we are a part of, there is a need to critically examine the curricula of accounting and finance education. While it goes without saying that students must have a solid understanding of the fundamentals, we believe that too much time and resources are devoted to details that, quite frankly, are not that important. Much greater effort should be directed towards instilling a mindset of life-long learning and ensuring that every student understands what it takes to progress from novice to expert—while also learning how to contribute to the development of society. To achieve this, grit, as well as a mindset that is critical, curious and ethically oriented, is necessary. In a world where scientific facts and reliable news sources are being questioned to an unprecedented extent, such a mindset is more important than ever—especially for expert fund managers who have a significant impact on the long-term (financial) sustainability of our society.

References

Alderotti G, Rapallini C, Traverso S (2023) The Big Five personality traits and earnings: a meta-analysis. J Econ Psychol 94:102570

Backman J, Grant M, Nilsson F (2024) Expertise in financial auditing. In: Marton J, Nilsson F, Öhman P (eds) Auditing transformation: regulation, digitalisation and sustainability. Routledge, Abingdon, New York, pp 338–359

Barker R, Hendry J, Roberts J, Sanderson P (2012) Can company-fund manager meetings convey informational benefits? Exploring the rationalisation of equity investment decision making by UK fund managers. Account Organ Soc 37:207–222

Barras L, Gagliardini P, Scaillet O (2022) Skill, scale, and value creation in the mutual fund industry. J Financ 77:601–638

Berk JB (2005) Five myths of active portfolio management. J Portfolio Manag 31:27–31

Bunnett ER (2020) Gender differences in perceived traits of men and women. In: Carducci BJ, Nave CS, Di Fabio A, Saklofske DH, Stough C (eds) The Wiley encyclopedia of personality and individual differences: personality processes and individual differences. Wiley, Hoboken, pp 179–184

Cao S, Jiang W, Wang J, Yang B (2024) From man vs. machine to man + machine: the art and AI of stock analyses. J Financ Econ 160:103910

Clare A, Sherman M, O'Sullivan N, Gao J, Zhu S (2022) Manager characteristics: predicting fund performance. Int Rev Financ Anal 80:102049

Cremers KM, Fulkerson JA, Riley TB (2019) Challenging the conventional wisdom on active management: a review of the past 20 years of academic literature on actively managed mutual funds. Financ Anal J 75:8–35

Flugum R, Souther ME (2025) Stakeholder value: a convenient excuse for underperforming managers? J Financ Quant Anal 60:135–168

Goldberg LR (1990) An alternative 'description of personality': the big-five factor structure. J Pers Soc Psychol 59:1216–1229

Gompers PA, Gornall W, Kaplan SN, Strebulaev IA (2020) How do venture capitalists make decisions? J Financ Econ 135:169–190

Grant M, Nilsson F (2020) The production of strategic and financial rationales in capital investments: judgments based on intuitive expertise. Br Account Rev 52:100861

Grant M, Nilsson F (2023) Intuitive expertise and financial decision-making. Routledge, Abingdon, New York

Kruger J, Dunning D (1999) Unskilled and unaware of it: how difficulties in recognizing one's own incompetence leads to inflated self-assessments. J Pers Soc Psychol 77:1121–1134

Mukherjee A, Panayotov G, Shon J (2021) Eye in the sky: private satellites and government macro data. J Financ Econ 141:234–254

Ross M (1989) Relation of implicit theories to the construction of personal histories. Psychol Rev 96:341–357

Schwarz N (2012) Why researchers should think "real-time": a cognitive rationale. In: Mehl MR, Conner TS (eds) Handbook of research methods for studying daily life. The Guilford Press, New York, pp 22–42

Taffler RJ, Spence C, Eshraghi A (2017) Emotional economic man: calculation and anxiety in fund management. Account Organ Soc 61:53–67

Tuckett D, Taffler RJ (2012) Fund management: an emotional finance perspective. CFA Institute Research Foundation. rf-v2012-n2-1.pdf. Accessed 13 Aug 2025

Appendix
Methodological Considerations

The appendix presents methodological considerations for chapters 'Performance and Fund Managers' Expertise,' 'Searching for Expert Fund Managers,' 'Judgments and Decisions by Expert Fund Managers,' 'Individual Foresight and Fund Management Expertise,' 'Artificial Intelligence in Discretionary Fund Management,' 'Integrating ESG Information in Active Fund Management,' and 'Analysing Fund Managers' Accountability,' as well as, how AI-tools have been used.[1]

Chapters 'Performance and Fund Managers' Expertise,' 'Searching for Expert Fund Managers,' and 'Judgments and Decisions by Expert Fund Managers'

The research design appendix covers chapters 'Performance and Fund Managers' Expertise,' 'Searching for Expert Fund Managers,' and 'Judgments and Decisions by Expert Fund Managers.' The study behind these chapters is explorative and based on semi-structured interviews. The overall objective is to gain knowledge of the concept of expertise in fund management by studying fund management recruiters' and other key stakeholders' perceptions of fund manager expertise. The qualitative method used provides a nuanced and rich description of fund manager expertise and aims to provide insights in key skills and characteristics of expert fund managers. Specifically, we targeted specialist recruiters, an investment fund association, and

---

[1] The use of AI-tools follows the Springer editorial principles on the use of AI-tools (see Artificial Intelligence (AI) | Springer—International Publisher, accessed 18 August 2025). That means that their use has been limited to what Springer allows, namely 'AI-assisted improvements to human-generated texts for readability and style, and to ensure that the texts are free of errors in grammar, spelling, punctuation and tone.' The output was reviewed and approved by the author(s) using the tool for copy-editing. Although Springer does not require this information to be disclosed, the decision has been made to do so in order to increase transparency.

F. Nilsson (ed.), *Exploring Fund Management Expertise*, Contributions to Finance and Accounting, https://doi.org/10.1007/978-3-032-08545-0

fund managers (fund CEO, and CIO) to get their description and perception of fund manager expertise.

We contacted a selection of recruiting firms, in Sweden and in the United Kingdom, to get recruiters specialised in the fund industry (the expertise domain). In total, we performed nine interviews with recruiters, fund managers, a rating agency, and the CEO and head of research at an investment fund association. The interviews were based on an interview guide comprising broad questions. To ensure consistency, each interview started with a presentation of our definition of expertise. The following themes were covered during the interviews:

- The interviewee's professional journey.
- Example of a typical assignment, recruiting an expert fund manager, identifying an expert, what is sought after.
- Examples of selection process and key drivers in selection.
- The importance of the physical meeting.
- Intuition as part of selection and judgments.
- Reasons for failures.
- The know-how of facing an expert.
- How to separate a good manager from a good fund (evaluation).

All interviews, except one which was conducted in a physical meeting, were carried out online (using Zoom). All interviews were recorded and transcribed. To ensure consistency in how the interviews were conducted, both authors (researchers) participated in the first five interviews. Subsequently, the first five interviews were all discussed among the researchers, and the way of conducting the remaining interviews was calibrated. Participants provided informed consent for the interviews, all data were anonymised, participants had the right to withdraw at any time. The interviews were 40–86 min long, with an average length of 59 min.

The analysis is founded on emergent findings in the data and the literature. The description of our analysis can be simplified into three main steps. First, the authors, together with the editor, read all interviews and identified over-arching concepts and themes related to recruiters and other key stakeholders' perception of expertise and how it can be identified. The authors used MAXQDA to further code all interviews based on the initial analysis. Next, the text was analysed in further detail, to identify categories and fine tune the coding structure. This part of the analysis was conducted jointly by both authors. In the third step, an additional analysis was done of the text and categories, resulting in the themes presented in the findings. It should be noted that the quotes are translated (except in two cases) from Swedish to English. Quotes are to a certain extent freely translated (Table A.1).

Table A.1 Description of interviewees

Interviewee	Years of experience	Position
1	>20	Specialist Recruiter Fund Industry
2	>10	Recruiter Banking/Fund Industry
3	>20	Rating Agency
4	>20	Specialist Recruiter Fund Industry
5	>20	Specialist Recruiter Fund Industry
6	>20	Fund CIO
7	>20	Fund CEO
8a	>20	CEO, Investment Fund Association
8b	>20	Head of Research, Investment Fund Association
9	>20	Specialist Recruiter Fund Industry

Notes Table shows the order of the interviews conducted and the years of experience of the interviewee. In addition, the position is listed, showing the perspective/knowledge expected from each interviewee. For interviewee 8a and 8b, the interviews were performed together, due to time constraints of the interviewees

Chapter 'Individual Foresight and Fund Management Expertise'

Anonymous commentary for this chapter was received from a key account manager of an Australian asset management firm with over 30 years' experience managing fund managers—thus referred to as an 'expert in fund management'. Other findings originate from a large qualitative study focused on lived experience of individuals experiencing the phenomenon of Individual Foresight (IF) in an organisational context (Innes 2023, 2024). Seeking an interpretive paradigm, Interpretive Phenomenological Analysis (IPA) was adopted. A purposive sampling approach of judgement sampling was used. In Phase One six HR experts provided insights to reveal two industries most appropriate for the study. Employees were provided with information about the study and requested to contact the researcher. The final sample comprised 27 IPA interviews between 40 and 60 min across managerial and non-managerial positions. Interviews were held with 12 employees from the finance and insurance industry (6 females and 6 males), and 15 employees from the utilities industry (3 females and 12 males) in Australia.

The interview protocol aligned with Bevan's (2014) work on the three key interview domains for descriptive phenomenological interviewing: Contextualisation, apprehending the phenomenon, and clarifying the phenomenon. Participants received an email prior to interviews to build shared understanding of the phenomenon of IF. They recalled two-three incidents in their working life where they drew on personal experience to make decisions about current actions, which then impacted on future job outcomes (i.e., using IF). Transcriptions were processed through Otter.ai (a web-based speech to text transcription technology software), checked for accuracy and de-identified. The research was conducted in accordance with University of the Sunshine Coast's Human Research Ethics Approval (#S191343). Table A.2 details the IPA analysis process advocated by Smith et al. (2009) and the activities undertaken to reveal emergent themes underpinning the IF Framework.

Chapter 'Artificial Intelligence in Discretionary Fund Management'

This research project covers seven semi-structured interviews with nine intervie-wees in fund management. It intends to explore how big data (BD) and artificial intelligence (AI) are implemented into fund management and how they can inter-play with human expertise by studying the perspective of key stakeholders, who are not limited to only fund/portfolio managers. The interviewees all use a discretionary strategy. Table A.3 provides details on the interviewees. Interviewees were identified through recommendations or existing connections. They were conducted between October and December 2024 in English, with an average duration of approximately 60 min. Most of them, except the interview with interviewee I, were done together with the topic on sustainability (chapter 'Integrating ESG Information in Active Fund Management' in this volume), either in person or online. Each interview was recorded, transcribed, and supplemented with necessary notes.

The semi-structured interviews in this chapter were designed around two key sessions, which align with the literature reviewed in this study. Interviewees received two to five key questions in advance. However, not all questions were asked, and additional questions emerged based on the context of the interview. The interviews began by exploring participants' perspectives on implementing BD and AI into their workflows and investment strategies. Fund managers were asked to provide examples of their investment processes. Those who did not systematically use BD and AI were asked to explain their reasoning. Finally, the interview went into how BD and AI not only influence their workflow but also interact with their expertise.

This research adopted a deductive approach at the beginning, as the two key interview sessions, which are related to the two questions in the literature review section, were derived from existing literature. And then, data analysis employed a combination of inductive and deductive coding. First, an inductive approach allowed themes and patterns to emerge directly from the data. Subsequently, a deductive approach was applied to align the identified themes with the pre-defined research questions.

Participants provided informed consent before the interviews, and all data were anonymised to protect their privacy. Participants retained the right to withdraw from the study at any time. All quotes used in the chapter have been approved by the interviewees. Some of the quotes have been slightly edited to increase readability.

Table A.2 Interpretive phenomenological analysis process for IF study

IPA analysis process	Analytical activities for this study
Step 1: Reading and re-reading **Step 2**[a]: Initial noting [a]Steps 1 and 2 merge following the initial transcript reading, such that reading, and note-taking will occur at the same time through the analysis	1. The researcher immersed themselves in the original data, beginning with the first original transcript 2. Interviews were recorded, researcher listened to the recording of the interview while reading transcript and imagining voice of participant for future readings 3. The researcher read and re-read the transcript to orient to a slower process of focusing on the participant as the focus of analysis 4. Immediately following each interview, the researcher undertook reflexive memoing (journaling) to contribute to the objective nature of the write-up of results. This aligned with Smith et al.'s (2009) recommendation that the researcher records their own observations about the interview recollection, and record the most striking observations in a journal to bracket them off while orienting to the participant experience during this initial stage 5. The researcher maintained an open mind and noted anything of interest within the transcript (this process became Step 2—initial noting) 6. This step represented a free textual analysis (i.e., there is no requirement at this stage to divide text into meaning units) 7. Initial noting was undertaken observing the following approach: **Descriptive comments**: production of a comprehensive and detailed set of notes and comments on the data (first level annotation) **Linguistic comments**: Focusing on language use to note when language use and content are clearly interrelated (for example use of repetition, change in tone, etc.) (second level annotation) **Conceptual comments**: Shifting in focus towards the participant's overarching understanding of issues they are discussing. This is a time-consuming process of conceptually interpreting the data through discussion, reflection, trial-and-error and refinement of ideas (third level annotation) 8. As part of Step 2, *Theoretical memoing* (Glaser and Strauss in Rennie 2000) was undertaken for each individual transcript where a log was kept to record 'hunches, speculations, [and] thoughts about the relations among categories'. This approach involved the researcher addressing the double hermeneutic process by developing theoretical memos after revisiting each transcript case

(continued)

Table A.2 (continued)

IPA analysis process	Analytical activities for this study
Step 3: Developing emergent themes	1. Utilising larger data set comprising original transcripts and notes, the researcher reduces the volume of detail (i.e., transcript and original notes) whilst maintaining complexity, in terms of mapping the interrelationships, connections and patterns between exploratory notes
	2. Focusing on discrete chunks of transcript the researcher analyzed exploratory comments
	3. The original whole of the interview became a set of parts (which comes together in a new whole at the end of the analysis in the write up)
	4. Emergent themes reflected the participants' original words and thoughts and the researcher's interpretation
Step 4: Searching for connections across emergent themes	1. Transcripts were transferred into NVivo where Emergent Themes (codes in NVivo) were developed and observed from one case to the next
	2. Researcher developed NVivo project maps for each case identifying connections across emergent themes *within each case* arriving at case-specific conceptual maps
	3. Working with the sets of themes developed, the researcher developed a sunburst chart for each case
	4. Researcher worked on how themes fit together (i.e., clustering related themes) developing tables representing an emergent theme (or set of themes)
	5. As per Smith et al. (2009) some themes were discarded (not all need be incorporated), dependent on RQ, the researcher's innovation and organization of analysis
	6. In searching for patterns and connections between emergent themes, the researcher included abstraction, subsumption, polarisation, and contextualisation of the themes to arrive at superordinate themes (refer to Smith et al. (2009) for further explanation of these suggestions)

(continued)

Table A.2 (continued)

IPA analysis process	Analytical activities for this study
Step 5: Moving to the next case	1. In studies with multiple cases Smith et al. (2009) suggest the researcher moves to the next case and repeats the process, treating each case on its own terms 2. Researcher repeated the process, bracketing ideas that emerged from the analysis of each case as they progressed the analysis (with reflexive memoing) 3. There is acknowledgment that during the repeated analyses of cases the researcher will be influenced by what they found in earlier cases, however, an important skill in IPA is to allow new themes to emerge with each case 4. Following the development and analysis of emergent theme, the researcher returned to the initial script for each case (now being aware of the final set of emergent themes), and without referring to the data from NVivo (a) developed a final reflexive memo notes for each case (in Excel), (b) identified the top three to five emergent themes relevant to each case (in Excel), and (c) compared these with the results from NVivo to check reliability of the process, and validity of the emergent themes 5. Although slight variations existed, this was deemed highly appropriate given the qualitative nature of the data, and the consideration of smaller, or less frequently coded themes that may be key to the case and emerged from the data 6. This process informed the development of superordinate themes observed across every case (see Step 6)
Step 6: Looking for patterns across cases	1. Researcher brought together emergent themes from steps 4 and 5 seeking connections between cases and themes 2. Questions in this step include What connections are there across cases? How do themes in one case illuminate a different case? Which themes are the most potent? 3. Utilising Excel and the themes emerging across cases, this led to the development of superordinate themes which were shared across cases 4. This step identified ways in which participants represented unique idiosyncratic instances and shared higher order superordinate themes within the group 5. The outcome of this step was a table summarising emergent themes as nested within superordinate themes–illustrating consideration of themes from each case

Table A.3 Description of interviewees

Interviewee	Years of experience	Position
A	>25	Head of Sustainability and Communication, asset management division, major Swedish bank
B	>10	Sustainability Products and Regulations Lead, asset management division, major Swedish bank
C	>20	Partner, large private equity fund in central Europe
D	>20	Vice President, large private equity fund in central Europe
E	>30	Co-founder, large Swedish fund management company
F	>25	Senior Portfolio Manager, large American hedge fund, Singapore office
G	>30	Chief Investment Officer and Chief Executive Officer, pension fund, major Swedish private healthcare provider
H	>30	General Secretary, financial analysts' association in a Nordic country
I	>30	Risk Manager, alternative investment fund in Europe

Chapter 'Integrating ESG Information in Active Fund Management'

In the research project conducted, eight experts in the field of fund management were interviewed (see Table A.4). The interviews were conducted between October and December 2024, with an average duration of approximately 60 min. The interviews were conducted in English and together with the interviews carried out for chapter 'Artificial Intelligence in Discretionary Fund Management.' Participants provided informed consent for the interviews and all data were anonymised. Participants had the right to withdraw at any time. All quotes used in the chapter have been approved by the interviewees. Some of the quotes have been slightly edited to increase readability. The following interview guide was used during the interviews:

1. Can you describe how ESG information is integrated in the valuation/investment process, and which type of ESG information is the most important?
2. What challenges do asset managers face when integrating ESG information in the valuation / investment process?
3. How often do you rely on ESG ratings and are there any challenges with using ESG ratings?
4. How do you find the balance between attracting ethical investors and ensuring financial returns for the fund? Do you believe investors can sacrifice returns for sustainability?
5. Do you believe a fund can impact ESG performance of portfolio companies and how?
6. How do you perceive the risks of 'greenwashing,' and how can these risks be managed?

7. How sustainability affects the skill set (i.e., expertise) needed in fund management?
8. Is ESG investing more based on intuition (e.g., memory-based inference, informal cue-integration) vs. analysis (e.g., explicit reasoning based on chosen criteria) compared with traditional investing

To analyse the data collected, thematic analysis was applied. The main stages of the analysis were:

1. The interviews were transcribed, and participants' personal data were anonymised.
2. Interview transcripts were read to identify recurring ideas.
3. Text from interviews was segmented into meaningful units, which were coded to reflect aspects of ESG signal analysis and the skills of active managers.
4. Themes identified were analysed and compared with the literature.

While our analysis focused on the emerging similarities across cases, we cannot exclude the possibility that a larger sample might also reveal differences among the various types of fund managers.

Only two of the interviewed fund managers had direct contact with ESG-labelled funds. Interviews with fund managers beyond ESG-labelled funds allowed us to validate statements by Edmans and Kacperczyk (2022) that ESG is no longer a niche concern but is integrated in mainstream financial decision-making of all funds irrespective of their goals.

Table A.4 Description of interviewees

Interviewee	Working experience	Position
A	>25	Head of Sustainability and Communication, asset management division, major Swedish bank
B	>10	Sustainability Products and Regulations Lead, asset management division, major Swedish bank
C	>20	Partner, large private equity fund in central Europe
D	>20	Vice President, large private equity fund in central Europe
E	>30	Co-founder, large Swedish fund management company
F	>25	Senior Portfolio Manager, large American hedge fund, Singapore office
G	>30	Chief Investment Officer, Chief Executive Officer, pension fund, major Swedish private healthcare provider
H	>30	General Secretary of financial analysts' association in a Nordic country

Chapter 'Analysing Fund Managers' Accountability'

The chapter utilises a conceptual research design to investigate accountability mechanisms in the light of expertise in fund management context. The methodology aligns with Jaakkola's (2020) approach of employing literature-based research to construct theories and gain new insights into complex phenomena. One method through which a conceptual paper can contribute to existing knowledge is by serving as a theory synthesis paper that integrates multiple theories or literature streams (Jaakkola 2020). This chapter identifies and analyses key themes and interactions of accountability in the fund management context. The chapter predominantly relies on secondary data from peer-reviewed books and journal articles. These sources provide insights into existing frameworks, stakeholder roles, and accountability mechanisms in the context of fund management. We chose this groundwork to give insights into different challenges actors face and how they deal with them. The literature review started by exploring the pivotal role of actors' accountability in the context of fund management. We established search strategies by identifying keywords relevant to the chapter topic, starting broadly with fund investment and identifying relevant actors within fund management using databases such as JSTOR, PubMed, Scopus, Google Scholar, and library catalogues. When finding relevant articles, we reviewed them and their reference lists to identify additional sources. The analysis is based on the fund management framework, emphasising the interconnectedness of expertise and accountability in a dynamic environment. It evaluates the role of fund managers in handling the many demands placed on them. The chapter provides insights into how fund managers' accountability to themselves and different stakeholders affects their practice of their expertise.

References

Bevan MT (2014) A method of phenomenological interviewing. Qual Health Res 24:136–144
Edmans A, Kacperczyk M (2022) Sustainable finance. Rev Financ 26:1309–1313
Innes M (2023) Exploring the lived experience of Individual Foresight in organisations. Doctoral dissertation, University of the Sunshine Coast, Queensland
Innes ML (2024) Exploring individual foresight: implications for organizational learning and innovation in firms. J Innov Knowl 9:100604
Jaakkola E (2020) Designing conceptual articles: four approaches. AMS Rev 10:18–26
Rennie, DL (2000) Grounded theory methodology as methodical hermeneutics: reconciling realism and relativism.Theory and Psychology 10: 481–502.
Smith J, Flowers P, Larkin M (2009) Interpretative phenomenological analysis: theory, method and research. Sage, London